ROMANTIC WOMEN POETS
1788 – 1848

MANCHESTER
UNIVERSITY PRESS

Romantic women poets
1788 – 1848

Volume II

edited by
Andrew Ashfield

Manchester University Press
Manchester and New York

distributed exclusively in the USA
by St. Martin's Press

Copyright © Andrew Ashfield 1998

Published by Manchester University Press
Oxford Road, Manchester M13 9NR, UK
and Room 400, 175 Fifth Avenue, New York, NY 10010, USA

Distributed exclusively in the USA by
St. Martin's Press, Inc., 175 Fifth Avenue, New York,
NY 10010, USA

Distributed exclusively in Canada by
UBC Press, University of British Columbia, 6344 Memorial Road,
Vancouver, BC, Canada V6T 1Z2

British Library Cataloguing-in-Publication Data
A catalogue record for this book is available from the British Library

Library of Congress Cataloging-in-Publication Data applied for

ISBN 0 7190 5292 0 *hardback*
    0 7190 5293 9 *paperback*

First published 1998

01 00 99 98   10 9 8 7 6 5 4 3 2 1

Typeset
by Bryan Williamson, Frome, Somerset

Printed in Great Britain
by Bell & Bain Ltd, Glasgow

Contents

Note	ix
Introduction	1

HELEN MARIA WILLIAMS (later Stone?) (1761–1827)
1. A Poem on the Bill Lately Passed for Regulating the Slave Trade — 12

HANNAH MORE (1745–1833)
2. Slavery, a Poem — 21
3. The Sorrows of Yamba — 27

ANN YEARSLEY (née Cromartie) (1752–1806)
4. A Poem on the Inhumanity of the Slave-Trade — 32

ANNA LAETITIA BARBAULD (née Aikin) (1743–1825)
5. Epistle to William Wilberforce — 43

MARY LEADBEATER (née Shackleton) (1758–1826)
6. The Triumph of Terror — 47
7. The Summer-Morning's Destruction — 48
8. The Ruined Cottage — 49

MARY ROBINSON (née Darby) (1758–1800)
9. The Maniac — 53
10. The Lascar — 56
11. Poor Marguerite — 64
12. Edmund's Wedding — 67
13. The Savage of Aveyron — 70

ANNE BANNERMAN (1765–1829)
14. Verses on an Illumination for a Naval Victory — 74
15. Ode I: The Spirit of the Air — 77
16. Ode II: The Mermaid — 80
17. The Soldier — 82
18. The Dark Ladie — 82

FANNY HOLCROFT (1780–1844)
19. Annabella — 88
20. The Penitent Mother — 89
21. Conscience the Worst of Tortures — 90
22. The Negro — 91
23. The Condemned Sailor — 92
24. The Debtor — 93
25. The Madagascar Mother — 94

JANE ELIZABETH ROSCOE (later Hornblower) (1797–1853)
26. Sonnet: 'Though to my living eye be still denied' — 96
27. The Visionary — 96
28. Llanberis Pass — 97

CONTENTS

29	Sonnet: 'Pent in the city's darkesome walls I pine'	98
30	Sonnet: 'Amidst the darkness of the ancient time'	98
31	Life	99
32	Sonnet: 'Yes! there are sympathies fate cannot part'	100
33	Solitary Imprisonment	100
34	Verses: 'Do I not love at midnight to gaze forth'	102
35	Verses: 'I was within a home, where nature smiled'	103

CAROLINE BOWLES (later Southey) (1786–1854)

36	There is a tongue in every leaf	105
37	On Reading 'The records of woman'	106
38	The Father's Tale	107
39	The Grandmother's Tale	112

FELICIA DOROTHEA HEMANS (née Browne) (1793–1835)

40	Bring Flowers	118
41	The American Forest-Girl	119
42	Corinne at the Capitol	121
43	The Grave of a Poetess	122
44	Woman on the Field of Battle	123
45	Woman and Fame	125
46	Arabella Stuart	126
47	The Spells of Home	133
48	The Beings of the Mind	134
49	The Land of Dreams	136
50	The Wings of the Dove	137
51	The Two Homes	139
52	The Dreaming Child	140
53	The Dreamer	141
54	To the Mountain Winds	142
55	The Return to Poetry	143
56	Intellectual Powers	143
57	Remembrances of Nature	143

MARIANNE PROWSE (née Jeffery) (1798–1850)

58	Nature	144
59	Home	145
60	On Visiting a Cataract	146
61	To *****	146
62	Written During a Storm at Night	147
63	The Desolate	148

LETITIA ELIZABETH LANDON (later Maclean) (1802–1838)

64	Corinna	151
65	The Enchanted Island	152
66	Stanzas on the Death of Mrs Hemans	153
67	[Fragment] 'The altar, 'tis of death! for there are laid'	156
68	[Fragment] 'Oh, what a waste of feeling and of thought'	156
69	The Polar Star	156

CONTENTS

CATHERINE GRACE GODWIN (née Garnett) (1798–1845)
70 Felicia Hemans   158
71 The Lady Jane Grey in her Study   160

MARY ANN BROWNE (later Gray) (1812–1845)
72 A World Without Water   163
73 Rocks   166
74 The Song of the Elements   166
75 A Vision of Power   170
76 Fragmentary Verses   174
77 The Embroideress at Midnight   176

MARIA ABDY (née Smith) (1797–1867)
78 The Enchanted Ground   179
79 The Poetess   180
80 Lines Written on the Death of Mrs Hemans   182
81 The Deserted Wife to her Sister   184
82 The Railway Tunnel   185
83 The Dressmaker   187
84 The Embroidery Frame   191

CAROLINE NORTON (née Sheridan, later Stirling-Maxwell) (1808–1877)
85 The Captive Heart   194
86 Sonnet: 'In the cold change which Time hath wrought on love' 195
87 A Voice from the Factories   195
88 Sonnet: 'Like an enfranchised bird, who wildly springs'   208
89 Sonnet: The Disdained Lover   208
90 The Poet's Choice   209

CAROLINE CLIVE (née Meysey-Wigley) (1801–1873)
91 The Grave   211
92 Written in Illness   213
93 Former Home   213

EMILY BRONTË (1818–1848)
94   'I'm happiest when most away'   216
95   'It's over now; I've known it all'   216
96   'Harp of wild and dream-like strain,'   217
97   'I am the only being whose doom'   217
98   'It is not pride, it is not shame'   218
99   'The wind, I hear it sighing'   219
100 The Night-Wind   219
101 'And like myself lone, wholly lone'   220
102 'Shall Earth no more inspire thee'   221
103 To Imagination   222
104 Remembrance   223
105 The Prisoner. A Fragment   224
106 'No coward soul is mine'   225
107 'Often rebuked, yet always back returning'   226

vii

CONTENTS

ANNE BRONTË (1820–1849)

108	The North Wind	227
109	To Cowper	228
110	Lines Composed in a Wood on a Windy Day	229
111	The Captive Dove	230
112	If This Be All	230
113	Dreams	231

CHARLOTTE BRONTË (later Nicholls) (1816–1855)

114	On the Death of Emily Jane Brontë	233
115	On the Death of Anne Brontë	233

ELIZABETH BARRETT BROWNING (née Barrett) (1806–1861)

116	Stanzas Addressed to Miss Landon	235
117	The Soul's Travelling	237
118	Cowper's Grave	242
119	The Cry of the Human	245
120	The Cry of the Children	248
121	Sonnet: The Soul's Expression	251
122	Sonnet: The Seraph and Poet	252
123	The Runaway Slave at Pilgrim's Point	252
124	Maude's Spinning	259
125	The Poet	260
126	Hiram Powers's Greek Slave	260

Notes	261
Appendix	
MARY BRYAN (née LANGDON) (1780–after 1823)	288
1 To W[illiam] W[ordsworth] Esq.	288
2 Sonnet: The Spinning Wheel	289
3 The Visit	290
4 On Seeing the Representation of a Victory	292
5 The Dream	293
Index of first lines	295
Selected thematic index	299

Note

In presenting poetry by women of this period, I have abandoned the traditional male markers and chosen dates which might be considered more appropriate for women. Volume I (1770–1838) therefore took 1770 as its starting point because significant women poets, Seward, Barbauld and More, started to produce important verse at around this time. The years 1770–1771 also saw the deaths of major male poets and the rise of national collections from which the women were excluded. The date 1838 marked the first major collection of Elizabeth Barrett, and the deaths of Hemans (1835) and Landon (1838) operate as important markers in the same way as 1744 or 1824 do for the male poets. In the case of the present volume, which charts different territory, 1788 saw the publication of three powerful indictments of slavery by women poets, and the theme resonates throughout the volume, sometimes mutating into other social concerns. The year 1848 closes the volume with Barrett Browning's important contribution to the the debate and marks the death of Emily Brontë, and social upheaval in Europe. Nevertheless, definitions of periods, though sometimes useful, are of strictly limited value and do not diminish the claims of 1824 or 1830 or 1832 for closing certain aspects of Romanticism.

As with the previous volume, texts have been lightly modernised, with contractions and elisions expanded and some archaic spellings replaced. One poet, Mary Bryan, about whom very little is known, has been placed in an appendix.

Introduction

By October 1856, two very different portraits of women readers were ready for the press. One went on to world-wide fame, the other fell into relative obscurity.[1] The first one tells us of a girl from the provinces, Emma Roualt, who read 'keepsakes' in a convent and trembled as she blew beneath the tissue paper covering engravings accompanying texts. It goes on to tell how her ascetic existence erupted into sensuality as she perversely interpreted church metaphors of Sick Lamb, Sacred Heart, Christ the Bridegroom, in a deeply personal way as powerful embodiments of the fine words she had found in romances—'bliss', 'passion', 'intoxication'.[2] The moral flaw of adultery is already deeply etched in her emotional economy:

> Accustomed to stillness, she turned towards its opposite in tumultuous scenes. She loved the sea only because of its storms and she never enjoyed greenery except when it was scattered among ruins. She valued things merely for a type of personal profit which she could draw from them, and rejected as useless everything that did not immediately contribute to the consummation of her heart—for she was by temperament sentimental rather than artistic, in search not of landscapes but of emotions.[3]

The second portrait of 1856 also takes up the theme of female sentimentality. Just as Emma Roualt suffers from a weakness for extracting 'personal profit' from experiences, Aurora Leigh is charged by her suitor with being too susceptible to 'the personal pang'. Women poets

> Will write of factories and of slaves, as if
> Your father were a negro, and your son
> A spinner in the mills. . . .
> Women as you are,
> Mere women, personal and passionate,
> You give us doting mothers, and perfect wives,
> Sublime Madonnas, and enduring saints!
> We get no Christ from you, and verily
> We shall not get a poet. . . .[4]

Elizabeth Barrett Browning's response to such a characterisation of the condition of women is characteristically hawkish and she gives us two other pictures of women readers very different from those trapped between tissue paper and the engraving. The first describes her early reading experiences and how she 'chanced upon the poets'. By temperament artistic rather than sentimental, she emerges from these reading experiences with a sense of her vocation as a poet and a sense of the destiny of poetry itself as 'imperative labour' often in stark opposition to industrial capitalism.

> Ay, and while your common men
> Lay telegraphs, gauge railroads, reign, reap, dine,,
> And dust the flaunty carpets of the world

INTRODUCTION

> For kings to walk on, or our president,
> The poet will suddenly catch them up
> With his voice like thunder, . . .
> . . . poetry, my life,
> My eagle, with both grappling feet still hot
> From Zeus's thunder, who hast ravished me
> Away from all the shepherds, sheep, and dogs,
> And set me in the Olympian roar and round
> Of luminous faces for a cup-bearer . . .[5]

The second portrait of a female reader Barrett Browning gives us is altogether grimmer. Marian Erle, a working-class seamstress, experiences poetry in fragments, 'some stray old volume' of Thomson or Shakespeare or stray leaves and half-leaves from Gray, Milton, Burns and other classics:

> 'Twas somewhat hard to keep the things distinct,
> And oft the jangling influence jarred the child
> Like looking at a sunset full of grace
> Through a pothouse window while the drunken oaths
> Went on behind her. . . .
> And thus she had grown, this Marian Erle of ours,
> To no book-learning, she was ignorant
> Of authors,—not in earshot of the things
> Outspoken o'er the heads of common men
> By men who are uncommon,—but within
> The cadenced hum of such, and capable
> Of catching from the fringes of the wing
> Some fragmentary phrases, here and there,
> Of that fine music, which being carried in
> To her soul, had reproduced itself afresh
> In finer motions of the lips and lids.[6]

Aurora Leigh, in Olympian roar, will go on to success as a woman poet and marry. Marian Erle, however, will move from the world of drunken oaths and fragmentary phrases to a Parisian brothel where she is drugged and raped and will live and die an outcast, unmarried mother.

These portraits of women readers given to us in the same year by Flaubert and Barrett Browning raise a number of important questions concerning the relations between canonical and non-canonical literature. Although he sails quite close to the wind on a number of occasions, Flaubert has generally been acquitted of malicious intent in his ruthless charting of the trajectory of sentimentality and *Madame Bovary* has entered into a constellation of 'great novels' of the nineteenth century. Whether Emma Bovary, Anna Karenina, Effie Brest or Tess Durbeyfield are humanist representations of tragic victims of pharisaic morality or post-modern victims of the novel's internal structure, unswervingly gravitating around death and adultery, remain important questions, not least because in the presence of 'power' in these nartives, liberal humanist and some post modern canons to some extent converge.[7] Yet whether we warm up in the exercise of moral drama or warm to the prospect of adultery and death, we acknowledge the power of the text and concede De Quincey's distinction between a literature of knowledge and a literature of power.[8] For this reason, in imaginative terms, Emma Bovary, and not Aurora Leigh or Marian Erle, seems 'representative' of woman in the nineteenth century.

The problem with this conception of an opposition between 'power' and 'knowledge' is that it rides roughshod over some complicated developments in eighteenth- and nineteenth-century culture which were central to many women poets' experiences, and in particular, their close links to dissenting culture and dissenting modes of inquiry. For Dissenters, power and knowledge were not disparate realms of experience but complex continuations of extreme conflicts and tensions they felt in attempting to reconcile reason and sentiment. The key arena in which they tried to harmonise reason and sentiment was education. Virtually all Dissenters were obsessed by promoting new approaches to education. Unitarians, for example, simultaneously promoted commercial education in conjunction with literary study, and, long before the tension between enquiry and culture surfaced powerfully in John Stuart Mill, they stressed cultivation of taste as a powerful palliative to the strains of commerce. At the same time, insistence on the right to free enquiry in matters of religion developed into a tendency to a project of enquiry itself and investigations into other 'injustices'. In the interregnum between the two great causes they supported, American Independence and the French Revolution, Dissenters and, in particular, Unitarians, were active in pushing for reforms in the slave-trade, prisons, hospitals, asylums, parliamentary franchise, education and public health. With the advent of the French Revolution and subsequent events, this relentless questioning of civic management and the unjust origins of social institutions ran into strong opposition. Edmund Burke saw in this wide-ranging and interconnected activity a form of Jacobinism which should be resisted by a 'majesty of terrors' since 'The foundations on which obedience to governments is founded are not to be constantly discussed . . . Otherwise we should dispute all the points of morality, before we can punish a murderer, robber, and adulterer; we should analyze all society.'[9] Burke's attack on the much-revered Richard Price also powerfully drew attention to the apocalyptic nature of much dissenting thought and raised the strong suspicion that the dark side of those impressive humanitarian reforms advocated by Dissenters might be an intelligentsia well prepared to be steeped in blood. With war and reaction the cultural programme of the radical Dissenters received a drubbing from which it would never fully recover. Their commercial ambitions flourished in the industrial cities of Manchester and Liverpool but the idea of harmonious development of culture

INTRODUCTION and commerce, central to eighteenth-century dissent failed to re-emerge in the rapidly industrialising society of the nineteenth century. So much so, that by the time Arnold published *Culture and anarchy* (1869), Dissenters were charged with provincialism and isolationism, sacrificing 'spontaneity of consciousness' to 'strictness of conscience'. Whether Burke and Arnold are correct in seeing the various forms of dissent as destructive to national character and the nation—in either vigorous enquiry or provincialism—is beyond the scope of this introduction. Nevertheless, these two powerful onslaughts on dissenting culture have important ramifications for the study of literature since they effectively promote a national, English literature, in which it is difficult to assign dissent a place. Burke's notion of the 'test of time', which throws a veil over injustices, and Arnold's notion of a 'study of perfection', which leads to a better self, both terminate in ennobling national monuments which are hostile to dissent in either its enquiring or provincial forms. Similarly, De Quincey's promotion of power over knowledge is equally problematic since 'knowledge' remained central to dissent.[10]

For De Quincey, in perusing works of imaginative power, we 'are startled into a feeling of the infinity of the world within' us. A literature of knowledge cannot do this and De Quincey cites parliamentary reports (among other works such as dictionaries) as an example. Yet it was precisely these parliamentary reports which exercised imaginative power over many women poets in the late eighteenth and first half of the nineteenth century, and to which they responded with a literature of power and knowledge. Following the parliamentary debates over the slave-trade in 1788, Helen Maria Williams, Hannah More and Ann Yearsley (1–3) published three of the most sustained poetic responses to the question. Anna Barbauld also responded to events in Parliament in 1791 (5). In the 1830s the various parliamentary reports on factory conditions drew attention to the plight of child labour and provoked important, though very different, poems from Caroline Bowles and Caroline Norton (38–39, 87). In the 1840s, further reports again highlighted the condition of working children and also drew attention to the miserable existence of female workers, particularly seamstresses. Mary Ann Browne, Maria Abdy and Elizabeth Barrett all published poems engaging various aspects of the reports (77, 83–84, 120, 124). These responses are not simply sentimental, treating social issues in a mere 'passionate and personal' way as Aurora Leigh's suitor contends. They are direct responses to careful readings of the parliamentary texts themselves. Caroline Bowles appended to her *Tales of the factories* (1833) a variety of printed sources documenting various aspects of the factory question. She includes the minutes from the *Factories' Labour Regulation Bill*, an address from a working-class meeting in Bradford, and Robert Southey's notes on 'The manufacturing system'. Elizabeth Barrett Browning's 'The cry of the children' similarly responds to the printed texts of the Commissioners' Report (in which her friend R. H. Horne played an important role). Caroline Norton claimed her *A voice from the factories* (1836) was based on printed reports and first-hand experience:

> I will only add, that I have in *no* instance overcharged or exaggerated, by poetical fictions, the picture drawn by the Commissioners appointed to inquire into this subject. I have strictly adhered to the printed Reports; to that which I believe to be the melancholy truth; and that which I have, in some instances, myself had the opportunity of witnessing.

All three of these poems respond in deeply personal ways to the question of child labour but do so, not as improvisation but as poetic responses to print knowledge. (It ought to be remembered that, shortly after the publication of her poem, Caroline Norton was to lose custody of her own children so her insistence on the public reports is all the more impressive.) The case is similar with the issue of slavery where there was indeed much sentimental and pious nonsense written. Yet Yearsley's early response in 1788 and Barrett's 1848 contribution to an American anti-slavery periodical also document the stark realities of slavery in the shadow of printed reports. It is of course true that in this period poetry enters into complex relations with other texts and often finds its starting point in other poems. The ubiquitous epigraph, usually a line or lines from another poem, takes off in this period as poetic texts spawn poetic responses. But this type of improvisation, the taking of a line or lines and spinning out the variations on the theme, a technique which Hemans and Landon used frequently, is only part of the story. Lines from Wordsworth, Byron and Shelley were frequently used to produce an improvisational poetry; passages from parliamentary reports to provide the basis for engagement with social themes. De Quincey's distinction between power and knowledge breaks down as women moved between the two realms, mixing magical lines and parliamentary prose.

Like many Dissenters, the women poets were quick to make connections between injustices and saw many of the issues as closely related. Caroline Norton clearly saw the linkages between anti-slavery, prison reform and factory legislation:

> Howard became immortally connected with the removal of the abuses which for centuries disgraced our prison discipline; as the perseverance of Wilberforce created the dawn of the long-delayed emancipation of the negroes;—so, my Lord [Ashley], I trust to see your name enrolled with the names of these great and good men, as the Liberator and Defender of those helpless beings, on whom are inflicted many of the evils both of slavery and imprisonment, without the odium of either. (**88n**)

Similarly, Caroline Bowles ironically juxtaposes the charitable collections to free negro slaves with 'no need to cross the sea / For your good work; on *this* side the salt waves, / No lack of Slavery, nor of *Infant Slaves*' (**38**). Barrett Browning, alluding to the abolition of slaves in Christian England, contrasts this with factory children who 'Are slaves, without the liberty of Christendom—' (**120**). Maria Abdy, contemplating the fate of seamstresses, sees them in 'chains of civic slavery' (**83**). In 'The embroidery frame' (**84**) she links the plight of the widowed but middle-class woman who embroiders to that of the working-class seamstress. With this consciousness of interconnected injustices, women naturally move on to the question of women's rights and freedom, although none of them manages to articulate fully what women's rights or freedom should or could be. Mary Ann Browne writes, 'I longed for fame—I longed to be / More than a women e'er had been' and 'flinging woman's fears away' she dreams of speaking 'of liberty, / Of slavish fear, of bonds of men, / Of justice, and of human laws' (**75**); yet the domestic pull of hearth and children's voices results in agony and stifles ambition. Although the women poets often correctly interpreted the indenture of child apprentices as slavery and extended this to female workers, they failed to free themselves from hearth and home to articulate a coherent position on women's rights. The temptation to adopt a form of martyrdom sketched along the lines of the unique purity of 'woman's love' often proved more alluring than liberty itself.

Linkages between important social issues, such as slavery, prisons or factory conditions, extended to linkages between the fate of the poetess and other women workers. The Corinne myth, central to Hemans and Landon, is shadowed by the image of the seamstress. By the time of the Commissioners' Report of 1843 (which first drew attention to the plight of seamstresses), the women poets who had been most seduced by the possibilities opened up by Corinne had all died in distant lands—Jewsbury in India, Hemans in Ireland, Landon in Africa. All three had worried incessantly about the cost of fame and poetic vocation. After their deaths, a darker side to female existence opened up and the notion of poetess as *grand improvisatrice* was undermined by a far more real comparison between the fate of the woman poet and the seamstress. Barrett Browning, in the figures of Aurora Leigh and Marian Erle, maintains both positions but for other poets such as Maria Abdy and Mary Ann Browne, the seamstress displaces Corinne as the emblem of female creativity. Fame for a woman poet is as precarious as the life of a seamstress. Just as seamstresses and embroideresses grow old and are abandoned, so too fame can vanish and leave the poetesses in the same condition as other women workers.[11] In 'The poetess' (**79**), Maria Abdy charts the progress of a woman poet from her first 'bright and wild imaginings' through success when she shone like 'a lovely meteor in the paths of men' to rejection by the man she loves and death. The woman poet who ventures on to enchanted ground becomes 'The sovereign of a desert waste of mind'. In 'The dressmaker' (**83**), the seamstress seems to suffer the same fate as the poetess. In early life 'her spirit was elate with buoyant hope' but the work has taken its toll and 'fled is her former smile'. And like the woman poet, she experiences the stress of domestic memory recalling her cottage home in childhood which is broken by her viewing 'The gay and glittering shreds that strew the ground' of her present condition. Just as the woman poet becomes a victim of fame and dies, so too the dressmaker, the 'helpless victim of the rich and great', finds repose only in the grave. Mary Ann Browne seems to draw close links between the poetess and the seamstress as embroiderers of flowers. One of the great ironies of women's poetry of this period is that the flowers which so obsessed Hemans and were variously deeply symbolic for her—accompaniments of early domestic happiness, marriage, sickness, funerals, shrines, conquests—terminate not in Corinne's garland but the discarded silken threads of the seamstress's embroidered flowers. The warmth and freedom of the south contract to a garret at midnight.

Earlier I drew attention to two different sources of power and knowledge as the starting points for women's poetry: lines of poetry taken as epigraphs and passages of parliamentary reports. It is not possible in this short introduction to document fully the complications that these two positions entail. Such an analysis would require detailed study of the epigraphs and the parliamentary reports. At a more general level, however, it is possible to trace a significant historical positioning connected to these two sources. The poetry taking its starting point from those magical lines of poetry Arnold was so fond of recommending produced not further works of perfection but often endless variations on a theme or never freed itself from the original epigraph. In this sense it might be argued that many of the women poets produce poems constantly constrained by the male Romantics such as Wordsworth, Coleridge and Byron, and never really throw off their sense of inferiority, so if we historically assess the women poets solely in relation to the major male Romantic figures, their importance is questionable. If, however, we look at the women poets as the continuation of a lost line in English poetry—the line from Cowper to Southey—we get a much clearer picture of what they were and what they were attempting to do. Unfortunately, the line from Cowper to Southey has fared little better in literary history than the women poets. Cowper has few fans and Southey has never been forgiven for apostasy; and while Wordsworth and Coleridge have been favoured with lavish scholarship, Southey's old inclusion in the Oxford Editions reduces his 'Poems concerning the slave trade', 'Botany Bay eclogues' and 'English eclogues' to an appendix of omitted works. These works, like many of the works of the women poets, also respond to a literature of knowledge surrounding the slave-trade, transportation and the English poor. It is against the 'Botany Bay eclogues' and 'English eclogues' that the outcast and marginalised figure of Mary Robinson (9–13) needs to be read. Although it is certainly true that these concerns with outcasts sometimes degenerated into sentimental sensationalism, as in the case of the youthful Fanny Holcroft's poems (**19–25**), the line from Cowper, the last great religious poet in English, to Southey, as champion of victims, is still the line that many of the women poets responded to. For both poets exemplified a poetics of desertion—by God or society—which powerfully undermined *improvisatrice* ambitions. The 'hunger, rebellion, and rage' Matthew Arnold found in Charlotte Brontë is more evident in the early Southey than in the other male Romantic poets and it was to Southey that Charlotte Brontë would turn for advice on her poems.[12] Caroline Bowles not only married Southey (who had earlier edited Cowper) but was herself termed 'the Cowper of our modern poetesses' by H. N. Coleridge. For Barrett Browning he seemed to embody 'the poet's high vocation' itself. The grim struggles against life-long depression manifesting themselves in beautiful hymns, uniquely simple natural description and the conscious eschewment of sublimities struck a deep chord with several women poets. Charlotte Smith found in Cowper 'infinite consolation' and 'enchantment'; Anne Brontë 'the language of my inmost heart' (**10**). Jane Elizabeth Roscoe's encounters with the sublimities and mysteries of life are likewise fraught with the influence of Cowper.

According to Flaubert, there were women like Emma Bovary in twenty French villages. This vision of sentimentality casting its giant shadow over provincial towns in the manner of Murnau's Faust is only partly true and largely fabulously false. Similarly, Arnold's charge of the provincialism of dissent is largely true and partly gravely false. Almost all the women poets in this volume emerged from the provinces and although they often lapsed into sentimentality, they were also largely responsible for keeping open one of the few real alternatives to visionary Romanticism—a poetics of desertion replete with hunger, rage and rebellion. *Aurora Leigh* may lack the emotional power of *Madame Bovary* but it is in many ways the culmination of a line of English poetry from Cowper to Southey and the women poets we have lost, and in losing this we have lost much of the sense of what poetry can, and sometimes does, do for us.

Notes

1 Gustave Flaubert's *Madame Bovary: moeurs de province* was first published in *Revue de France*, 1 October to 15 December 1856, and published in book form the following year.

   Elizabeth Barrett Browning's *Aurora Leigh* was completed in October 1956 and issued in late December with a postdated imprint of 1857.

2 *Madame Bovary: moeurs de provinces* (1857), ed. Maurice Nadeau, Paris: Gallimard 1972, pp.64, 67, 65.

3 *Ibid.*, pp.65-6. In a further prelude to criminal conversation, she later invokes sea and storms, 'Does it not seem to you that the spirit spreads its wings more freely over the limitless expanse of ocean, the contemplation of which elevates the soul and gives it ideas of the infinite and the ideal?' *Ibid.*, p.122.

4 *Aurora Leigh*, Second Book, lines 194-6, 220-5.

5 *Ibid.*, First Book, lines 869-74, 918-23.

6 *Ibid.*, Third Book, lines 983-7, 998-1008.

7 On adultery and the novel, see Tony Tanner, *Adultery and the novel*, Baltimore: The Johns Hopkins University Press 1979. On death and the novel, see Walter Benjamin, 'Der Erzähler', in *Gesammelte Schriften*, Frankfurt: Suhrkamp 1977, ii.2, 438-65.

8 For De Quincey on the distinction between power and knowledge, see 'Oliver Goldsmith', 'Letters to a young man whose education has been neglected', and 'The poetry of Pope', *The collected writings of Thomas De Quincey*, ed. David Mason, 14v. Edinburgh 1889-90, iv.308-13, x.46-52, xi.52-62, 96-7.

9 Edmund Burke, 'Speech on the petition of the Unitarians' (1793), *The works*, London 1906, iii.324.

10 For the contribution of Dissent to female education, see Ruth Watts, 'The Unitarian contribution to the development of female education 1790–1850', *History of Education*, 9 (1980), 173–86, and 'Knowledge is power – Unitarians, gender and education in the eighteenth and early nineteenth centuries', *Gender and Education*, I (1989), 35–50.

11 The employment of women as governesses was equally problematic. Mary Wollstonecraft, Fanny Holcroft and Anne Brontë were all dismissed from their posts.

12 Matthew Arnold, *Letters*, ed. G. W. E. Russell, London 1895, i.29.

HELEN MARIA WILLIAMS (later STONE?) (1761–1827)

She was born in London on 17 June 1761, the daughter of Charles Williams, an army officer, and Helen (née Hay). After her father's death in 1769, the family moved to Berwick-upon-Tweed, possibly to be nearer her mother's relatives. She came to London in 1781, and with the help of a leading Dissenter, Andrew Kippis, published *Edwin and Eltruda. A legendary tale*, London 1782. This was followed by *An ode on the peace*, London 1783 and *Peru, a poem. In six cantos*, London 1784, the latter being the first work she put her name to. She achieved widespread recognition with the publication of *Poems*, 2v. London 1786, a subscription edition with over 1500 names. A second expanded edition was printed in 1791. In 1788 she visited France for the first time and stayed with her elder sister, Cecilia, who had married Athanase Coquerel, a French Protestant minister. By this time, she was acquainted with many of the leading literary figures of the day: Boswell, Johnson, Hayley, Rogers, Kippis, Price, Joseph and Thomas Warton, Hannah More, Elizabeth Montague, Anna Seward, Charlotte Smith and Hester Thrale. She visited France again after the Revolution and her enthusiastic account of it in *Letters written in France in the summer of 1790*, London 1790, marked the beginning of her alienation from English society. Her novel, *Julia*, 2v. London 1790, was reviewed and admired by Mary Wollstonecraft and also contained a pro-revolutionary poem, 'The Bastille, a vision' (ii. 218–23). At this time she was living in a house in Southampton Row, which she thought had once been inhabited by Gray. She left England again, signalling her departure in *A farewell for two years, to England*, London 1791. In France, she soon came into contact with John Hurford Stone (1763–1818), a Unitarian radical who hosted dinners for British residents. He was arrested with his wife, Rachel Coope, in April 1794 but soon released. He appears to have divorced her in June and eloped with Helen Maria Williams to Switzerland, with Rachel Coope following then, possibly because of the dubious legality of the divorce. On 4 October 1794 Daniel Lyson wrote to Hester Thrale that Stone had married Williams and 'avail'd himself of the summary laws of France to divorce himself'. However, by 20 April 1795, Hester Thrale noted that 'Helena Williams's Friends are all ashamed of *her*. When Stone's *real* Wife followed her Husband to Basle in Switzerland, whither He had fled with his newer Connexion, fair Helen,—leaving the first poor Soul behind; in hope that She would by Guillotined by the Terrorists: *his* Conscience smote him, and he would at least have behaved civilly, but the second Lady stormed and cried, and obliged him to drive Mrs Stone from his Door, at which She intreated for Bread' (*Thraliana*, ii.922). Hester Thrale's disapproval of Williams's liaison with Stone was constant, but earlier, at the end of 1792, while she noted that Williams was 'sacrificing her Reputation' she simply put it down to 'an old classical connexion between Helen and Paris'. Her later report of the *ménage à trois* is so tinged with Burkean melodrama—a wife abandoned to execution, begging for bread—that there must be some doubt as to its reliability.

In October 1793 Williams herself was imprisoned, although this may only have been house-arrest. During her period of confinement she translated Bernardin St Pierre, published (with additional sonnets) as *Paul and Virginia*, [Paris] 1795. She continued to produce her prose reports on the course of the Revolution in France (although Stone and Thomas Christie contributed much of the material) and much later on the effects of the Restoration. Her visit to Switzerland is described in

HELEN MARIA WILLIAMS

A tour in Switzerland, 2v. 1798, which included 'A hymn written among the Alps' and contains historically important passages on the sublime and revolutionary sentiment. Her later work consisted mostly of translations, presumably undertaken to support her and Stone, whose publishing business had failed. She and Stone became naturalised in 1817, although he died the following year. By 1819 Crabb Robinson (who had visited her in the company of the Clarksons in September 1814 and had tried to help her with publishing difficulties with Longmans) reported that she was in financial need and had sold all her property. In 1820 he introduced Wordsworth to her who paid her several visits, during one of which Wordsworth recited her 'Sonnet. To Hope' 'from memory, after a lapse of many years'. (Much earlier, in 1791, Wordsworth had visited Charlotte Smith in Brighton, and asked her for a letter of introduction to Williams but failed to meet her at this time.) She moved briefly to Amsterdam, where her nephew, Athanese Laurent Charles Coquerel, was minister to the French Protestant congregation, but soon returned to Paris, living on an annuity from her nephew. She died in Paris on 15 December 1827, and was buried beside Stone at Père-Lachaise.

1   A POEM ON THE BILL LATELY PASSED
    FOR REGULATING THE SLAVE TRADE

> *The quality of mercy is not strained;*
> *It droppeth, as the gentle rain from heaven*
> *Upon the place beneath. It is twice blessed;*
> *It blesseth him that gives, and him that takes.*   Shakespeare

The hollow winds of Night, no more
In wild, unequal cadence pour
On musing Fancy's wakeful ear,
The groan of agony severe
From yon dark vessel, which contains
The wretch new bound in hopeless chains;
Whose soul with keener anguish bleeds,
As Afric's lessening shore recedes—
No more where Ocean's unseen bound
Leaves a drear world of waters round,
Between the howling gust, shall rise
The stifled Captive's latest sighs—;
No more shall suffocating death
Seize the pent victim's sinking breath;
The pang of that convulsive hour
Reproaching Man's insatiate power;
Man! who to Afric's shore has passed
Relentless, as the annual blast
That sweeps the Western Isles, and flings
Destruction from its furious wings—
And Woman, she, too weak to bear
The galling chain, the tainted air;
Of mind too feeble to sustain
The vast, accumulated pain;
No more, in desperation wild,

HELEN
MARIA
WILLIAMS

Shall madly strain her gasping child;
With all the mother at her soul,
With eyes where tears have ceased to roll,
Shall catch the livid infant's breath;
Then sink in agonizing death.
   Britain! the noble, blessed decree
That soothes despair, is framed by Thee!
Thy powerful arm has interposed,
And *one* dire scene for ever closed;
Its horror shall no more belong
To that foul drama, deep with wrong.
Oh, first of Europe's polished lands,
To ease the Captive's iron bands!
Long as thy glorious annals shine,
This proud distinction shall be thine:
Not first alone when Valour leads,
To rush on Danger's noblest deeds;
When Mercy calls thee to explore
A gloomy path, untrod before,
Thy ardent spirit springs to heal,
And, greatly generous, dares to feel!—
Valour is like the meteor's light,
Whose partial flash leaves deeper night;
While Mercy, like the lunar ray,
Gilds the thick shade with softer day.
   For this, in Fame's immortal shrine,
A double wreath, O Pitt, is thine!
For this! while distant ages hear
With Admiration's sacred tear,
Of powers, whose energy sublime
Disdained to borrow force from Time,
With no gradations marked their flight,
But rose, at once, to Glory's height;
The deeds of Mercy, that embrace
A distant sphere, an alien-race,
Shall Virtue's lips record, and claim
The fairest honours of thy name!
'Tis ever Nature's generous view;
Great minds, should noble ends pursue;
As the clear sun-beam, when most bright,
Warms, in proportion to its light.—
And Richmond, he! who, high in birth,
Adds the unfading rays of worth;
Who stoops, from scenes in radiance dressed,
To ease the mourner's aching breast;
The tale of private woe to hear,
And wipe the friendless orphan's tear!—
His bosom for the Captive bleeds,
He, Guardian of the injured! pleads

HELEN MARIA WILLIAMS

With all the force that Genius gives,
And warmth that but with Virtue lives;
For Virtue, with divine control,
Collects the various powers of soul;
And lends, from her unsullied source,
The gems of thought their purest force.
　Oh blessed decree! whose lustre seems
Like the sweet Morn's reviving beams,
That chase the hideous forms of night,
And promise day more richly bright;
Great deed! that met consenting minds
In all, but those whom Avarice binds;
Who creep in Interest's crooked ways,
Nor ever pass her narrow maze;
Or those, whom hard Indifference steels
To every pang another feels.
For *Them* has Fortune, round their bowers,
Twined (partial nymph!) her lavish flowers;
For *Them*, from unsunned caves, she brings
Her summer ice; for *Them*, she springs
To climes, where hotter suns produce
The richer fruits delicious juice:
While *They* whom wasted blessings tire,
Nor leave *one* want, to feed desire;
With cool, insulting ease, demand
Why for yon hopeless, Captive Band,
Is asked, to mitigate despair,
The mercy of the common air?
The boon of larger space to breathe,
While cooped that hollow deck beneath?
A lengthened plank, on which to throw
Their shackled limbs, while fiercely glow
The beams direct, that on each head
The fury of contagion shed?—
And dare presumptuous, guilty man,
Load with offence his fleeting span?
Deform Creation with the gloom
Of crimes, that blot its cheerful bloom;
Darken a work so perfect made,
And cast the Universe in shade!—
Alas, to Afric's fettered race
Creation wears no form of grace!
To Them, Earth's pleasant vales are found
A blasted waste, a sterile bound;
Where the poor wanderer must sustain
The load of unremitted pain!
A region, in whose ample scope
His eye discerns no gleam of hope;
Where Thought no kind asylum knows,

On which its anguish may repose,
But Death, that to the ravaged breast
Comes not in shapes of terror dressed.
Points to green hills where Freedom roves,
And minds renew their former loves;
Or, lowering in the troubled air,
Hangs the fierce spectre of Despair,
Whose soul abhors the gifts of life,
Who steadfast grasps the reeking knife,
Bids the charged heart in torrents bleed,
And smiles in frenzy, at the deed.
So, when rude winds the sailor urge
On polar seas, near Earth's last verge;
Long with the blast he struggles hard,
To save his bark, in ice imbarred;
But finds at length, o'ercome with pain,
The conflict with his fate is vain;
Then heaves no more the useless groan,
But hardens like the wave to stone.
   Ye noble minds! who o'er a sky
Where clouds are rolled, and tempests fly,
Have bid the lambent lustre play
Of *one* pure, lovely, azure ray;
Oh, far diffuse its opening bloom,
And the wide hemisphere illume!
Ye, who *one* bitter drop have drained
From Slavery's cup, with horror stained;
Oh, let no fatal dregs be found,
But dash her chalice on the ground:
Oh, while she links her impious chain,
And calculates the price of pain;
Weighs Agony in sordid scales,
And marks if Death, or Life prevails;
In one short moment, seals the doom
Of years, which anguish shall consume;
Decides how near the mangling scourge
May to the grave its victim urge,
Yet for awhile, with prudent care
The half-worn wretch, if useful, spare;
And speculates with skill refined,
How deep a wound will stab the mind;
How far the spirit can endure
Calamity, that hopes no cure;—
Ye! who can selfish cares forgo,
To pity those which others know;
As Light, that from its centre strays,
To glad all Nature with its rays;
Oh! ease the pangs ye stoop to share,
And rescue millions from despair!—

HELEN MARIA WILLIAMS

HELEN
MARIA
WILLIAMS

For you, while Morn in graces gay,
Wakes the fresh bloom of opening Day;
Gilds with her purple light your dome,
Renewing all the joys of home;
Of home! dear scene, whose ties can bind
With sacred force the human mind,
That feels each little absence pain
And lives but to return again;
To that loved spot, however far,
Points, like the needle to its star;
That native shed which first we knew,
Where first the sweet affections grew;
Alike the willing heart can draw,
If framed of marble, or of straw;
Whether the voice of pleasure calls,
And gladness echoes through its walls;
Or, to its hallowed roof we fly,
With those we love to pour the sigh;
The load of mingled pain to bear,
And soften every pang we share!—
Ah, think how desolate *His* state,
How *He* the cheerful light must hate,
Whom, severed from his native soil,
The Morning wakes to fruitless toil;
To labours, hope shall never cheer,
Or fond domestic joy endear;
Poor wretch! on whose despairing eyes
His cherished home shall never rise!
Condemned, severe extreme, to live
When all is fled that life can give!—
And ah! the blessings valued most
By human minds, are blessings lost!
Unlike the objects of the eye,
Enlarging, as we bring them nigh,
Our joys, at distance strike the breast,
And seem diminished when possessed.
   Who, from his far-divided shore,
The half-expiring Captive bore?
Those, whom the traffic of their race
Has robbed of every human grace;
Whose hardened souls no more retain
Impressions Nature stamped in vain;
All that distinguishes their *kind*,
For ever blotted from their mind;
As streams, that once the landscape gave
Reflected on the trembling wave,
Their substance change, when locked in frost,
And rest, in dead contraction lost;—
Who view unmoved, the look, that tells

HELEN MARIA WILLIAMS

The pang that in the bosom dwells;
Heed not the nerves that terror shakes,
The heart convulsive anguish breaks;
The shriek that would their crimes upbraid,
But deem despair a part of trade.—
Such only, for detested gain,
The barbarous commerce would maintain.
The generous sailor, he, who dares
All forms of danger, while he bears
The British Flag o'er untracked seas,
And spreads it on the polar breeze;
He, who in Glory's high career,
Finds agony, and death are dear;
To whose protecting arm we owe
Each blessing that the happy know;
Whatever charms the softened heart,
Each cultured grace, each finer art,
E'en thine, most lovely of the train!
Sweet Poetry! thy heaven-taught strain—
His breast, where nobler passions burn,
In honest poverty would spurn
The wealth, Oppression can bestow,
And scorn to wound a fettered foe.
True courage in the unconquered soul
Yields to Compassion's mild control;
As, the resisting frame of steel
The magnet's secret force can feel.
   When borne at length to Western Lands,
Chained on the beach the Captive stands,
Where Man, dire merchandise! is sold,
And bartered life is paid for gold;
In mute affliction, see him try
To read his new possessor's eye;
If one blest glance of mercy there,
One half-formed tear may check despair!—
Ah, if that eye with sorrow sees
His languid look, his quivering knees,
Those limbs, which scarce their load sustain,
That form, consumed in wasting pain;
Such sorrow melts his ruthless eye
Who sees the lamb, he doomed to die,
In pining sickness yield his life,
And thus elude the sharpened knife.—
Or, if where savage habit steels
The vulgar mind, one bosom feels
The sacred claim of helpless woe—
If Pity in that soil can grow;
Pity! whose tender impulse darts
With keenest force on nobler hearts;

HELEN MARIA WILLIAMS

As flames that purest essence boast,
Rise highest when they tremble most.—
Yet *why* on one poor chance must rest
The interests of a kindred breast?
Humanity's devoted cause
Recline on Humour's wayward laws?
To Passion's rules must Justice bend,
And life upon Caprice depend?—
   Ah ye, who one fixed purpose own,
Whose untired aim is *Self* alone;
Who think in gold the essence lies
From which extracted bliss shall rise;
To whose dull sense, no charm appears
In social smiles; or social tears;
As mists that o'er the landscape sail,
Its beauteous variations veil;
Or, if in some relenting hour,
When nature re-assumes her power,
Your alms to Penury ye lend,
Or serve, for once, a suffering friend;
Whom no weak impulse e'er betrayed
To give that friend incautious aid;
Who with exact precision, pause
At that nice point which Interest draws;
Your watchful footsteps never found
To stray beyond that guarded bound;—
Does fleeting Life proportion bear
To all the wealth ye heap with care?
When soon your days in measured flight
Shall sink in Death's terrific night;
Then seize the moments in your power,
To Mercy consecrate the hour!
Risk something in her cause at last,
And thus atone for all the past;
Break the hard fetters of the Slave;
And learn the luxury to save!—
Does Avarice, your god, delight
With agony to feast his sight?
Does he require that victims slain,
And human blood, his altars stain?
Ah, not alone of power possessed
To check each *virtue* of the breast;
As when the numbing frosts arise,
The charm of vegetation dies;
His sway the hardened bosom leads
To Cruelty's remorseless deeds;
Like the blue lightning when it springs
With fury on its livid wings,
Darts to its goal with baleful force,

HELEN MARIA WILLIAMS

Nor heeds that ruin marks its course.—
   Oh! Eloquence, prevailing art!
Whose force can chain the listening heart;
The throb of Sympathy inspire,
And kindle every great desire;
With magic energy control
And reign the sovereign of the soul!
That dreams while all its passions swell,
It shares the power it feels so well;
As visual objects seem possessed
Of those clear hues by light impressed;
Oh, skilled in every grace to charm,
To soften, to appal, to warm;
Fill with thy noblest rage the breast,
Bid on those lips thy spirit rest,
That shall, in Britain's Senate, trace
The wrongs of Afric's Captive Race!—
But Fancy o'er the tale of woe
In vain one heightened tint would throw;
For ah, the Truth, is all we guess
Of anguish in its last excess:
Fancy may dress in deeper shade
The storm that hangs along the glade,
Spreads o'er the ruffled stream its wing,
And chills awhile the flowers of Spring:
But, where the wintry tempests sweep
In madness, o'er the darkened deep;
Where the wild surge, the raging wave,
Point to the hopeless wretch a grave;
And Death surrounds the threatening shore—
Can Fancy add one horror more?
   Loved Britain! whose protecting hand
Stretched o'er the Globe, on Afric's strand
The honoured base of Freedom lays,
Soon, soon the finished fabric raise!
And when surrounding realms would frame,
Touched with a spark of generous flame,
Some pure, ennobling, great design,
Some lofty act, almost divine;
Which Earth may hail with rapture high,
And Heaven may view with favouring eye;
Teach them to make all Nature free,
And shine by emulating Thee!—

(1788)

HANNAH MORE (1745–1833)

She was born on 2 February 1745, at Stapleton, near Bristol, the fourth of five daughters of Jacob More, schoolmaster, and Mary (née Grace). All the daughters were educated to become teachers and in 1758 the three eldest set up at a boarding school in Trinity Street, Bristol, which Hannah More attended and later had a share in. She was a precocious child and eventually her father taught her Latin, to which she later added Italian and Spanish. Around 1767 she entered into a protracted and complicated engagement to Edward Turner which he eventually broke off, offering compensation of £200 a year which she refused. The money was secretly paid into a trust and she was later persuaded to accept it. Turner also left her £1000 on his death. The experience appears to have resulted in a firm resolution never to marry. In 1773–1774 she visited London, met Johnson, Burke and Reynolds and formed a lasting friendship with Garrick and his wife. She stayed with them for some months in 1776, and regularly stayed with Mrs Garrick after Garrick's death in 1779. During this period she wrote a number of successful and mostly very profitable plays. On Garrick's death, she appears to have lost interest in or access to the theatre and, increasingly, wrote didactic and educational works: *Essays on various subjects*, London 1777, *Sacred dramas*, London 1782, *Thoughts on the importance of the manners of the great to general society*, London 1788, *An estimate of the religion of the fashionable world*, London 1791, *Strictures on the modern system of female education*, London 1799. These, together with her poems and other pieces, were collected in *The Works*, 11v. London 1830, although there are numerous omissions.

In 1784 she discovered and prepared for publication the poems of Ann Yearsley, a Bristol milkwoman. Together with Elizabeth Montagu she helped raise over 1000 subscribers for *Poems on several occasions*, London 1785. Initially, Hannah More and Elizabeth Montagu acted as trustees of the subscription money but an acrimonious dispute followed and eventually, it seems, the money was handed over to Yearsley. This experience of 'blackest ingratitude' probably heightened an already well-developed sense of conservatism and the natural order of society and, combined with her increasing sense of piety following the break with the theatre, almost certainly laid the grounds for an increased interest in religion and conservative politics. Although in the main High Church, in 1787, she came under the powerful influence of John Newton (1725–1807) and William Wilberforce (1759–1833) (as did the poet William Cowper at about the same time) and her thought began to exhibit strains of High Church conservatism with strong elements of Methodist zeal, an odd mixture of piety and passion that several women poets developed. The Unitarian and radical Amelia Opie (1769–1853) similarly renounced the theatre under the influence of Quakerism but retained a passionate commitment to the anti-slavery campaigns. After a visit to Cheddar with her sister, Martha, and Wilberforce in 1789, during which she was appalled at the lack of religious education, she became increasingly concerned with the Sunday School movement. After 1789 and the revolutionary threat of France, she wrote a series of didactic *Cheap repository tracts* in simple English designed to impress Christian morality and subservience to the natural order on working-class readers. An urn commemorating John Locke, given to her by Mrs Montagu in 1787, was in her garden at Cowslip Green, near Bristol, throughout the period of these mad tracts, but Locke appears not to have replied.

In 1802 she moved to a house in Barley Wood, very near to where

Locke was born. Her sisters and the urn soon joined her. In 1828 in poor health, she sold Barley Wood and moved to 4 Windsor Terrace, Clifton. She died of mad cow's disease on 7 September 1833 and left £30,000 to an array of religious societies and charities. All the sisters were buried at Wrington and the urn seems finally to have been set free.

2 SLAVERY, A POEM

> – O great design!
> Ye Sons of Mercy! O complete your work;
> Wrench from Oppression's hand the iron rod,
> And bid the cruel feel the pains they give.   Thomson's *Liberty*

If Heaven has into being deigned to call
Thy light, O Liberty! to shine on all;
Bright intellectual Sun! why does thy ray
To earth distribute only partial day?
Since no resisting cause from spirit flows
Thy penetrating essence to oppose;
No obstacles by Nature's hand impressed,
Thy subtle and ethereal beams arrest;
Nor motion's laws can speed thy active course,
Nor strong repulsion's powers obstruct thy force;
Since there is no convexity in Mind,
Why are thy genial beams to parts confined?
While the chill North with thy bright ray is blessed,
Why should fell darkness half the South invest?
Was it decreed, fair Freedom! at thy birth,
That thou shouldst ne'er irradiate *all* the earth?
While Britain basks in thy full blaze of light,
Why lies sad Afric quenched in total night?
  Thee only, sober Goddess! I attest,
In smiles chastised, and decent graces dressed.
Not that unlicensed monster of the crowd,
Whose roar terrific bursts in peals so loud,
Deafening the ear of Peace: fierce Faction's tool;
Of rash Sedition born, and mad Misrule;
Whose stubborn mouth, rejecting Reason's rein,
No strength can govern, and no skill restrain;
Whose magic cries the frantic vulgar draw
To spurn at Order, and to outrage Law;
To tread on grave Authority and Power,
And shake the work of ages in an hour:
Convulsed her voice, and pestilent her breath,
She raves of mercy, while she deals out death:
Each blast is fate; she darts from either hand
Red conflagration o'er the astonished land;
Clamouring for peace, she rends the air with noise,
And to reform a part, the whole destroys.
  O, plaintive Southerne! whose impassioned strain
So oft has waked my languid Muse in vain!

HANNAH MORE

Now, when congenial themes her cares engage,
She burns to emulate thy glowing page;
Her failing efforts mock her fond desires,
She shares thy feelings, not partakes thy fires.
Strange power of song! the strain that warms the heart
Seems the same inspiration to impart;
Touched by the kindling energy alone,
We think the flame which melts us is our own;
Deceived, for genius we mistake delight,
Charmed as we read, we fancy we can write.

  Though not to me, sweet Bard, thy powers belong,
Fair Truth, a hallowed guide! inspires my song
Here Art would weave her gayest flowers in vain,
For Truth the bright invention would disdain.
For no fictitious ills these numbers flow,
But living anguish, and substantial woe;
No individual griefs my bosom melt,
For millions feel what Oronoko felt:
Fired by no single wrongs, the countless host
I mourn, by rapine dragged from Afric's coast.

  Perish the illiberal thought which would debase
The native genius of the sable race!
Perish the proud philosophy, which sought
To rob them of the powers of equal thought!
Does then the immortal principle within
Change with the casual colour of a skin?
Does matter govern spirit? or is mind
Degraded by the form to which 'tis joined?

  No: they have heads to think, and hearts to feel,
And souls to act, with firm, though erring zeal;
For they have keen affections, kind desires,
Love strong as death, and active patriot fires;
All the rude energy, the fervid flame,
Of high-souled passion, and ingenuous shame:
Strong, but luxuriant virtues boldly shoot
From the wild vigour of a savage root.

  Nor weak their sense of honour's proud control,
For pride is virtue in a pagan soul;
A sense of worth, a conscience of desert,
A high, unbroken haughtiness of heart;
That self-same stuff which erst proud empires swayed,
Of which the conquerors of the world were made.
Capricious fate of man! that very pride
In Afric scourged, in Rome was deified.

  No Muse, O Qua-shi! shall thy deeds relate,
No statue snatch thee from oblivious fate!
For thou wast born where never gentle Muse
On Valour's grave the flowers of Genius strews;
And thou wast born where no recording page

Plucks the fair deed from Time's devouring rage.
Had Fortune placed thee on some happier coast,
Where polished souls heroic virtue boast,
To thee, who sought'st a voluntary grave,
The uninjured honours of thy name to save,
Whose generous arm thy barbarous Master spared,
Altars had smoked, and temples had been reared.

   Whene'er to Afric's shores I turn my eyes,
Horrors of deepest, deadliest guilt arise;
I see, by more than Fancy's mirror shewn,
The burning village, and the blazing town:
See the dire victim torn from social life,
The shrieking babe, the agonizing wife!
She, wretch forlorn! is dragged by hostile hands,
To distant tyrants sold, in distant lands!
Transmitted miseries, and successive chains,
The sole sad heritage her child obtains!
Ev'n this last wretched boon their foes deny,
To weep together, or together die.
By felon hands, by one relentless stroke,
See the fond links of feeling Nature broke!
The fibres twirling round a parent's heart,
Torn from their grasp, and bleeding as they part.

   Hold, murderers, hold! nor aggravate distress;
Respect the passions you yourselves possess;
Ev'n you, of ruffian heart, and ruthless hand,
Love your own offspring, love your native land.
Ah! leave them holy Freedom's cheering smile,
The heaven-taught fondness for the parent soil;
Revere affections mingled with our frame,
In every nature, every clime the same;
In all, these feelings equal sway maintain;
In all the love of Home and Freedom reign:
And Tempe's vale, and parched Angola's sand,
One equal fondness of their sons command.
The unconquered Savage laughs at pain and toil,
Basking in Freedom's beams which gild his native soil.

   Does thirst of empire, does desire of fame,
(For these are specious crimes) our rage inflame?
No: sordid lust of gold their fate controls,
The basest appetite of basest souls;
Gold, better gained, by what their ripening sky,
Their fertile fields, their arts and mines supply.

   What wrongs, what injuries does Oppression plead
To smooth the horror of the unnatural deed?
What strange offence, what aggravated sin?
They stand convicted—of a darker skin!
Barbarians, hold! the opprobrious commerce spare,
Respect *his* sacred image which they bear.

HANNAH MORE

Though dark and savage, ignorant and blind,
They claim the common privilege of kind;
Let Malice strip them of each other plea,
They still are men, and men should still be free.
Insulted Reason loathes the inverted trade—
Dire change! the agent is the purchase made;
Perplexed, the baffled Muse involves the tale;
Nature confounded, well may language fail!
The outraged Goddess with abhorrent eyes
Sees Man the traffic, Souls the merchandise!
    Plead not, in reason's palpable abuse,
Their sense of feeling callous and obtuse:
From heads to hearts lies Nature's plain appeal,
Though few can reason, all mankind can feel.
Though wit may boast a livelier dread of shame,
A loftier sense of wrong refinement claim,
Though polished manners may fresh wants invent,
And nice distinctions nicer souls torment;
Though these on finer spirits heavier fall,
Yet natural evils are the same to all.
Though wounds there are which reason's force may heal,
There needs no logic sure to make us feel.
The nerve, howe'er untutored, can sustain
A sharp, unutterable sense of pain;
As exquisitely fashioned in a slave,
As where unequal fate a sceptre gave.
Sense is as keen where Congo's sons preside,
As where proud Tiber rolls his classic tide.
Rhetoric or verse may point the feeling line,
They do not whet sensation, but define.
Did ever slave less feel the galling chain,
When Zeno proved there was no ill in pain?
Their miseries philosophic quirks deride,
Slaves grown in pangs disowned by Stoic pride.
    When the fierce Sun darts vertical his beams,
And thirst and hunger mix their wild extremes;
When the sharp iron wounds his inmost soul,
And his strained eyes in burning anguish roll;
Will the parched negro find, ere he expire,
No pain in hunger, and no heat in fire?
    For him, when fate his tortured frame destroys,
What hope of present fame, or future joys?
For *this*, have heroes shortened nature's date;
For *that*, have martyrs gladly met their fate;
But him, forlorn, no hero's pride sustains,
No martyr's blissful visions sooth his pains;
Sullen, he mingles with his kindred dust,
For he has learned to dread the Christian's trust;
To him what mercy can that Power display,

Whose servants murder, and whose sons betray?
Savage! thy venial error I deplore,
They are *not* Christians who infest thy shore.
　O thou sad spirit! whose preposterous yoke
The great deliverer Death, at length, has broke!
Released from misery, and escaped from care,
Go, meet that mercy men denied thee here.
In thy dark home, sure refuge of the oppressed,
The wicked vex not and the weary rest.
And, if some notions vague and undefined,
Of future terrors have assailed thy mind;
If such thy masters have presumed to teach,
As terrors only they are prone to preach;
(For should they paint eternal Mercy's reign,
Where were the oppressor's rod, the captive's chain?)
If, then, thy troubled soul has learned to dread
The dark unknown thy trembling footsteps tread;
On Him, who made thee what thou art, depend;
He, who withholds the means, accepts the end.
Not *thine* the reckoning dire of Light abused,
Knowledge disgraced, and Liberty misused;
On *thee* no awful judge incensed shall sit
For parts perverted, and dishonoured wit.
Where ignorance will be found the sorest plea,
How many learned and wise shall envy *thee*!
　And thou, White Savage! whether lust of gold,
Or lust of conquest, rule thee uncontrolled!
Hero, or robber!—by whatever name
Thou plead thy impious claim to wealth or fame;
Whether inferior mischiefs be thy boast,
A petty tyrant rifling Gambia's coast:
Or bolder carnage track thy crimson way,
Kings dispossessed, and Provinces thy prey;
Panting to tame wide earth's remotest bound;
All Cortez murdered, all Columbus found;
O'er plundered realms to reign, detested Lord,
Make millions wretched, and thyself abhorred;—
In Reason's eye, in Wisdom's fair account,
Your sum of glory boasts a like amount;
The means may differ, but the end's the same;
Conquest is pillage with a nobler name.
Who makes the sum of human blessings less,
Or sinks the stock of general happiness,
No solid fame shall grace, no true renown,
His life shall blazon, or his memory crown.
　Had those adventurous spirits who explore
Through ocean's trackless wastes, the far sought shore;
Whether of wealth insatiate, or of power,
Conquerors who waste, or ruffians who devour:

HANNAH MORE

Had these possessed, O Cook! thy gentle mind,
Thy love of arts, thy love of humankind;
Had these pursued thy mild and liberal plan,
Discoverers had not been a curse to man!
Then, blessed Philanthropy! thy social hands
Had linked dissevered worlds in brothers bands;
Careless, if colour, or if clime divide;
Then, loved, and loving, man had lived, and died.

    The purest wreaths which hang on glory's shrine,
For empires founded, peaceful Penn! are thine;
No blood-stained laurels crowned thy virtuous toil,
No slaughtered natives drenched thy fair-earned soil.
Still thy meek spirit in thy flock survives,
Consistent still, *their* doctrines rule their lives;
Thy followers only have effaced the shame
Inscribed by Slavery on the Christian name.

    Shall Britain, where the soul of Freedom reigns,
Forge chains for others she herself disdains?
Forbid it, Heaven! O let the nations know
The liberty she loves she will bestow;
Not to herself the glorious gift confined,
She spreads the blessing wide as humankind;
And, scorning narrow views of time and place,
Bids all be free in earth's extended space.

    What page of human annals can record
A deed so bright as human rights restored?
O may that god-like deed, that shining page,
Redeem our fame, and consecrate our age!

    And see, the cherub Mercy from above,
Descending softly quits the sphere of love!
On feeling hearts she sheds celestial dew,
And breathes her spirit o'er the enlightened few;
From soul to soul the spreading influence steals,
Till every breast the soft contagion feels.
She bears, exulting, to the burning shore
The loveliest office Angel ever bore;
To vindicate the power in Heaven adored,
To still the clank of chains, and sheathe the sword;
To cheer the mourner, and with soothing hands
From bursting hearts unbind the Oppressor's bands;
To raise the lustre of the Christian name,
And clear the foulest blot that dims its fame.

    As the mild Spirit hovers o'er the coast,
A fresher hue the withered landscape boast;
Her healing smiles the ruined scenes repair,
And blasted Nature wears a joyous air.
She spreads her blessed commission from above,
Stamped with the sacred characters of love;
She tears the banner stained with blood and tears,

And, Liberty! thy shining standard rears: HANNAH
As the bright ensign's glory she displays, MORE
See pale Oppression faints beneath the blaze!
The giant dies! no more his frown appals,
The chain untouched, drops off; the fetter falls.
Astonished echo tells the vocal shore,
Oppression's fallen, and Slavery is no more!
The dusky myriads crowd the sultry plain,
And hail that mercy long invoked in vain.
Victorious Power! she bursts their two-fold bands,
And Faith and Freedom spring from Mercy's hands.

(1788)

3 THE SORROWS OF YAMBA, OR,
   THE NEGRO WOMAN'S LAMENTATION

'In St. Lucie's distant isle,
   Still with Afric's love I burn;
Parted many a thousand mile,
   Never, never to return.

Come kind death! and give me rest,
   Yamba has no friend but thee;
Thou canst ease my throbbing breast,
   Thou canst set the Prisoner free.

Down my cheeks the tears are dripping,
   Broken is my heart with grief;
Mangled my poor flesh with whipping,
   Come kind death! and bring relief.

Born on Afric's Golden Coast,
   Once I was as blessed as you;
Parents tender I could boast,
   Husband dear, and children too.

Whity man he came from far,
   Sailing o'er the briny flood,
Who, with help of British Tar,
   Buys up human flesh and blood.

With the Baby at my breast
   (Other two were sleeping by)
In my Hut I sat at rest,
   With no thought of danger nigh.

From the Bush at even tide
   Rushed the fierce man-stealing Crew;
Seized the Children by my side,
   Seized the wretched Yamba too.

HANNAH MORE

Then for love of filthy Gold
   Straight they bore me to the Sea;
Crammed me down a Slave Ship's hold,
   Where were Hundreds stowed like me.

Naked on the Platform lying,
   Now we cross the tumbling wave;
Shrieking, sickening, fainting, dying.
   Deed of shame for Britons brave.

At the savage Captain's beck
   Now like Brutes they make us prance.
Smack the Cat about the Deck,
   And in scorn they bid us dance.

Nauseous horse-beans they bring nigh,
   Sick and sad we cannot eat;
Cat must cure the Sulks they cry,
   Down their throats we'll force the meat.

I in groaning passed the night,
   And did roll my aching head;
At the break of morning light,
   My poor Child was cold and dead.

Happy, happy, there she lies,
   Thou shalt feel the lash no more.
Thus full many a Negro dies
   Ere we reach the destined shore.

Thee, sweet infant, none shall sell,
   Thou hast gained a watery Grave;
Clean escaped the Tyrants fell,
   While thy mother lives a Slave.

Driven like Cattle to a fair,
   See they sell us young and old;
Child from Mother too they tear,
   All for love of filthy Gold.

I was sold to Massa hard,
   Some have Massas kind and good;
And again my back was scarred,
   Bad and stinted was my food.

Poor and wounded, faint and sick,
   All exposed to burning sky,
Massa bids me grass to pick,
   And I now am near to die.

HANNAH
MORE

What and if to death he send me,
    Savage murder though it be,
British Law shall ne'er befriend me,
    They protect not Slaves like me.'

Mourning thus my wretched state,
    (Ne'er may I forget the day)
Once in dusk of evening late
    Far from home I dared to stray;

Dared, alas! with impious haste
    Towards the roaring Sea to fly,
Death itself I longed to taste,
    Longed to cast me in and Die.

There I met upon the Strand
    English Missionary Good,
He had Bible book in hand,
    Which poor me no understood.

Led by pity from afar
    He had left his native ground;
Thus if some inflict a scar,
    Others fly to cure the wound.

Straight he pulled me from the shore,
    Bid me no self-murder do;
Talked of state when life is o'er,
    All from Bible good and true.

Then he led me to his Cot,
    Soothed and pitied all my woe;
Told me 'twas the Christian's lot
    Much to suffer here below.

Told me then of God's dear Son,
    (Strange and wondrous is the story;)
What sad wrong to him was done,
    Though he was the Lord of Glory.

Told me too, like one who knew him,
    (Can such love as this be true?)
How he died for them that slew him,
    Died for wretched Yamba too.

Freely he his mercy proffered,
    And to Sinners he was sent:
E'en to Massa pardon's offered:
    O if Massa would repent!

HANNAH MORE

Wicked deed full many a time
    Sinful Yamba too hath done;
But she wails to God her crime,
    But she trusts his only Son.

O ye slaves whom Massas beat,
    Ye are stained with guilt within;
As ye hope for mercy sweet,
    So forgive your Massas' sin.

And with grief when sinking low,
    Mark the Road that Yamba trod;
Think how all her pain and woe
    Brought the Captive home to God.

Now let Yamba too adore
    Gracious Heaven's mysterious Plan;
Now I'll count my mercies o'er,
    Flowing through the guilt of man.

Now I'll bless my cruel capture,
    (Hence I've known a Saviour's name)
Till my Grief is turned to Rapture,
    And I half forget the blame.

But though here a Convert rare
    Thanks her God for Grace divine,
Let not man the glory share,
    Sinner, still the guilt is thine.

Here an injured Slave forgives,
    There a Host for vengeance cry;
Here a single Yamba lives,
    There a thousand droop and die.

Duly now baptised am I
    By good Missionary Man:
Lord my nature purify
    As no outward water can!

All my former thoughts abhorred,
    Teach me now to pray and praise:
Joy and Glory in my Lord,
    Trust and serve him all my days.

Worn indeed with Grief and Pain,
    Death I now will welcome in:
O the Heavenly Prize to gain!
    O to escape the power of Sin!

HANNAH MORE

True of heart, and meek and lowly,
   Pure and blameless let me grow!
Holy may I be, for Holy,
   Is the place to which I go.

But though death this hour may find me,
   Still with Afric's love I burn,
(There I've left a spouse behind me)
   Still to native land I turn.

And when Yamba sinks in death,
   This my latest prayer shall be,
While I yield my parting breath,
   O that Afric might be free.

Cease, ye British Sons of murder!
   Cease from forging Afric's chain;
Mock your Saviour's name no further,
   Cease your savage lust of gain.

Ye that boast '*Ye rule the waves,*'
   Bid no Slave Ship soil the sea,
Ye that '*never will be slaves,*'
   Bid poor Afric's land be free.

Where ye gave to war its birth,
   Where your traders fixed their den,
There go publish '*Peace on Earth,*'
   Go proclaim '*good-will to men.*'

Where ye once have carried slaughter,
   Vice, and Slavery, — and Sin;
Seized on Husband, Wife, and Daughter,
   Let the Gospel enter in.

Thus where Yamba's native home,
   Humble Hut of Rushes stood,
Oh if there should chance to roam
   Some dear Missionary good;

Thou in Afric's distant land,
   Still shalt see the man I love;
Join him to the Christian band,
   Guide his Soul to Realms above.

There no Fiend again shall sever
   Those whom God hath joined and blessed:
There they dwell with Him for ever,
   There '*the weary are at rest.*'

(1795)

ANN YEARSLEY

ANN YEARSLEY (née CROMARTIE) (1752–1806)

She was christened on 15 July 1752 in Clifton Parish Church, the daughter of John and Ann Cromartie. She had little or no education and was taught to read by her brother. Her mother delivered milk and she followed suit. In June 1774 she married a labourer, John Yearsley. In 1784 Hannah More was shown some of her poems by her cook and together with Elizabeth Montagu organised a subscription volume which appeared as *Poems on several occasions*, London 1785. There were over a thousand subscribers and the work went through four editions by the following year. It had been agreed that Hannah More and Elizabeth Montagu would act as trustees of the profits of the book and in June 1785 £350 was invested to provide an annuity of £18. Yearsley thought differently, however, and an acrimonious dispute ensued, with Yearsley eventually obtaining the money to use as she saw fit. She later published *A second book of poems on various subjects*, London 1787, *Stanzas of woe*, London 1790, *Reflections on the death of Louis XVI*, Bristol 1793, *An elegy on Marie Antoinette of Austria*, Bath [1795?], *The rural lyre*, London 1796, and a novel, *The royal captives*, 4v. London 1796 for which she was paid £200. By early 1793 she had established a circulating library at 4 Hot Wells Crescent and received some assistance from Joseph Cottle, the bookseller, Ralph Griffiths, editor of the *Monthly Review*, and Thomas Beddoes, a local physician. Her health declined towards the end of the 1790s and her husband died in 1803. She probably moved to Melksham, Wiltshire at about this time, presumably to be near her son John who was a clothier at Trowbridge. She died at Melksham on 8 May 1806 and was buried at Clifton.

4   A POEM ON THE INHUMANITY OF THE SLAVE-TRADE

Bristol, thine heart hath throbbed to glory.—Slaves,
E'en Christian slaves, have shook their chains, and gazed
With wonder and amazement on thee. Hence
Ye grovelling souls, who think the term I give,
Of Christian slave, a paradox! to *you*
I do not turn, but leave you to conception
Narrow; with that be blessed, nor dare to stretch
Your shackled souls along the course of *Freedom*.

Yet, Bristol, list! nor deem Lactilla's soul
Lessened by distance; snatch her rustic thought,
Her crude ideas, from their panting state,
And let them fly in wide expansion; lend
Thine energy, so little understood
By the rude million, and I'll dare the strain
Of Heaven-born Liberty till Nature moves
Obedient to her voice. Alas! my friend,
Strong rapture dies within the soul, while Power
Drags on his bleeding victims. Custom, Law,
Ye blessings, and ye curses of mankind,
What evils do ye cause? We feel enslaved,
Yet move in your direction. Custom, thou

ANN YEARSLEY

Wilt preach up filial piety; thy sons
Will groan, and stare with impudence at Heaven,
As if they did abjure the act, where Sin
Sits full on Inhumanity; the church
They fill with mouthing, vaporous sighs and tears,
Which, like the guileful crocodile's, oft fall,
Nor fall, but at the cost of human bliss.

Custom, thou hast undone us! led us far
From God-like probity, from truth, and heaven.

But come, ye souls who feel for human woe,
Though dressed in savage guise! Approach, thou son,
Whose heart would shudder at a father's chains,
And melt o'er thy loved brother as he lies
Gasping in torment undeserved. Oh, sight
Horrid and insupportable! far worse
Than an immediate, an heroic death;
Yet to this sight I summon thee. Approach,
Thou slave of avarice, that canst see the maid
Weep o'er her inky fire! Spare me, thou God
Of all-indulgent Mercy, if I scorn
This gloomy wretch, and turn my tearful eye
To more enlightened beings. Yes, my tear
Shall hang on the green furze, like pearly dew
Upon the blossom of the morn. My song
Shall teach sad Philomel a louder note,
When Nature swells her woe. O'er suffering *man*
My soul with sorrow bends! Then come, ye few
Who feel a more than cold, material essence;
Here ye may vent your sighs, till the bleak North
Find its adherents aided.—Ah, no more!
The dingy youth comes on, sullen in chains;
He smiles on the rough sailor, who aloud
Strikes at the spacious heaven, the earth, the sea,
In breath too blasphemous; yet not to *him*
Blasphemous, for *he* dreads not either:—lost
In dear internal imagery, the soul
Of Indian Luco rises to his eyes,
Silent, not inexpressive: the strong beams
With eager wildness yet drink in the view
Of his too humble home, where he had left
His mourning father, and his Incilanda.

Curse on the toils spread by a Christian hand
To rob the Indian of his freedom! Curse
On him who from a bending parent steals
His dear support of age, his darling child;
Perhaps a son, or a *more tender* daughter,

ANN YEARSLEY

Who might have closed his eyelids, as the spark
Of life gently retired. Oh, thou poor world!
Thou fleeting good to individuals! see
How much for thee they care, how wide they ope
Their helpless arms to clasp thee; vapour thou!
More swift than passing wind! thou leav'st them nought
Amid the unreal scene, but a *scant grave.*

I know the crafty merchant will oppose
The plea of nature to my strain, and urge
His toils are for his children: the lost plea
Dissolves my soul—*but when I sell a son,
Thou God of nature, let it be my own!*

Behold that Christian! see what horrid joy
Lights up his moody features, while he grasps
The wished-for gold, purchase of human blood!
Away, thou seller of mankind! Bring on
Thy daughter to this market! bring thy wife!
Thine aged mother, though of little worth,
With all thy ruddy boys! Sell them, thou wretch,
And swell the price of Luco! Why that start?
Why gaze as thou wouldst fright me from my challenge
With look of anguish? Is it *Nature* strains
Thine heart-strings at the image? Yes, my charge
Is full against her, and she rends thy soul,
While I but strike upon thy pitiless ear,
Fearing her rights are violated.—Speak,
Astound the voice of *Justice*! bid thy tears
Melt the unpitying power, while thus she claims
The pledges of thy love. Oh, throw thine arm
Around thy little ones, and loudly plead
Thou *canst not* sell thy children.—Yet, beware
Lest Luco's groan be heard; should *that* prevail,
Justice will scorn thee in her turn, and hold
Thine *act* against thy *prayer.* Why clasp, she cries,
That blooming youth? Is it because thou lov'st him?
Why Luco was beloved: then wilt thou feel,
Thou selfish Christian, for thy private woe,
Yet cause such pangs to him that is a father?
Whence comes thy right to barter for thy fellows?
Where are thy statutes? Whose the iron pen
That gave thee precedent? Give me the seal
Of virtue, or religion, for thy trade,
And I will ne'er upbraid thee; but if force
Superior, hard brutality alone
Become thy boast, hence to some savage haunt,
Nor claim protection from my social laws.

ANN YEARSLEY

Luco is gone; his little brothers weep,
While his fond mother climbs the hoary rock
Whose point o'er-hangs the main. No Luco there,
No sound, save the hoarse billows. On she roves,
With love, fear, hope, holding alternate rage
In her too anxious bosom. Dreary main!
Thy murmurs now are riot, while she stands
Listening to every breeze, waiting the step
Of gentle Luco. Ah, return! return!
Too hapless mother, thy indulgent arms
Shall never clasp thy fettered Luco more.
See Incilanda! artless maid, my soul
Keeps pace with thee, and mourns. Now o'er the hill
She creeps, with timid foot, while Sol embrowns
The bosom of the isle, to where she left
Her faithful lover: here the well-known cave,
By Nature formed amid the rock, endears
The image of her Luco; here his pipe,
Formed of the polished cane, neglected lies,
No more to vibrate; here the useless dart,
The twanging bow, and the fierce panther's skin,
Salute the virgin's eye. But where is Luco?
He comes not down the steep, though he had vowed,
When the sun's beams at noon should sidelong gild
The cave's wide entrance, he would swift descend
To bless his Incilanda. Ten pale moons
Had glided by, since to his generous breast
He clasped the tender maid, and whispered love.

Oh, mutual sentiment! thou dangerous bliss!
So exquisite, that Heaven had been unjust
Had it bestowed less exquisite of ill;
When thou art held no more, thy pangs are deep,
Thy joys convulsive to the soul; yet all
Are meant to smooth the uneven road of life.

For Incilanda, Luco ranged the wild,
Holding her image to his panting heart;
For her he strained the bow, for her he stripped
The bird of beauteous plumage; happy hour,
When with these guiltless trophies he adorned
The brow of her he loved. Her gentle breast
With gratitude was filled, nor knew she aught
Of language strong enough to paint her soul,
Or ease the great emotion; whilst her eye
Pursued the generous Luco to the field,
And glowed with rapture at his wished return.

ANN YEARSLEY

Ah, sweet suspense! betwixt the mingled cares
Of friendship, love, and gratitude, so mixed,
That ev'n the soul may cheat herself.—Down, down,
Intruding Memory! bid thy struggles cease,
At this soft scene of innate war. What sounds
Break on her ear? She, starting, whispers 'Luco.'
Be still, fond maid; lift to the tardy step
Of leaden-footed woe. A father comes,
But not to seek his son, who from the deck
Had breathed a last adieu: no, he shuts out
The soft, fallacious gleam of hope, and turns
Within upon the mind: horrid and dark
Are his wild, unenlightened powers: no ray
Of *forced* philosophy to calm his soul,
But all the anarchy of wounded nature.

Now he arraigns his country's gods, who sit,
In his bright fancy, far beyond the hills,
Unriveting the chains of slaves: his heart
Beats quick with stubborn fury, while he doubts
Their justice to his child. Weeping old man,
Hate not a Christian God, whose record holds
Thine injured Luco's name. Frighted he starts,
Blasphemes the Deity, whose altars rise
Upon the Indian's helpless neck, and sinks,
Despising comfort, till by grief and age
His angry spirit is forced out. Oh, guide,
Ye angel-forms, this joyless shade to worlds
Where the poor *Indian*, with the *sage*, is proved
The work of a Creator. Pause not here,
Distracted maid! ah, leave the breathless form,
On whose cold cheek thy tears so swiftly fall,
Too unavailing! On this stone, she cries,
My Luco sat, and to the wandering stars
Pointed my eye, while from his gentle tongue
Fell old traditions of his country's woe.
Where now shall Incilanda seek him? Hence,
Defenceless mourner, ere the dreary night
Wrap thee in added horror. Oh, Despair,
How eagerly thou rend'st the heart! She pines
In anguish deep, and sullen: Luco's form
Pursues her, lives in restless thought, and chides
Soft consolation. Banished from his arms,
She seeks the cold embrace of death; her soul
Escapes in one sad sigh. Too hapless maid!
Yet happier far than he thou lov'dst; his tear,
His sigh, his groan avail not, for they plead
Most weakly with a Christian. Sink, thou wretch,
Whose act shall on the cheek of Albion's sons

ANN YEARSLEY

Throw Shame's red blush: thou, who hast frighted far
Those simple wretches from thy God, and taught
Their erring minds to mourn his partial love,
Profusely poured on thee; while they are left
Neglected to *thy* mercy. Thus deceived,
How doubly dark must be *their* road to death!

   Luco is borne around the neighbouring isles,
Losing the knowledge of his native shore
Amid the pathless wave; destined to plant
The sweet luxuriant cane. He strives to please,
Nor once complains, but greatly smothers grief.
His hands are blistered, and his feet are worn,
Till every stroke dealt by his mattock gives
Keen agony to life; while from his breast
The sigh arises, burthened with the name
Of Incilanda. Time inures the youth,
His limbs grow nervous, strained by willing toil;
And resignation, or a calm despair,
(Most useful either) lulls him to repose.

A Christian renegade, that from his soul
Abjures the tenets of our schools, nor dreads
A future punishment, nor hopes for mercy,
Had fled from England, to avoid those laws
Which must have made his life a retribution
To violated justice, and had gained,
By fawning guile, the confidence (ill placed)
Of Luco's master. O'er the slave he stands
With knotted whip, lest fainting nature shun
The talk too arduous, while his cruel soul,
Unnatural, ever feeds, with gross delight,
Upon his sufferings. Many slaves there were,
But none who could suppress the sigh, and bend,
So quietly as Luco: long he bore
The stripes, that from his manly bosom drew
The sanguine stream (too little prized); at length
Hope fled his soul, giving her struggles o'er,
And he resolved to die. The sun had reached
His zenith—pausing faintly, Luco stood,
Leaning upon his hoe, while memory brought,
In piteous imagery, his aged father,
His poor fond mother, and his faithful maid:
The mental group in wildest motion set
Fruitless imagination; fury, grief,
Alternate shame, the sense of insult, all
Conspire to aid the inward storm; yet words
Were no relief, he stood in silent woe.

ANN YEARSLEY

Gorgon, remorseless Christian, saw the slave
Stand musing, 'mid the ranks, and, stealing soft
Behind the studious Luco, struck his cheek
With a too-heavy whip, that reached his eye,
Making it dark for ever. Luco turned,
In strongest agony, and with his hoe
Struck the rude Christian on the forehead. Pride,
With hateful malice, seize on the Gorgon's soul,
By nature fierce; while Luco sought the beach,
And plunged beneath the wave; but near him lay
A planter's barge, whose seamen grasped his hair,
Dragging to life a wretch who wished to die.

   Rumour now spreads the tale, while Gorgon's breath
Envenomed, aids her blast: imputed crimes
Oppose the plea of Luco, till he scorns
Even a just defence, and stands prepared.
The planters, conscious that to fear alone
They owe their cruel power, resolve to blend
New torment with the pangs of death, and hold
Their victims high in dreadful view, to fright
The wretched number left. Luco is chained
To a huge tree, his fellow-slaves are ranged
To share the horrid sight; fuel is placed
In an increasing train, some paces back,
To kindle slowly, and approach the youth,
With more than native terror. See, it burns!
He gazes on the growing flame, and calls
For 'water, water!' The small boon's denied.
E'en Christians throng each other, to behold
The different alterations of his face,
As the hot death approaches. (Oh, shame, shame
Upon the followers of Jesus! shame
On him that dares avow a God!) He writhes,
While down his breast glide the unpitied tears,
And in their sockets strain their scorched balls.
'Burn, burn me quick! I cannot die!' he cries:
'Bring fire more close!' The planters heed him not,
But still prolonging Luco's torture, threat
Their trembling slaves around. His lips are dry,
His senses seem to quiver, e'er they quit
His frame for ever, rallying strong, then driven
From the tremendous conflict. Sigh no more
Is Luco's, his parched tongue is ever mute;
Yet in his soul his Incilanda stays,
Till both escape together. Turn, my muse,
From this sad scene; lead Bristol's milder soul
To where the solitary spirit roves,
Wrapped in the robe of innocence, to shades

ANN YEARSLEY

Where pity breathing in the gale, dissolves
The mind, when fancy paints such real woe.

   Now speak, ye Christians (who for gain enslave
A soul like Luco's, tearing her from joy
In life's short vale; and if there be a hell,
As ye believe, to *that* ye thrust her down,
A blind, involuntary victim), where
Is your true offence of religion? where
Your proofs of righteousness, when ye conceal
The knowledge of the Deity from those
Who would adore him *fervently*? Your God
Ye rob of worshippers, his altars keep
Unhailed, while driving from the sacred font
The eager slave, lest *he* should hope in *Jesus*.

   Is this your piety? Are these your laws,
Whereby the glory of the Godhead spreads
O'er barbarous climes? Ye hypocrites, disown
The Christian name, nor shame its cause: yet where
Shall souls like yours find welcome? Would the Turk,
Pagan, or wildest Arab, ope their arms
To gain such proselytes? No; he that owns
The name of Mussulman would start, and shun
Your worse than serpent touch; *he* frees his slave
Who turns to Mahomet. The Spaniard stands
Your brighter contrast; he condemns the youth
For ever to the mine; but ere the wretch
Sinks to the deep domain, the hand of Faith
Bathes his faint temples in the sacred stream,
Bidding his spirit hope. Briton, dost thou
Act up to this? If so, bring on thy slaves
To Calvary's mount, raise high their kindred souls
To him who died to save them: this alone
Will teach them calmly to obey thy rage,
And deem a life of misery but a day,
To long eternity. Ah, think how soon
Thine head shall on earth's dreary pillow lie,
With thy poor slaves, each silent, and unknown
To his once furious neighbour. Think how swift
The sands of time ebb out, for him and *thee*.
Why groans that Indian youth, in burning chains
Suspended o'er the beach? The labouring sun
Strikes from his full meridian on the slave
Whose arms are blistered by the heated iron,
Which still corroding, seeks the bone. What crime
Merits so dire a death? Another gasps
With strongest agony, while life declines
From recent amputation. Gracious God!

39

ANN YEARSLEY

Why thus in mercy let thy whirlwinds sleep
O'er a vile race of Christians, who profane
Thy glorious attributes? Sweep them from earth,
Or check their cruel power: the savage tribes
Are angels when compared to brutes like these.

   Advance, ye Christians, and oppose my strain:
Who dares condemn it? Prove from laws divine,
From deep philosophy, or social love,
That ye derive your privilege. I scorn
The cry of Avarice, or the trade that drains
A fellow-creature's blood: bid Commerce plead
Her public good, her nation's many wants,
Her sons thrown idly on the beach, forbade
To seize the image of their God and sell it:—
I'll hear her voice, and Virtue's hundred tongues
Shall sound against her. Hath our public good
Fell rapine for its basis? Must our wants
Find their supply in murder? Shall the sons
Of Commerce shivering stand, if not employed
Worse than the midnight robber? Curses fall
On the destructive system that shall need
Such base supports! Doth England need them? No;
Her laws, with prudence, hang the meagre thief
That from his neighbour steals a slender sum,
Though famine drove him on. O'er *him* the priest,
Beneath the fatal tree, laments the crime,
Approves the law, and bids him calmly die.
Say, doth this law, that dooms the thief, protect
The wretch who makes another's life his prey,
By hellish force to take it at his will?
Is this an English law, whose guidance fails
When crimes are swelled to magnitude so vast,
That *Justice* dare not scan them? Or does *Law*
Bid *Justice* an eternal distance keep
From England's great tribunal, when the slave
Calls loud on *Justice only*? Speak, ye few
Who fill Britannia's senate, and are deemed
The fathers of your country! Boast your laws,
Defend the *honour* of a land so fallen,
That Fame from every battlement is flown,
And Heathens start, even at a Christian's name.

   Hail, social love! true soul of *order*, hail!
Thy softest emanations, pity, grief,
Lively emotion, sudden joy, and pangs,
Too deep for language, are thy own: then rise,
Thou gentle angel! spread thy silken wings
O'er drowsy *man*, breathe in his *soul*, and give

ANN YEARSLEY

Her God-like powers thy animating force,
To banish Inhumanity. Oh, loose
The fetters of his mind, enlarge his views,
Break down for him the bound of avarice, lift
His feeble faculties beyond a world
To which he soon must prove a stranger! Spread
Before his ravished eye the varied tints
Of future glory; bid them live to *Fame,*
Whose banners wave for ever. Thus inspired,
All that is great, and good, and sweetly mild,
Shall fill his noble bosom. He shall melt,
Yea, by thy sympathy unseen, shall feel
Another's pang: for the lamenting maid
His heart shall heave a sigh; with the old slave
(Whose head is bent with sorrow) he shall cast
His eye back on the joys of youth, and say,
'Thou *once* couldst feel, as I do, love's pure bliss;
Parental fondness, and the dear returns
Of filial tenderness were thine, till torn
From the dissolving scene.'—Oh, social love,
Thou universal good, thou that canst fill
The vacuum of immensity, and live
In endless void! thou that in motion first
Set'st the long lazy atoms, by thy force
Quickly assimilating, and restrained
By strong attraction; touch the soul of man;
Subdue him; make a fellow-creature's woe
His own by heart-felt sympathy, whilst wealth
Is made subservient to his soft disease.

And when thou hast to high perfection wrought
This mighty work, say, *'such is Bristol's soul.'*

(1788)

ANNA LAETITIA BARBAULD (née AIKIN) (1743–1825)

She was born at Kibworth, Leicestershire on 20 June 1743, the only daughter and eldest child of John Aikin D.D. and Jane (Jennings). She was christened at Saint Ives, in Huntingdon on 6 July 1743. Her early education was described by her niece, Lucy Aikin, as 'entirely domestic, and principally conducted by her excellent mother'. Despite strong initial opposition from her father, she was allowed to learn modern languages, Latin and Greek, and was probably educated in the English classics as well since this was a significant feature of dissenting education. This may have been as a result of her father's move to Warrington in 1758 as tutor in languages and *belles lettres*, which would have brought the family into close contact with leading figures of the Midlands Enlightenment in an innovative pedagogical environment. She remained in Warrington for

ANNA LAETITIA BARBAULD

fifteen years and formed long friendships with some of her father's colleagues and their families, most notably Joseph Priestley and William Enfield. Her long-standing admiration for John Howard, the prison reformer, who was frequently in Warrington, probably dates from this period and there is some evidence that she might have considered marrying him. In 1773 she published *Poems*, which went through four editions in the same year, and with her brother, John Aikin, *Miscellaneous pieces in prose*, 1773. On first encountering her poems as a young girl, Mary Robinson 'read them with rapture; I thought them the most beautiful Poems I had ever seen, and considered the woman who could invent such poetry, as the most to be envied of human creatures' (*Memoirs*, i.102). In 1774 she married a former Warrington student, Rochemont Barbauld (1749–1808), and they settled in Palgrave, Suffolk, where they opened a school and he was minister to the dissenting congregation. In 1777, having no children of their own, they adopted Charles Rochemont Aikin (b. 1775), her brother's third son. During this period, she produced a series of educational works for children, *Lessons for children*, 1778–1779, *Hymns for children*, 1781. In September 1785 they gave up the school and toured France, returning to London in June 1786. By 1807 they had settled in Hampstead with Rochemont Barbauld securing another post as dissenting minister and she continuing to teach young children. However, he had probably been suffering from mental illness for some time, culminating in an incident of domestic violence in January 1808 and they separated in March. On 11 November 1808 he was found drowned in a river, with suicide suspected. She wrote a memoir of his life (*Monthly Repository*, iii (1808), 706–9). Following bereavement, she appears to have thrown herself into editorial work, and published *The British novelists*, 50v. London 1810, and *The female speaker*, London 1811. The following year she published a fierce attack on commerce and empire, *Eighteen hundred and eleven*, London 1812, which provoked the hostility of reviewers. Her remaining years were marred by the loss of her closest friends and she died in Stoke Newington on 9 March 1825.

Barbauld has sometimes been seen as a withdrawn and self-critical talent resembling Thomas Gray. As a poet, it is true she exercises classical restraint in restricted and chaste diction, and has clear links to Gray, Goldsmith and, to a lesser extent Pope. However, ideologically, she is much closer to the energetic republicanism which Thomson and Akenside were sometimes thought to embody. These two poets were certainly much in favour at Warrington Academy and Barbauld's first known poem, 'Corsica', written in 1769 and published in 1773, takes its lead from Thomson. She later edited Akenside's *The pleasures of imagination . . .*, London 1794. She retained a certain strain of fiery and defiant republicanism throughout her life and this certainly distances her from Gray and Goldsmith. With the advent of the French Revolution in 1789, followed shortly by renewed efforts in early 1790 to repeal the Test and Corporation Acts (which deprived Dissenters of certain religious and civic rights), like many Dissenters, she abandoned classical restraint in favour of an apocalyptic vision of the furthering of the Glorious Revolution of 1688, clearly linking events in France with the Repeal of the Test and Corporation Acts in England. Her *Address to the opposers of the repeal of the Corporation and Test Acts*, London 1790, is in many ways, a defence and continuation of Richard Price's *A discourse on the love of our country*, London 1789, which had provoked Edmund Burke to dizzy rage. Together with Helen Maria Williams' *Letters written in*

France, London 1790, it remains one of the most fervent and enthusiastic endorsements of the French Revolution, sketching deep analogies between the inspiring and sublime revolutions of nature and the Revolution in France (see **5n**). Not surprisingly, this line of thinking touched a raw nerve in Burke, who saw strong links between the enterprising and industrious talents of the Dissenters and the French 'ethics of vanity', both attempting 'a regeneration of the moral constitution of man' but turning into 'revolution harpies' in the process. Burke succinctly expressed his objections to the Dissenters' project of inquiry in his *Speech on the petition of the Unitarians* (1792): 'The foundations on which obedience to governments is founded are not to be constantly discussed . . . Otherwise we should dispute all the points of morality, before we can punish a murderer, a robber, and adulterer; we should analyze all society.' Indignation and the apocalyptic strain in Barbauld's thinking resurfaced in *Eighteen hundred and eleven*, London 1812, with its vision of London in ruins. She was equally defiant (and generous) in her remark to Crabb Robinson in 1814 that Helen Maria Williams would be quite welcome to stay with her. (Williams had by this time long been held a traitor, had a poor moral reputation, and was completely unacceptable to large sections of English society.) The *Literary Gazette* (24 September 1825, 611), in reviewing *The works*, 2v. London 1825, drew attention to the fact that Barbauld's 'fiery democracy sometimes carried her almost the length of profanation'. All this and considerably more evidence point to the fact that she was much closer in spirit to the revolutionary fervour of the 1790s than her affinities to Gray and Goldsmith might suggest.

5   EPISTLE TO WILLIAM WILBERFORCE, ESQ. ON THE
    REJECTION OF THE BILL FOR ABOLISHING
    THE SLAVE TRADE

Cease, Wilberforce, to urge thy generous aim!
Thy Country knows the sin, and stands the shame!
The Preacher, Poet, Senator in vain
Has rattled in her sight the Negro's chain;
With his deep groans assailed her startled ear,
And rent the veil that hid his constant tear;
Forced her averted eyes his stripes to scan,
Beneath the bloody scourge laid bare the man,
Claimed Pity's tear, urged Conscience' strong control,
And flashed conviction on her shrinking soul.
The Muse too, soon awaked, with ready tongue
At Mercy's shrine applausive paeans rung;
And Freedom's eager sons, in vain foretold
A new Astrean reign, an age of gold:
She knows and she persists—Still Afric bleeds,
Unchecked, the human traffic still proceeds;
She stamps her infamy to future time,
And on her hardened forehead seals the crime.
   In vain, to thy white standard gathering round,
Wit, Worth, and Parts and Eloquence are found:
In vain, to push to birth thy great design,

ANNA LAETITIA BARBAULD

Contending chiefs, and hostile virtues join;
All, from conflicting ranks, of power possessed
To rouse, to melt, or to inform the breast.
Where seasoned tools of Avarice prevail,
A Nation's eloquence, combined, must fail:
Each flimsy sophistry by turns they try;
The plausive argument, the daring lie,
The artful gloss, that moral sense confounds,
The acknowledged thirst of gain that honour wounds:
Bane of ingenuous minds, the unfeeling sneer,
Which, sudden, turns to stone the falling tear:
They search assiduous, with inverted skill,
For forms of wrong, and precedents of ill;
With impious mockery wrest the sacred page,
And glean up crimes from each remoter age:
Wrung Nature's tortures, shuddering, while you tell,
From scoffing fiends burst forth the laugh of hell;
In Britain's senate, Misery's pangs give birth
To jests unseemly, and to horrid mirth—
Forbear!—thy virtues but provoke our doom,
And swell the account of vengeance yet to come;
For, not unmarked in Heaven's impartial plan,
Shall man, proud worm, condemn his fellow-man?
And injured Afric, by herself redressed,
Darts her own serpents at her Tyrant's breast.
Each vice, to minds depraved by bondage known,
With sure contagion fastens on his own;
In sickly languors melts his nerveless frame,
And blows to rage impetuous Passion's flame:
Fermenting swift, the fiery venom gains
The milky innocence of infant veins;
There swells the stubborn will, damps learning's fire,
The whirlwind wakes of uncontrolled desire,
Sears the young heart to images of woe,
And blasts the buds of Virtue as they blow.
   Lo! where reclined, pale Beauty courts the breeze,
Diffused on sofas of voluptuous ease;
With anxious awe, her mental train around,
Catch her faint whispers of half-uttered sound;
See her, in monstrous fellowship, unite
At once the Scythian, and the Sybarite;
Blending repugnant vices, misallied,
Which *frugal* nature purposed to divide;
See her, with indolence to fierceness joined,
Of body delicate, infirm of mind,
With languid tones imperious mandates urge;
With arm recumbent wield the household scourge;
And with unruffled mien, and placid sounds,
Contriving torture, and inflicting wounds.

ANNA LAETITA BARBAULD

Nor, in their palmy walks and spicy groves,
The form benign of rural Pleasure roves;
No milk-maid's song, or hum of village talk,
Soothes the lone Poet in his evening walk:
No willing arm the flail unwearied plies,
Where the mixed sounds of cheerful labour rise;
No blooming maids, and frolic swains are seen
To pay gay homage to their harvest queen:
No heart-expanding scenes their eyes must prove
Of thriving industry, and faithful love:
But shrieks and yells disturb the balmy air,
Dumb sullen looks of woe announce despair,
And angry eyes through dusky features glare.
Far from the sounding lash the Muses fly,
And sensual riot drowns each finer joy.
   Nor less from the gay East, on essenced wings,
Breathing unnamed perfumes, Contagion springs;
The soft luxurious plague alike pervades
The marble palaces, and rural shades:
Hence, thronged Augusta builds her rosy bowers,
And decks in summer wreaths her smoky towers;
And hence, in summer bowers, Art's costly hand
Pours courtly splendours o'er the dazzled land:
The manners melt—One undistinguished blaze
O'erwhelms the sober pomp of elder days;
Corruption follows with gigantic stride,
And scarce vouchsafes his shameless front to hide:
The spreading leprosy taints every part,
Infects each limb, and sickens at the heart.
Simplicity! most dear of rural maids,
Weeping resigns her violated shades:
Stern Independence from his glebe retires,
And anxious Freedom eyes her drooping fires;
By foreign wealth are British morals changed,
And Afric's sons, and India's, smile avenged.
   For you, whose tempered ardour long has borne
Untired the labour, and unmoved the scorn;
In Virtue's fasti be inscribed your fame,
And uttered your's with Howard's honoured name,
Friends of the friendless—Hail, ye generous band!
Whose efforts yet arrest Heaven's lifted hand,
Around whose steady brows, in union bright,
The civic wreath, and Christian's palm unite:
Your merit stands, no greater and no less,
Without, or with the varnish of success;
But seek no more to break a Nation's fall,
For ye have saved yourselves—and that is all.
Succeeding times your struggles, and their fate,
With mingled shame and triumph shall relate,

ANNA
LAETITIA
BARBAULD

While faithful History, in her various page,
Marking the features of this motley age,
To shed a glory, and to fix a strain,
Tells how you strove, and that you strove in vain.

(1791)

MARY LEADBEATER (née SHACKLETON) (1758–1826)

She was born on 1 December 1758 at Ballitore, Co. Kildare, to Richard Shackleton (1726–1792) and his second wife Elizabeth (née Carleton), both Quakers. The family had a long connection with Edmund Burke. Her grandfather, Abraham Shackleton, had been Burke's schoolmaster and her father had been a fellow student at Trinity College Dublin. She also maintained a long correspondence with him, and wrote several poems to and about him. She visited Burke with her father in London in 1784 and later at Beaconsfield. In England she also visited Quakers in Selby, Yorkshire. In 1791 she married William Leadbeater, a former pupil of her father's, and they remained in Ballitore where she ran the village post office. She had begun writing poetry in the early 1770s and contributed to Joshua Edkins' anthology, *A collection of poems, mostly original*, 2v. Dublin 1789–1790. She published further poems in her *Extracts and original anecdotes for the improvement of youth*, Dublin 1794. Her *Poems*, Dublin 1808, was her last collection of verse and much of her work still remains in manuscript with important collections in the National Library of Ireland, the Royal Irish Academy, Newbridge County Library and several other repositories. Other important manuscripts exist, notably her diary (45v.), essays and extensive correspondence (which included George Crabbe and Maria Edgeworth).

She and her husband remained in Ballitore and lived through the Irish rebellion and its suppression of 1798, witnessing some of the atrocities and in considerable danger themselves. She wrote a history of Ballitore covering the period 1766–1823, *Annals of Ballitore*, 4v. Religious Society of Friends, Dublin Mss, posthumously published as *The Leadbeater papers*, 2v. London 1862) which includes an important eye-witness account of the political violence of 1798. She also published important prose works preserving various Irish customs, *Cottage dialogues among the Irish peasantry*, Dublin 1811, *Tales for cottagers*, Dublin 1814, *Cottage biography, being a collection of lives of the Irish peasantry*, Dublin 1822. She also published a memoir of her parents and a history of the Quakers in Ireland. She died at Ballitore on 27 June 1826 and was buried there in the Quaker graveyard.

6 THE TRIUMPH OF TERROR

MARY LEADBEATER

On the morning in which Ballitore was given up to the military, the life of an old man was attacked: he was rescued by his daughter: but epileptic fits were the consequences of the shock which she received, and which caused her untimely death.

The morning, unconscious of horrors, arose,
   The whispering Zephyr breathed soft through the shade;
And Nature, awakened from balmy repose,
   Her charms all bespangled with dew-drops displayed.

But hark! in the vale so secluded and sweet,
   The cries of destruction and misery blend;
And 'mid the green boughs, once of peace the retreat,
   The pitiless flames, winged with vengeance, ascend.

Oh what wrought this change? 'twas a people misled
   In deeds of rebellion and strife to engage:—
Yet listen to mercy;—the guilty are fled;
   Oh let not the guiltless fall victims to rage!

'Oh stay thy hand, soldier,—Oh pity my sire,
   And from his hoar head turn thy weapon aside;
Or, if thou a sacrifice seek to thine ire,
   Then deep in my breast let thy weapon be died!'

Filial Piety pleaded;—the soldier withdrew;
   And Ferdinand rose, while his beating heart glowed:
Then swift to his daughter's fond bosom he flew,
   For now to each other existence they owed.

But ah! that fond bosom had agony seized,
   With a gripe too severe e'en for Hope to unbind;
And what though the tumults of war were appeased,
   The fatal impression still dwelt on her mind.

'Twas then that the triumph of Terror began,
   And youth's sprightly grace from that moment decayed:
Her eyes lost their lustre; and withered and wan
   Was that cheek on which Health once in dimples had played.

Her delicate nerves by convulsions were strained,
   Her eye-balls all haggard so wildly would rove;
Yet Reason unshaken her empire maintained,
   Undiminished the duties of filial love.

To cheer the lone couch where her parent was laid,
   When sickness oppressed him, each effort she tried;
To cheer his lone cot, and his labours to aid,
   His food and his raiment her cares would provide.

MARY LEADBEATER

In this pious act to the streamlet she came,
    To prepare coarse viands which nature required;
When sudden distemper assailed her worn frame,
    And 'mid stifling waters poor Polly expired!

Fair maids of the valley, ye mourned for her woes,
    To you may the wretched with confidence come:
Down your cheek the soft current of tenderness flows,
    And Pity your bosoms has claimed for her home.

                                              (Wr. 1798, pub. 1808)

7   THE SUMMER-MORNING'S DESTRUCTION

Now falls the thick-descending rain,
    Where late the hostile squadron stood:
Ye showers, ye have not washed the stain
    Of lost Horatio's precious blood.

The earth, which drank his blood so dear,
    The earth his murder will not hide,
And torn Maria's streaming tear:—
    O shall those tears be ever dried?

The tender pledges of their love
    In life's first dawn feel sorrow's smart;
And, whilst a parent's loss they prove,
    Keen anguish wrings the infant heart.

Her trumpet dire Bellona blows;
    The echoing hills repeat the sound:
With blood the blighted valley flows,
    And Death and Horror rage around.

Ah where is now the peaceful scene,
    Where the soft Muse attuned her lay;
The tranquil bower, the cheerful green,
    The rural sports at closing day?

The bowers were wrapped in ruthless fires,
    Prone on their fields the peasants bled:
The Muses dropped their golden lyres,
    And from the scene of slaughter fled.

Yet ere they bled, one sacred tear,
    Horatio, on thy grave must fall:
To thee the Muse's song was dear;
    Thy soul awoke at Pity's call.

MARY
LEADBEATER

Thine was the voice, whose cheering sound
   Spoke comfort to the couch of pain:—
And were these gentle accents found
   To plead for life—and plead in vain?

High flashed the brandished swords in air;
   Brave, though unarmed, their victim stood:
Descending deaths remorseless tear
   That breast, which thirsted not for blood.

O hide the melancholy hour;
   O veil it deep in shades of night:
Yet the broad sun displayed its power,
   And shone in morning-glories bright.

Sweet smiled the war-devoted vale,
   In summer's radiant robes arrayed:
How soon did sorrow load the gale!
   How soon did every beauty fade!

Where are thy simple village pleasures,
   Sweet employments, guiltless leisures?—
Where are thy joys, which charmed when o'er?
   Fled are thy joys, O Ballitore!

                  (Wr. 1798, pub. 1808)

8   THE RUINED COTTAGE

Ye trees, does your foliage delay,
   Refusing to veil with its shade
That spot—once so cheerful and gay,
   That cottage—in ruin now laid?

While others arise on the plain,
   These walls in sad silence repose;
As never expecting again
   Such social delights to enclose.

Fair decency, cheerful content,
   By industry honest were won:
Here quiet his days Owen spent,
   And counted his blessings his own.

His forge knew no weapons of blood,
   Devoted to peaceful employ;
The stranger partook of his food,
   Nor want chilled the bosom of joy.

MARY
LEADBEATER

Yet, torn from his babes, and his home,
  From his consort so fond and so fair,
He must change, for a prison's dark gloom,
  This balmy, salubrious air.

Her infant new-born at her breast,
  His Doro beheld him depart;
She sunk, with her sorrows oppressed,
  (Ah more—thou must ten times more smart!)

'And O if the lashes', she cried,
  'My Owen be forced to endure,
With his blood if the scourges be died,
  His life will sink under it sure!'

See her Owen returning again,
  His neighbours all smiling around,
His innocence free from a stain,
  And no lash has inflicted a wound!

How changed the glad prospect, how soon!
  See the clouds of Rebellion arise!
The prison had then been a boon
  Most grateful to Owen's sad eyes.

What, though from the maddening train,
  As soon as he might he retired;
In his cottage resolved to remain,
  While innocence courage inspired!

But innocence cannot avail,
  When danger like this is so nigh:
This Doro, all weeping and pale,
  Revolved, and implored him to fly.

For see, breathing vengeance and dread,
  The disciplined armies appear;
The bands so tumultuous are fled,
  And the cannon's dire thunder they hear!

But resolved in his cottage to stay,
  In his cottage mild Owen they found;
Like furies they seize on their prey,
  And his bosom receives the death wound.

The firebrands his dwelling invade,
  The smoke—it ascends to the sky;
There innocence injured may plead!
  There heard is the sufferer's cry!

MARY LEADBEATER

Then Doro, her infants around,
   Beheld her loved home wrapped in fire;
They heard the explosion's dread sound,
   And in agony called on their sire.

Her stores by hard industry gained,
   To rapine and flames were a prey:
But ah—if her Owen remained
   Of how little value are they!

She darts through the furious crowd,
   Resolving his fate to explore:
She calls on her Owen aloud;—
   She sees him—all bathed in his gore!

Oh then, on his corse as she lay,
   Her babe all unconscious beside,
In vain she invoked the cold clay;
   Her Owen no longer replied.

The warriors, reproached by her moans,
   Their bosoms all poisoned with strife,
With insults reply to her groans,
   And threaten her innocent life.

Oh what was her life in that hour!—
   The load she had gladly resigned;
Nor insults, nor threats could have power
   To quell the fierce pangs of her mind.

She lives for her fatherless train,
   She lives, though her comfort is dead.
Chill poverty's gripe to sustain,
   And strive for a morsel of bread.

Humanity weeps at the tale;
   Yet frequent such scenes will appear,
Till Concord's soft voice shall prevail,
   Which angels delighted will hear.

(Wr. 1798, pub. 1808)

MARY ROBINSON (née DARBY) (1758–1800)

She was born on 27 November 1758 at College Green, Bristol, the daughter of Captain John Darby and Maria (née Seys). She was initially educated at the school run by Hannah More's sisters in Trinity Street, Bristol, and later at various schools in London. She married Thomas Robinson on 12 April 1774 at the age of fifteen. A daughter, Mary Elizabeth, was born on 18 November 1774. The following year her husband was arrested for debt and she spent ten months in prison with him where she began to write verse. Two early collections, *Poems*, London 1775, and *Captivity, a poem. And Celadon and Lydia, a tale*, London [1777], give little indication of her later development. At this time she also began to act and appeared as Juliet at Drury Lane in December 1776. Playing the role of Perdita in *The winter's tale*, she attracted the attentions of the Prince of Wales and became his mistress. He discarded her after about a year and she demanded £25,000 for the return of his letters. She eventually settled for £5,000 and in 1782 Charles James Fox secured a further annuity of £500 for her. In 1782 she formed a liaison with Colonel Banastre Charleton, an army officer, which lasted, with a number of separations, until 1798 when he married an heiress. In 1788 she began to contribute to the Della Cruscan poetry magazines, *The World* and *The Oracle*, under the signatures 'Laura' and 'Laura Maria' and this seems to have opened up new avenues and areas to her, particularly in the investiture of personification with identifiable human characteristics. Her next collections register an important stage on the way to later Romantic verse. Her *Poems*, 2v. London 1791–1793, and *Sight, the cavern of woe, and solitude. Poems*, London 1793, extend the eighteenth-century ode on such subjects as melancholy, despair, genius and nightingales into sustained treatments with the self at the centre yet always in interaction with clearly identifiable objects. Under the pressure of newly emerged and much more personal subject matter, such as maniacs, abandoned women, the figures of Chatterton and Werther, personification in the ode gradually breaks down as emblems turn human. At the same time, Robinson's verse exhibits important and different relations to society from those of Blake, Wordsworth and Coleridge, and still retains links with eighteenth-century satire. This simultaneous push towards human figures (often outcasts) and retention of satirical modes of thinking distinguishes her from mainstream Romanticism, and links her more closely to Robert Southey. Two other publications at this time, *Ainsi va le monde*, London 1790, and *Modern manners, a poem. In two cantos*, London 1793, demonstrate her lingering debts to the Della Cruscans and her satirical social concerns.

Often in financial difficulty, despite the Prince of Wales' settlement and the annuity, she turned to novel writing and published a series of profitable novels which have attracted almost no critical attention, although several of them examine important themes and ideas of the 1790s: *Vacenza*, 2v. London 1792, *The widow* 2v. London 1794, *Hubert de Seyrac*, 3v. London 1796, *Angelina*, 3v. London 1796, *Walsingham*, 4v. London 1797, *The false friend*, 4v. London 1799, and *The natural daughter*, 2v. London 1799. Under the name of Anne Frances Randall, she also published an important feminist tract, *A letter to the women of England, on the injustice of mental subordination*, London 1799, and a collection of sonnets, *Sappho and Phaon . . . with thoughts on poetical subjects, and anecdotes of the Grecian poetess*, London 1796.

From 1798 to 1800 she became a regular contributor of poems to *The*

Morning Post, alongside Southey and Coleridge. The full extent of her contributions is not widely available and remains unpublished, although there are at least two lists which have been compiled, by Judith Pascoe in America and Martin J. Levy in Britain. As with her earlier Della Cruscan contributions, she used various pseudonyms: 'Laura', 'Laura Maria', 'Lesbia', 'Oberon', 'Tabitha Bramble', 'Titania', and so on. Some of this verse was collected by her daughter and published in the *Memoirs of the late Mrs Robinson, written by herself. With some posthumous pieces* (ed. Maria Elizabeth Robinson), 4v. London 1801, and *The wild wreath* (ed. Maria Eliza Robinson), London 1804, with a more extensive, though still incomplete selection appearing in *The poetical works* (ed. Maria Elizabeth Robinson), 3v. London 1806.

Her *Lyrical tales*, London 1800, is closer to Southey's humanitarian concerns and subject matter at this time than to Wordsworth's figures in *Lyrical ballads* and also contains important, technically innovative poems such as 'The haunted beach'. (Together with the now forgotten Frank Sayers, Robinson's technical virtuosity and variety have largely been ignored, although they were widely recognised at the time.) In her novels and the feminist tract, she is much closer to the Godwin circle and the radicalism of the 1790s than her reputation as an actress and mistress would suggest. Similarly, the later poetry of the *Lyrical tales* is a catalogue of outcast marginalised figures—widows, fugitives, negroes, orphans— far removed from the catalogue of corruptions of London society she documented in 'January 1795', 'Stanzas' and other poems. She died on 26 December 1800 at Englefield Green where she was buried on 31 December, with William Godwin one of the few mourners who attended her funeral.

9   THE MANIAC

    Ah! what art thou, whose eye-balls roll
    Like *Heralds* of the wandering soul,
While down thy cheek the scalding torrents flow?
    Why does that agonizing shriek
    The mind's unpitied anguish speak!—
O tell me, Thing Forlorn! and let me share thy woe.

    Why dost thou rend thy matted hair,
    And beat thy burning bosom bare?
Why is thy lip so parched? thy groan so deep?
    Why dost thou fly from cheerful light,
    And seek in caverns, mid-day night,
And cherish thoughts untold, and banish gentle sleep?

    Why dost thou from thy scanty bed
    Tear the rude straw to crown thy head,
And nod with ghastly smile, and wildly sing?
    While down thy pale distorted face,
    The crystal drops each other chase,
As though thy brain were drowned in one eternal Spring?

MARY ROBINSON

Why dost thou climb yon craggy steep,
  That frowns upon the clamorous deep,
And howl, responsive to the waves below?
    Or on the margin of the rock,
    Thy Sovereign Ore exulting mock,
And waste the freezing night in pacing to and fro?

Why dost thou strip the fairest bowers,
  To dress thy scowling brow with flowers,
And fling thy tattered garment to the wind?
    Why madly dart from cave to cave,
    Now laugh and sing, then weep and rave,
And round thy naked limbs fantastic fragments bind?

Why dost thou drink the midnight dew,
  Slow trickling from the baneful Yew,
Stretched on a pallet of sepulchral stone;
    While, in her solitary tower,
    The *Minstrel of the witching hour*
Sits half congealed with fear, to hear thy dismal moan?

Thy form upon the cold earth cast,
  Now grown familiar with the blast,
Defies the biting Frost and scorching Sun:
    All Seasons are alike to thee;
    Thy sense, unchained by Destiny,
Resists, with dauntless pride, all miseries but one!

Fix not thy steadfast gaze on me,
  Shrunk atom of Mortality!
Nor freeze my blood with thy distracted groan;
    Ah! quickly turn those eyes away,
    They fill my soul with dire dismay!
For dead and dark they seem, and almost chilled to Stone!

Yet, if thy precious senses stray,
  Where Reason scorns to lend a ray,
Or if Despair supreme usurps her throne,
    Oh! let me all thy sorrows know;
    With thine my mingling tear shall flow,
And I will share thy pangs, and make thy griefs my own.

Hath Love unlocked thy feeling breast,
  And stolen from thence the balm of rest?
Then far away, on purple pinions borne,
    Left only keen *regret* behind,
    To tear with poisoned fangs thy mind,
While barbarous Memory lives, and bids thee hopeless mourn?

MARY ROBINSON

   Does Fancy, to thy straining arms,
   Give the false Nymph in all her charms,
And with her airy voice beguile thee so,
   That Sorrow seems to pass away,
   Till the blithe harbinger of day
Awakes thee from thy dream, and yields thee back to woe?

   Say, have the bonds of Friendship failed,
   Or jealous pangs thy mind assailed;
While black Ingratitude, with rancorous tooth,
   Pierced the fine fibres of thy heart,
   And festering every sensate part,
Dimmed with contagious breath, the crimson glow of youth?

   Or has stern Fate, with ruthless hand,
   Dashed on some wild untrodden strand,
Thy little Bark, with all thy fortunes fraught;
   While thou didst watch the stormy night
   Upon some black rock's fearful height,
Till thy hot brain consumed with desolating Thought?

   Ah! Wretch forlorn, perchance thy breast,
   By the cold fangs of Avarice pressed,
Grew hard and torpid by her touch profane;
   Till Famine pinched thee to the bone,
   And mental torture made thee own
That thing the most accursed, who drags her endless chain?

   Or say, does flushed Ambition's wing
   Around thy feverish temples fling
Dire incense, smoking from the ensanguined plain,
   That drained from bleeding warriors hearts,
   Swift to thy shattered sense imparts
The Victor's savage joy, that thrills through every vein?

   Does not the murky gloom of night
   Give to thy view some murderous Sprite,
Whose poniard gleams along thy cell forlorn;
   And when the Sun expands his ray,
   Dost thou not shun the jocund day,
And mutter curses deep, and *hate* the ruddy Morn?

   And yet the Morn on rosy wing
   Could once to thee its raptures bring,
And Mirth's enlivening song delight thine ear!
   While Hope thin eye-lids could unclose,
   From the sweet slumbers of repose,
To tell thee Love's gay throng of tender joys were near!

MARY
ROBINSON

Or hast thou stung with poignant smart,
The Orphan's and the Widow's heart,
And plunged them in cold Poverty's abyss;
 While Conscience, like a Vulture stole,
 To feed upon they tortured soul,
And tear each barbarous Sense from transitory Bliss?

Or hast thou seen some gentle Maid,
 By thy deluding voice betrayed,
Fade like a flower, slow withering with remorse?
 And didst thou then refuse to save
 Thy Victim from an early grave,
Till at thy feet she lay, a pale and ghastly Corse?

Oh! tell me, tell me all thy pain;
Pour to mine ear thy frenzied strain,
And I will share thy pangs, and soothe thy woes!
 Poor Maniac! I will dry thy tears,
 And bathe thy wounds, and calm thy fears,
And with soft Pity's balm enchant thee to repose.

(1793)

10 THE LASCAR

PART FIRST

I

'Another day, Ah! me, a day
 Of dreary Sorrow is begun!
And still I loath the tempered ray,
 And still I hate the sickly Sun!
Far from my Native Indian shore,
I hear our wretched race deplore;
I mark the smile of taunting Scorn,
And curse the hour, when I was born!
I weep, but no one gently tries
To stop my tear, or check my sighs;
For, while my heart beats mournfully,
Dear Indian home, I sigh for Thee!

II

'Since, gaudy Sun! I see no more
 Thy hottest glory gild the day;
Since, severed from my burning shore,
 I waste the vapid hours away;
O! darkness come! come, deepest gloom!
Shroud the young Summer's opening bloom;
Burn, tempered Orb, with fiercer beams
This northern world! and drink the streams

That through the fertile valleys glide
To bathe the feasted Fiends of Pride!
Or, hence, broad Sun! extinguished be!
For endless night encircles Me!

III

'What is, to me, the City gay?
  And what, the board profusely spread?
I have no home, no rich array,
  No spicy feast, no downy bed!
I, with the dogs am doomed to eat,
To perish in the peopled street,
To drink the tear of deep despair;
The scoff and scorn of fools to bear!
I sleep upon a bed of stone,
I pace the meadows, wild—alone!
And if I curse my fate severe,
Some Christian Savage mocks my tear!

IV

'Shut out the Sun, O! pitying Night!
  Make the wide world my silent tomb!
O'ershade this northern, sickly light,
  And shroud me, in eternal gloom!
My Indian plains, now smiling glow,
There stands my Parent's hovel low,
And there the towering aloes rise
And fling their perfumes to the skies!
There the broad palm Trees covert lend,
There Sun and Shade delicious blend;
But here, amid the blunted ray,
Cold shadows hourly cross my way!

V

'Was it for this, that on the main
  I met the tempest fierce and strong,
And steering o'er the liquid plain,
  Still onward, pressed the waves among?
Was it for this, the Lascar brave
Toiled, like a wretched Indian Slave;
Preserved your treasures by his toil,
And sighed to greet this fertile soil?
Was it for this, to beg, to die,
Where plenty smiles, and where the Sky
Sheds cooling airs; while feverish pain,
Maddens the famished Lascar's brain?

VI

'Oft, I the stately Camel led,
  And sung the short-houred night away;
And oft, upon the top-mast's head,
  Hailed the red Eye of coming day.
The Tanyan's back my mother bore;
And oft the wavy Ganges' roar
Lulled her to rest, as on she past—
'Mid the hot sands and burning blast!
And oft beneath the Banyan tree
She sate and fondly nourished me;
And while the noontide hour past slow,
I felt her breast with kindness glow.

VII

'Where'er I turn my sleepless eyes,
  No cheek so dark as mine, I see;
For Europe's Suns, with softer dyes
  Mark Europe's favoured progeny!
Low is my stature, black my hair,
The emblem of my Soul's despair!
My voice no dulcet cadence flings,
To touch soft pity's throbbing strings!
Then wherefore cruel Briton, say,
Compel my aching heart to stay?
To-morrow's Sun—may rise, to see—
The famished Lascar, blessed as thee!'

VIII

The morn had scarcely shed its rays
  When, from the City's din he ran;
For he had fasted, four long days,
  And faint his Pilgrimage began!
The Lascar, now, without a friend,—
Up the steep hill did slow ascend;
Now o'er the flowery meadows stole,
While pain, and hunger, pinched his Soul;
And now his feverish lip was dried,
And burning tears his thirst supplied,
And, ere he saw the Evening close,
Far off, the City dimly rose!

IX

Again the Summer Sun flamed high
  The plains were golden, far and wide;
And fervid was the cloudless sky,
  And slow the breezes seemed to glide:
The gossamer, on briar and spray,
Shone silvery in the solar ray;

MARY
ROBINSON

And sparkling dew-drops, falling round
Spangled the hot and thirsty ground;
The insect myriads, hummed their tune
To greet the coming hour of noon,
While the poor Lascar Boy, in haste,
Flew, frantic, o'er the sultry waste.

X

And whither could the wanderer go?
  Who would receive a stranger poor?
Who, when the blasts of night should blow,
  Would ope to him the friendly door?
Alone, amid the race of man,
The sad, the fearful alien ran!
None would an Indian wanderer bless;
None greet him with fond caress;
None feed him, though with hunger keen
He at the Lordly gate were seen,
Prostrate, and humbly forced to crave
A shelter, for an Indian Slave.

XI

The noon-tide Sun, now flaming wide,
  No cloud its fierce beam shadowed o'er,
But what could worse to him betide
  Than begging, at the proud man's door?
For closed and lofty was the gate,
And there, in all the pride of State,
A surly Porter turned the key,
A man of sullen soul was he—
His brow was fair; but in his eye
Sat pampered scorn, and tyranny;
And, near him, a fierce mastiff stood,
Eager to bathe his fangs in blood.

XII

The weary Lascar turned away,
  For trembling fear his heart subdued,
And down his cheek the tear would stray,
  Though burning anguish drank his blood!
The angry Mastiff snarled, as he
Turned from the house of luxury;
The sultry hour was long, and high
The broad-sun flamed athwart the sky—
But still a throbbing hope possessed
The Indian wanderer's feverish breast,
When from the distant dell a sound
Of swelling music echoed round.

XIII

It was the church-bell's merry peal;
   And now a pleasant house he viewed:
And now his heart began to feel
   As though, it were not quite subdued!
No lofty dome, shewed loftier state,
No pampered Porter watched the gate,
No Mastiff, like a tyrant stood,
Eager to scatter human blood;
Yet the poor Indian wanderer found,
E'en where Religion smiled around—
That tears had little power to speak
When trembling, on a sable cheek!

XIV

With keen reproach, and menace rude,
   The Lascar Boy away was sent;
And now again he seemed subdued,
   And his soul sickened, as he went.
Now, on the river's bank he stood;
Now, drank the cool refreshing flood;
Again his fainting heart beat high;
Again he raised his languid eye;
Then, from the upland's sultry side,
Looked back, forgave the wretch, and sighed!
While the proud Pastor bent his way
To preach of Charity—and Pray!

PART SECOND

I

The Lascar Boy still journeyed on,
   For the hot Sun, he well could bear,
And now the burning hour was gone,
   And Evening came, with softer air!
The breezes kissed his sable breast,
While his scorched feet the cold dew pressed;
The waving flowers soft tears displayed,
And songs of rapture filled the glade;
The South-wind quivered, o'er the stream
Reflecting back the rosy beam,
While, as the purpling twilight closed,
On a turf bed—the Boy reposed!

II

And now, in fancy's airy dream,
   The Lascar Boy his Mother spied;
And, from her breast, a crimson stream
   Slow trickled down her beating side:

And now he heard her wild, complain,
As loud she shrieked—but shrieked in vain!
And now she sunk upon the ground,
The red stream trickling from her wound,
And near her feet a murderer stood,
His glittering poniard tipped with blood!
And now, 'farewell, my son!' she cried,
Then closed her fainting eyes—and died!

        III
The Indian Wanderer, waking, gazed
  With grief, and pain, and horror wild;
And though his feverish brain was crazed,
  He raised his eyes to Heaven, and smiled!
And now the stars were twinkling clear,
And the blind Bat was whirling near;
And the lone Owlet shrieked, while He
Still sate beneath a sheltering tree;
And now the fierce-toned midnight blast
Across the wide heath, howling past,
When a long cavalcade he spied
By torch-light near the river's side.

        IV
He rose, and hastening swiftly on,
  Called loudly to the Sumptuous train,—
But soon the cavalcade was gone—
  And darkness wrapped the scene again.
He followed still the distant sound;
He saw the lightning flashing round;
He heard the crashing thunder roar;
He felt the whelming torrents pour;
And, now beneath a sheltering wood
He listened to the tumbling flood—
And now, with faltering, feeble breath,
The famished Lascar, prayed for Death.

        V
And now the flood began to rise
  And foaming rushed along the vale;
The Lascar watched, with steadfast eyes,
  The flash descending quick and pale;
And now again the cavalcade
Passed slowly near the upland glade;—
But He was dark, and dark the scene,
The torches long extinct had been;
He called, but, in the stormy hour,
His feeble voice had lost its power,
Till, near a tree, beside the flood,
A night-bewildered Traveller stood.

VI

The Lascar now with transport ran
   'Stop! stop!' he cried—with accents bold;
The Traveller was a fearful man—
   And next his life he prized his gold!—
He heard the wanderer madly cry;
He heard his footsteps following nigh;
He nothing saw, while onward pressed,
Black as the sky, the Indian's breast;
Till his firm grasp he felt, while cold
Down his pale cheek the big drop rolled;
Then, struggling to be free, he gave—
A deep wound to the Lascar Slave.

VII

And now he groaned, by pain oppressed,
   And now crept onward, sad and slow:
And while he hid his bleeding breast,
   He feebly poured the plaint of woe!
'What have I done?' the Lascar cried—
'That Heaven to me the power denied
To touch the soul of man, and share
A brother's love, a brother's care;
Why is this dingy form decreed
To bear oppression's scourge and bleed?—
Is there a God, in yon dark Heaven,
And shall such monsters be forgiven?

VIII

'Here, in this smiling land we find
   Neglect and misery sting our race;
And still, whate'er the Lascar's mind,
   The stamp of sorrow marks his face!'
He ceased to speak; while from his side
Fast rolled life's swiftly-ebbing tide,
And now, though sick and faint was he;
He slowly climbed a tall Elm tree,
To watch, if, near his lonely way,
Some friendly Cottage lent a ray,
A little ray of cheerful light,
To gild the Lascar's long, long night!

IX

And now he hears a distant bell,
   His heart is almost rent with joy!
And who, but such a wretch can tell,
   The transports of the Indian boy?
And higher now he climbs the tree,
And hopes some sheltering Cot to see;

Again he listens, while the peal
Seems up the woodland vale to steal;
The twinkling stars begin to fade,
And dawnlight purples o'er the glade—
And while the severing vapours flee,
The Lascar boy looks cheerfully!

            X
And now the Sun begins to rise
    Above the Eastern summit blue;
And o'er the plain the day-breeze flies,
    And sweetly bloom the fields of dew!
The wandering wretch was chilled, for he
Sate, shivering in the tall Elm tree;
And he was faint, and sick, and dry,
And bloodshot was his feverish eye;
And livid was his lip, while he
Sate silent in the tall Elm tree—
And parched his tongue; and quick his breath,
And his dark cheek, was cold as Death!

            XI
And now a Cottage low he sees,
    The chimney smoke, ascending grey,
Floats lightly on the morning breeze
    And o'er the mountain glides away.
And now the Lark, on fluttering wings,
Its early Song, delighted sings;
And now, across the upland mead,
The Swains their flocks to shelter lead;
The sheltering woods, wave to and fro;
The yellow plains, far distant, glow;
And all things wake to life and joy,
All! but the famished Indian Boy!

            XII
And now the village throngs are seen,
    Each lane is peopled, and the glen
From every opening path-way green,
    Sends forth the busy hum of men.
They cross the meads, still, all alone,
They hear the wounded Lascar groan!
Far off they mark the wretch, as he
Falls, senseless, from the tall Elm tree!
Swiftly they cross the river wide
And soon they reach the Elm tree's side,
But, ere the sufferer they behold,
His withered Heart, is dead,—*and* cold!

(1800)

11 POOR MARGUERITE

Swift, o'er the wild and dreary waste
A nut-brown Girl was seen to haste;
Wide waving was her unbound hair,
And sun-scorched was her bosom bare;
For Summer's noon had shed its beams
While she lay wrapped in feverish dreams;
While, on the withered hedge-row's side,
By turns she slept, by turns she cried,
'Ah! where lies hid the balsam sweet,
To heal the wounds of Marguerite?'

Dark was her large and sunken eye
Which wildly gazed upon the sky;
And swiftly down her freckled face
The chilling dews began to pace:
For she was lorn, and many a day,
Had, all alone, been doomed to stray,
And, many a night, her bosom warm,
Had throbbed, beneath the pelting storm,
And still she cried, 'the rain falls sweet,
It bathes the wounds of Marguerite.'

Her garments were by briars torn,
And on them hung full many a thorn;
A thistle crown, she muttering twined,
Now darted on,—now looked behind—
And here, and there, her arm was seen
Bleeding the tattered folds between;
Yet, on her breast she oft displayed
A faded branch, that breast to shade:
For though her senses were astray,
She felt the burning beams of day:
She felt the wintry blast of night,
And smiled to see the morning light,
For then she cried, 'I soon shall meet
The plighted love of Marguerite.'

Across the waste of printless snow,
All day the nut-brown Girl would go;
And when the winter moon had shed
Its pale beams on the mountain's head,
She on a broomy pillow lay
Singing the lonely hours away;
While the cold breath of dawnlight flew
Across the fields of glittering dew:—
Swift o'er the frozen lake she passed
Unmindful of the driving blast,

And then she cried 'the air is sweet—
It fans the breast of Marguerite.'

MARY
ROBINSON

The weedy lane she loved to tread
When stars their twinkling lustre shed;
While from the lone and silent Cot
The watchful Cur assailed her not,
Though at the beggar he would fly,
And fright the Traveller passing by:
But she, so kind and gentle seemed,
Such sorrow in her dark eyes beamed,
That savage fierceness could not greet
With less than love,—Poor Marguerite!

Oft, by the splashy brook she stood
And sung her Song to the waving wood;
The waving wood, in murmurs low,
Filled up the pause of weary woe;
Oft, to the Forest tripped along
And inly hummed her frantic Song;
Oft danced mid shadows Evening spread
Along the whispering willow-bed.
    And wild was her groan,
    When she climbed, alone—
    The rough rock's side,
    While the foaming tide,
Dashed rudely against the sandy shore,
And the lightning flashed mid the thunder's roar.

And many a time she chased the fly,
And mocked the Beetle, humming by;
And then, with loud fantastic tone
She sang her wild strain, sad—alone.
And if a stranger wandered near
Or paused the frantic Song to hear,
The burthen she would soft repeat,
'Who comes to soothe Poor Marguerite?'

And why did she with sun-burnt breast,
So wander, and so scorn to rest?
Why did the nut-brown Maiden go
O'er burning plains and wastes of snow?
What bade her feverish bosom sigh,
And dimmed her large and hazel eye?
What taught her o'er the hills to stray
Fearless by night, and wild by day?
What stole the hour of slumber sweet—
From the scorched brain of Marguerite.

MARY ROBINSON

Soon shalt thou know; for see how lorn
She climbs the steep of shaggy thorn—
Now on the jutting cliff she stands,
And clasps her cold,—but snow-white hands.
And now aloud she chants her strain
While fiercely roars the troublous main.
Now the white breakers curling shew
The dread abyss that yawns below,
And still she sighs, 'the sound is sweet,
It seems to say, Poor Marguerite!'

'Here will I build a rocky shed,
And here I'll make my sea-weed bed;
Here gather, with unwearied hands—
The orient shells that deck the sands,
And here will I skim o'er the billows so high,
And laugh at the moon and the dark frowning sky.
And the Sea-birds, that hover across the wide main,
Shall sweep with their pinions, the white bounding plain.—
And the shivering sail shall the fierce tempest meet,
Like the storm, in the bosom of Poor Marguerite!

'The setting Sun, with golden ray,
Shall warm my breast, and make me gay.
The clamours of the roaring Sea
  My midnight serenade shall be!
The Cliff that like a Tyrant stands
Exulting o'er the wave-lashed sands,
With its weedy crown, and its flinty crest,
Shall, on its hard bosom, rock *me* to rest;
And I'll watch for the Eagle's unfledged brood,
And I'll scatter their nest, and I'll drink their blood;
And under the crag I will kneel and pray
And silver my robe, with the moony ray:
And who shall scorn the lone retreat
Which Heaven has chose, for Marguerite?

'Here, did the exiled Henry stray
Forced from his native land, away;
Here, here upon a foreign shore,
His parents, lost, awhile deplore;
Here find, that pity's holy tear
Could not an *alien wanderer* cheer;
And now, in fancy, he would view,
Shouting aloud, the rabble crew—
The rabble crew, whose impious hands
Tore asunder nature's bands!—
I see him still,—He waves me on!
And now to the dark abyss he's gone—

He calls—I hear his voice, so sweet,—
It seems to say—Poor Marguerite!'

Thus, wild she sung! when on the sand
She saw her long lost Henry, stand:
Pale was his cheek, and on his breast
His icy hand he, silent, pressed;
And now the Twilight shadows spread
Around the tall cliff's weedy head;
Far o'er the main the moon shone bright,
She marked the quivering stream of light—
It danced upon the murmuring wave
It danced upon—her Henry's Grave!
It marked his visage, deathly pale,—
His white shroud floating in the gale;
His speaking eyes—his smile so sweet
That won the love—of Marguerite!

And now he beckoned her along
The curling moonlight waves among;
No footsteps marked the slanting sand
Where she had seen her Henry stand!
She saw him o'er the billows go—
She heard the rising breezes blow;
She shrieked aloud! The echoing steep
Frowned darkness on the troubled deep;
The moon in cloudy veil was seen,
And louder howled the night blast keen!—
And when the morn, in splendour dressed,
Blushed radiance on the Eagle's nest,
That radiant blush was doomed to greet—
The lifeless form—of Marguerite!

(1800)

12 EDMUND'S WEDDING

By the side of the brook, where the willow is waving
    Why sits the wan Youth, in his wedding-suit gay!
Now sighing so deeply, now frantically raving
    Beneath the pale light of the moon's sickly ray.
Now he starts, all aghast, and with horror's wild gesture,
Cries, 'Agnes is coming, I know her white vesture!
See! see! how she beckons me on to the willow,
Where, on the cold turf, she has made our rude pillow.

'Sweet girl! yes I know thee; thy cheek's living roses
    Are changed and grown pale, with the touch of despair:
And thy bosom no longer the lily discloses—
    For thorns, my poor Agnes, are now planted there!

MARY ROBINSON

Thy blue, starry Eyes! are all dimmed by dark sorrow;
No more from thy lip, can the flower fragrance borrow;
For cold does it seem, like the pale light of morning,
And thou smil'st, as in sadness, thy fond lover, scorning!

'From the red scene of slaughter thy Edmund returning,
   Has dressed himself gaily, with May-blooming flowers;
His bosom, dear Agnes! still faithfully burning,
   While, madly impatient, his eyes beam in showers!
O! many a time have I thought of thy beauty—
When cannons, loud roaring, taught Valour its duty;
And many a time, have I sighed to behold thee—
When the sulphur of War, in its cloudy mist rolled me!

'At the still hour of morn, when the Camp was reposing,
   I wandered alone on the wide dewy plain:
And when the gold curtains of Evening were closing,
   I watched the long shadows steal over the Main!
Across the wild Ocean, half frantic they bore me,
Unheeding my groans, from Thee, Agnes, they tore me;
But, though my poor heart might have bled in the battle,
Thy name should have echoed, amidst the loud rattle!

'When I gazed on the field of the dead and the dying—
   O Agnes! my fancy still wandered to Thee!
When around, my brave Comrades in anguish were lying
   I longed on the death-bed of Valour to be.
For, severed from Thee, my Sweet Girl, the loud thunder
Which tore the soft fetters of fondness asunder—
Had only one kindness, in mercy to shew me,
To bid me *die bravely*, that thou, Love, may'st *know me!*'

His arms now are folded, he bows as in sorrow,
   His tears trickle fast, down his wedding-suit gay;
'My Agnes will bless me,' he murmurs, 'to-morrow,
   As fresh as the breezes that welcome the day!'
Poor Youth! know thy Agnes, so lovely and blooming,
Stern Death has embraced, all her beauties entombing!
And, pale as her shroud in the grave she reposes,
Her bosom of snow, all besprinkled with Roses!

Her Cottage is now in the dark dell decaying,
   And shattered the casements, and closed is the door,
And the nettle now waves, where the wild Kid is playing,
   And the neat little garden with weeds is grown o'er!
The Owl builds its nest in the thatch, and there, shrieking,
(A place all deserted and lonely bespeaking)
Salutes the night traveller, wandering near it,
And makes his faint heart, sicken sadly to hear it.

Then Youth, for thy habit, henceforth, thou should'st borrow
   The Raven's dark colour, and mourn for thy dear:
Thy Agnes for thee, would have cherished her Sorrow,
   And dressed her pale cheek with a lingering tear:
For, soon as thy steps to the Battle departed,
She drooped, and poor Maiden! she died, broken hearted;
And the turf that is bound with fresh garlands of roses,
Is now the cold bed, where her sorrow reposes!

The gay and the giddy may revel in pleasure,—
   May think themselves happy, their short summer-day;
May gaze, with fond transport, on fortune's rich treasure,
   And, carelessly sporting,—drive sorrow away:
But the bosom, where feeling and truth are united—
From folly's bright tinsel will turn, undelighted—
And find, at the grave where thy Agnes is sleeping,
That the proudest of hours, is the lone hour of weeping!

The Youth now approached the long branch of the willow;
   And stripping its leaves, on the turf threw them round.
'Here, here, my sweet Agnes! I make my last pillow,
   My bed of long slumber, shall be the cold ground!
The Sun, when it rises above thy low dwelling,
Shall gild the tall Spire, where my death-toll is knelling.
And when the next twilight its soft tears is shedding,
At thy Grave shall the Villagers—witness *our* Wedding!'

Now over the Hills he beheld a group coming,
   Their arms glittered bright, as the Sun slowly rose;
He heard them their purposes, far distant, humming,
   And welcomed the moment, that ended his woes!—
And now the fierce Comrade, unfeeling, espies him,
He darts through the thicket, in hopes to surprise him;
But Edmund, of Valour, the dauntless defender,
Now *smiles*, while his Corporal bids him—'Surrender!'

Soon, proved a Deserter, Stern Justice prevailing,
   He Died! and his Spirit to Agnes is fled:—
The breeze, on the mountain's tall summit now sailing
   Fans lightly the dew-drops, that spangle their bed!
The Villagers, thronging around, scatter roses,
The grey wing of Evening the western sky closes,—
And Night's sable pall, o'er the landscape extending,
Is the mourning of Nature! the solemn Scene ending.

(1800)

13 THE SAVAGE OF AVEYRON

'Twas in the mazes of a wood,
　　The lonely wood of Aveyron,
　　I heard a melancholy tone,
　　It seemed to freeze my blood!
A torrent tear was flowing fast,
And hollow was the morning blast,
As o'er the leafless woods it passed,
　　While terror-fraught it stood!
O! mazy woods of Aveyron!
O! wilds of dreary solitude!
Amid thy thorny alleys rude
　　I thought myself alone!
　　I thought no living thing could be
　　So weary of the world as me,
While on my winding path the pale moon shone.

Sometimes the tone was loud and sad,
　　And sometimes dulcet, faint, and slow;
　　And then a tone of frantic woe,
　　It almost made me mad.
The burthen was 'alone! alone!'
And then the heart did feebly groan,
Then suddenly a cheerful tone
　　Proclaimed a spirit glad!
'O! mazy woods of Aveyron!
O! wilds of dreary solitude,
Amid your thorny alleys rude
I wished myself—a traveller alone!'

'Alone,' I heard the wild boy say,
　　And swift he climbed a blasted oak,
　　And there while Morning's herald woke,
　　He watched the opening day;
Yet dark and sunken was his eye,
Like a lorn maniac's, wild and shy,
And scowling like a winter's sky,
　　Without one beamy ray!
Then mazy woods of Aveyron,
　　Then wilds of dreary solitude,
　　Amid thy thorny alleys rude,
I sighed to be—a traveller alone!

'Alone! alone!' I heard him shriek,
　　'Twas like the shriek of dying man!
　　And then to mutter he began,
　　But, O! *he could not speak!*

MARY ROBINSON

I saw him point to Heaven, and sigh,
The big drop trembled in his eye,
And slowly from the yellow sky,
    I saw the pale moon break:
I saw the woods of Aveyron,
    Their wilds of dreary solitude!
    I marked their thorny alleys rude,
And wished to be a traveller alone!

His hair was long and black, and he
    From infancy *alone* had been!
    For since his fifth year he had seen
        None marked his destiny!
No mortal ear had heard his groan,
For him no beam of hope had shone,
While sad he sighed—'alone, alone!'
        Beneath the blasted tree!
And there, O! woods of Aveyron!
    O! wilds of dreary solitude!
    Amid your thorny alleys rude,
I thought myself a traveller alone.

And now upon the blasted tree
    He carved *three* notches, broad and long,
    And all the while he sang a song
        Of Nature's melody!
And though of words he little knew,
And though his dulcet tones were few,
Across the yielding bark he drew,
        Deep sighing, notches three!
O! mazy woods of Aveyron!
    O! wilds of dreary solitude,
    Amid your thorny alleys rude,
Upon this blasted oak, no sun shone!

And now he pointed one, two, three,
    And now he shrieked with wild dismay!
    And now he paced the thorny way,
        Quitting the blasted tree.
It was a dark December morn,
The dew was frozen on the thorn,
But to a wretch so sad, so lorn,
        All days alike would be!
Yet, mazy woods of Aveyron!
    Yet, wilds of dreary solitude!
    Amid your frosty alleys rude,
I wished to be—a traveller alone!

MARY
ROBINSON

I followed him along the wood,
    To a small grot his hands had made,
    Deep in a black rock's sullen shade,
        Beside a tumbling flood!
Upon the earth I saw him spread,
    Of withered *leaves* a narrow bed,
    Yellow as gold, and streaked with red;
        They looked like streaks of blood!
Fallen from the woods of Aveyron,
    And scattered o'er the solitude
    By midnight whirlwinds, strong and rude,
To pillow the scorched brain, that throbbed alone!

Wild berries were his winter food,
    With them his sallow lip was dyed!
    On chestnuts wild he fed beside,
        Steeped in the foamy flood.
Chequered with scars, his breast was seen,
Wounds, streaming fresh with anguish keen!
And marks where other wounds had been,
        Torn by the brambles rude.
Such was the Boy of Aveyron,
    The tenant of that solitude,
    Where still by misery unsubdued,
He wandered *nine long winters*, all alone!

Before the step of his rude throne
    The *squirrel* sported, tame and gay;
    The *dormouse* slept its life away,
        Nor heard his midnight groan:
About his form a garb he wore,
Ragged it was, and marked with gore;
And yet, whene'er 'twas folded o'er,
        Full many a spangle shone!
Like little stars, O! Aveyron!
    They gleamed amid thy solitude!
    Or like, along thy alleys rude,
The summer dew-drops, sparking in the sun!

It once had been a lady's vest,
    White as the whitest mountain snow!
    Till ruffian hands had taught to flow
        The fountain of her breast!
Remembrance bade the wild Boy trace
Her beauteous form, her angel face,
Her eye that beamed with heavenly grace,
        Her fainting voice, that blessed!
When in the woods of Aveyron,
    Deep in their deepest solitude,

   Three barbarous ruffians shed her blood,
And mocked, with cruel taunts, her dying groan.

  Remembrance traced the summer bright,
    When all the trees were fresh and green,
    When lost the alleys long between,
      The lady past the night;
She past the night bewildered wild,
She past it with her fearless child,
Who raised his little arms, and smiled,
    To see the morning light!
While in the woods of Aveyron,
  Beneath the broad oak's canopy,
  She marked aghast the ruffians three,
Waiting to seize the traveller alone!

Beneath the broad oak's canopy
    The lovely lady's bones were laid;
    But since that hour no breeze has played
      About the blasted tree!
The leaves all withered ere the sun
His next day's rapid course had run,
And ere the summer day was done,
    It winter seemed to be!
And still, O! woods of Aveyron,
  Amid thy dreary solitude
  The oak, a sapless trunk, has stood,
To mark the spot where murder foul was done!

  From her the wild Boy learnt 'alone:'
    She tried to say, *my babe will die*;
    But angels caught her parting sigh,
      The babe her *dying tone*!
And from that hour the Boy has been
Lord of the solitary scene,
Winding the dreary shades between,
    Making his dismal moan!
Till, mazy woods of Aveyron!
  Dark wilds of dreary solitude!
  Amid your thorny alleys rude,
    I thought myself alone;
And could a wretch more wretched be,
More wild and fancy-fraught, than he,
Whose melancholy tale would pierce an heart of stone.

                (Wr. 1800, pub. 1801)

ANNE BANNERMAN

ANNE BANNERMAN (1765–1829)

She was born in Edinburgh on 31 October 1765, the eldest child of William Bannerman and Isobel (née Dick). Little is known of her early life other than she did not marry and appears to have always lived with her mother. She published *Poems*, Edinburgh 1800, containing original odes, sonnets and translations, together with a poem to Robert Anderson, an important literary figure in Edinburgh in the 1790s. She also published *Tales of superstition and chivalry*, London 1802. When her mother died in December 1803, Anderson noted that 'Her health is at all times so uncertain and so ill-prepared to stand such a shock as it has been exposed to, that my fears are great; but when to her uncertain health, add the feverish inability of her mind, heightened by constitutional causes,— her total inability, from health and inclination, to pursue the ordinary means by which those of her sex are usually enabled to secure a livelihood, her entire want of relations, . . . my fears rise to a very painful height.' By September 1804 Anderson had learned of the death of her brother in Jamaica and raised the question with Bishop Percy and William Richardson whether some form of public support could be secured for her. Richardson and Anderson probably then arranged for an application to the Royal Literary Fund in 1805 and began to organise the publication of a further volume of her poems by subscription. However, Anderson again noted that 'her mind is so lofty and unaccommodating, that it is exceedingly difficult, at all times, to do her any reasonable service'. Nevertheless, money was raised (including a contribution from Bishop Percy), the subscription volume appeared as *Poems. New edition*, Edinburgh 1807 (with 250 subscribers), and a post as governess to Lady Frances Beresford's daughter was secured for her and she moved to Exeter. How long she remained in the post is unclear. With Anderson's strong hints of mental instability and inability to cope with daily life, she may well have shared the same fate as the 'romantic' Fanny Holcroft and may have been soon dismissed. In any event, she died an impoverished invalid, possibly in a state of poor mental health, at Portobello, Edinburgh on 29 September 1829.

14 VERSES ON AN ILLUMINATION FOR A NAVAL VICTORY

> Quels traits me présentent vos fastes,
>   Impitoyables conquerans?
> —Des murs, que la flamme ravage,
> —Des vainqueurs, fumans de carnage,
>   Un peuple au fér abandonné.
> Juges insensés que nous sommes,
> Nous admirons de tels exploits. [J. B. Rousseau]

Hark! 'tis the note of joy; the trumpet's voice
Swells in the wind, and bids the world rejoice;
From street to street, in artificial light,
The blaze of torches glitters on the night;
Loud peals of triumph rend the startled sky:
Rejoice; it is the shout of victory!
Rejoice o'er thousands in untimely graves;
Rejoice! for Conquest rides the crimsoned waves.
Is this a time for triumph and applause,

ANNE BANNERMAN

When shrinking Nature mourns her broken laws?
Wide o'er the bloody scene, while glory flies
To heap the pile of human sacrifice;
Hid in some dark retreat, the widow weeps
Her heart's best treasure buried in the deeps;
The frantic mother's cries of Heaven implore
Some youthful warrior—she shall meet no more:
From the first beam, that wakes the golden day,
To lingering twilight's melancholy ray,
No respite comes, their breaking hearts to cheer,
Or, from the fount of misery, steal a tear!
  Rough as the storm that rends the icy seas,
The uncultured savage spurns the arts of peace;
Impelled by hatred, and revenge his guide,
He leaves his native mountain's sheltering side,
Through trackless deserts holds his bloody way,
With toil unwearied, through the tedious day;
At night, reposing on the blasted heath,
In dreams, his fancy points the stroke of death,
Exults horrific o'er his prostrate foe,
And aims anew the visionary blow.
Starting he wakes: afar he sees a form,
Half-viewless, stalking through the misty storm;
Nearer he comes; his frantic eye-balls glare,
And yells inhuman ring along the air:
They meet, engage; affrighted Nature flies;
A fearful darkness dims the lowering skies;
Revenge beside them points the envenomed stings,
And murder shrouds them, with his gory wings!
  'Accursed the deed!' the Sons of Europe cry,
While the tear starting, trembles in their eye;
Yes! ye may boast, from feeling's source sublime,
That milder mercy gilds your favoured clime;
With eager joy, you bid oppression cease,
And lull the jarring universe to peace!
Alas! Humanity would shroud the sight,
And wrap Destruction in his native night;
With breasts begirt with steel, in dread array,
The glittering legions flash upon the day;
Brothers in Science, at the trumpet's sound,
Like demons meet, and scatter death around.
Unmoved they stand, and view the living tide
Pour, with a torrent's force, on every side.
On Andes' cliffs, untutored Murder lowers,
But all its keener, deadlier arts—are ours.
  O! could some Spirit, from the fields of day,
To this fair planet wing his venturous way,
Inhale the freshness of the vernal breeze,
And mark the sun, reflected in the seas,

ANNE BANNERMAN

View where, abundant, on a thousand shores,
The waving harvests yield their golden stores;
Gay Beauty smiling in the sweets of morn,
The opening violet, and the flowering thorn,
The expanding fields of every varied hue,
And the clear concave of unclouded blue!
  Then let Him stand, where hostile armies join,
By the red waters of the rushing Rhine,
Amid thick darkness, hear the trumpets blow,
And the last shriek of Nature quiver low,
Mark the full tide of Desolation spread,
And count, at eve, the dying and the dead:
How would he pause! How seek, in vain, to find
Some trace, in Man, of an immortal mind;
Man, who can glory in a scene like this,
Yet look to brighter worlds, for endless bliss!
  O! for a lodge, where Peace might love to dwell,
In some sequestered, solitary dell!
Some fairy isle, beyond the Southern wave,
Where War ne'er led his victims to the grave;
Where, mid the tufted groves, when twilight pale
Peoples with shadowy forms the dewy dale,
The lone Enthusiast, wrapped in trance sublime,
Might soar, unfettered by the bounds of time,
Might bask in Fancy's reign, where scenes appear
Of blooms perpetual, through the vernal year;
Where heavenly odours scent the zephyr's wing,
And fruits and flowers, in wild luxuriance spring!
  Such were the dreams, that soothed the pensive breast,
And lulled the soul to visionary rest.
  Such were the scenes, the poet's fancy drew,
While Rapture hailed the moments, as they flew:
Till mad Ambition bade the battle rage,
And Man with Man eternal warfare wage.
  Ah! did our years through circling ages flow,
Or Fate secure the heart from private woe;
Did strength for ever in the arm reside,
Or the firm frame retain its youthful pride;
The eye that saw the embattled hosts extend,
Might also hope to see their discord end;
The heart, which Sorrow never taught to feel,
Might point, with surer aim, the avenging steel:
Ah! when a few short years have rolled away,
The foes shall rest, unjarring, in the clay.
The Tartar-Chief, expiring on the plain,
Amid the multitudes his arm has slain,
Yields his fierce soul, ere half his years are run,
And ends his fiery course, when scarce begun.
The polished youth, whom Europe rears to arms,

And glory flatters, with deceitful charms,
Chills each fine impulse of the glowing soul,
And, pressing onward to the laurelled goal,
Forgets that feeling ever warmed his breast,
Or Pity pleaded for the heart oppressed.
   All hail, ye joys! to genuine feeling dear,
The heart's warm transport, and the gushing tear!
Welcome the sigh, from pity's altar stole,
Ye calm the tumult of the troubled soul.
O! on whatever shore, by fortune cast,
My shattered bosom finds a home at last;
Whatever ills, in sorrow's ample reign,
May wring my heart, with aggravated pain;
Still, at those hours, when, hushed in deep repose,
The happy lose their joys, the sad their woes,
May fancy lead me to the desert steep,
Stupendous frowning o'er the sullen deep;
To hear the ship-wrecked mariner deplore
His doom relentless, on the rocky shore!
Even when the winds their awful fury urge,
And, heaped like mountains, raves the foaming surge,
Less dread the terrors of the turbid main,
Than Carnage, stalking o'er the ensanguined plain!
   And ye, who, bending o'er the untimely urn,
Will see nor joy, nor happiness return;
Through your changed homes, who wildly seek in vain
For those who slumber in the stormy main;
May piercing anguish spare his arrows keen,
And pity soothe you, as ye weep unseen!
May peace pervade, where faithful sorrow reigns,
And charm the grief, that not an eye profanes!
Ah! think, though lingering years unblessed decay,
To troubled night succeeds untroubled day!
Time's feeble barrier bounds the painful course,
But joy shall reign, eternal as its source.

(1800)

15   ODE I: THE SPIRIT OF THE AIR

I

Be hushed, ye angry winds, that sweep,
   Resistless o'er the polar coast:
Thou swell'st no more, tremendous deep!
   I lock thee in eternal frost.
My will supreme, mine awful sway,
The earth, the air, the sea obey;

ANNE BANNERMAN

My glance pervades the realms of space;
Each hidden spring, this arm can trace;
O'er all the prostrate world my power extends,
Alike on Zembla's ice, on Zaara's burning sands.

II

Amid the lightning's forky flame,
　　While, driven on high, the billows roll;
'Tis mine to loose the struggling frame,
　　And mind to soothe the parting soul:
I come, on viewless winds reclined,
To cheer the wretch, whom fetters bind,
To crush the oppressor's giant crest,
To hurl destruction on his breast,
Amid the spoils his abject soul adores;
And trembling earth recoils along her utmost shores.

III

What form is that, half-hid in air,
　　Round whose pale brow, the torrents roar?
'Tis Freedom! mark her deep despair;
　　She points to Afric's bleeding shore.
Hark! what a groan!—with horror wild,
I see the mother clasp her child;
'My son, my son!' she madly cries;—
Spare, monsters, spare her agonies.—
Too late, for, rapid, to the vessel's side
She flies, and, plunging, sinks beneath the billowy tide.

IV

Proceed unmoved, ye men of blood!
　　Your course along the waters urge;
No winds shall vex the unruffled flood,
　　Nor toss on high the deafening surge.
Now, for your happy homes prepare;
But, curb your joy, I meet you there.
Then, as your friends, your infant race,
Rush wildly to your fond embrace,
Before your eyes a ghastly form shall stand,
And o'er her infant weep, and wave her beckoning hand.

V

Fierce through the desert's frightful sand,
　　When Cancer rules the burning day,
The Arab leads his daring band,
　　Exulting on their perilous way.
'Prepare,' he cries, 'prepare for war:
Mark yonder sandy cloud afar;
We share the blood, we share the toil,

And we shall share the glorious spoil;
Collect your courage, now the foe is nigh;
Victorious, we return;—subdued, revenge and die.'

VI
But, vengeful, on the rushing wind,
   I come to toss the sandy waves;
To whelm the spoilers of their kind,
   Inglorious, in untimely graves.
Yon livid flame, that flings on high
Its terrors through the reddening sky;
Glares on your van, in awful state,
The herald of impending fate.
I speak—the suffocating blast descends
In clouds of fluid fire; and nature's conflict ends.

VII
Where the wild ocean's heaving waves
   Boil round Magellan's stormy coast;
When long and loud the tempest raves,
   I mark the straining vessel tossed,
By night along unfathomed seas,
I see the living current freeze;
As horror grasps each fainting form,
High mid the fury of the storm;
Till the tall masts in scattered fragments lie,
And, plunged amid the surge, the sufferers sink, and die.

VIII
Soft be your bed, and sweet your rest,
   Ye luckless tenants of the deep!
And, o'er each cold and shroudless breast,
   May spirits of the waters weep!
And still, when awful midnight reigns,
My harp shall join in solemn strains;
My voice shall echo to the waves,
That dash above your coral graves;
Blessed be the gloom, that wraps each sacred head,
And blessed the unbroken sleep, and silence of the dead!

IX
High on yon cloud's cerulean seat,
   I ride sublime through ether blue,
To fling, while reigns the power of heat,
   On fainting earth the summer dew:
I bid the rose in crimson glow,
And spread the lily's robe of snow;
I waft from heaven the balmy breeze,
That sighs along the sleeping seas;

ANNE BANNERMAN

What time the spirit of the rock is nigh,
To pour upon the night his heaven-taught melody.

X

But, far beyond the solar blaze,
   Again I wing my rapid flight;
Again I cleave the liquid maze,
   Exulting in immortal might.
O'er me nor cold, nor heat, prevails,
Nor poison from malignant gales;
I glide along the trackless coast,
That binds the magazines of frost;
Encompassed by the raging storm,
I smile at danger's threatening form;
I mock destruction on his towering seat,
And leave the roaring winds, contending at my feet.

(1800)

16 ODE II: THE MERMAID

When at last they retired to rest, Ajut went down to the beach, where finding a fishing-boat, she entered it without hesitation, and, telling those who wondered at her rashness, that she was going in search of Anningait, rowed away with great swiftness, and was seen no more.

The fate of these lovers gave occasion to various fictions and conjectures. Some are of the opinion that they were changed into stars; others imagine, Anningait was seized in his passage by the Genius of the Rocks, and that Ajut was transformed into a *Mermaid*, and still continues to seek her lover in the deserts of the seas. [Rambler, No. 187]

I

Blow on, ye death-fraught whirlwinds! blow,
   Around the rocks, and rifted caves;
Ye demons of the gulf below!
   I hear you, in the troubled waves.
High on this cliff, which darkness shrouds
In night's impenetrable clouds,
My solitary watch I keep,
And listen, while the turbid deep
Groans to the raging tempests, as they roll
Their desolating force, to thunder at the pole.

II

Eternal world of waters, hail!
   Within thy caves my lover lies;
And day and night alike shall fail,
   Ere slumber lock my streaming eyes.
Along this wild untrodden coast,
Heaped by the gelid hand of frost;

ANNE BANNERMAN

Through this unbounded waste of seas,
    Where never sighed the vernal breeze;
Mine was the choice, in this terrific form,
To brave the icy surge, to shiver in the storm.

III
Yes, I am changed.—My heart, my soul,
    Retain no more their former glow.
Hence, ere the blackening tempests roll,
    I watch the bark, in murmurs low,
(While darker lowers the thickening gloom)
To lure the sailor to his doom;
Soft from some pile of frozen snow
I pour the siren-song of woe;
Like the sad mariner's expiring cry,
As, faint and worn with toil, he lays him down to die.

IV
Then, while the dark and angry deep
    Hangs his huge billows high in air;
And the wild wind, with awful sweep,
    Howls in each fitful swell—beware!
High on the rent and crashing mast,
I lend new fury to the blast;
I mark each hardy cheek grow pale,
And the proud sons of courage fail;
Till the torn vessel drinks the surging waves,
Yawns the disparted main, and opes its shelving graves.

V
When Vengeance bears along the wave
    The spell, which heaven and earth appals;
Alone, by night, in darksome cave,
    On me the gifted wizard calls.
Above the ocean's boiling flood
Through vapour glares the moon, in blood:
Low sounds along the waters die,
And shrieks of anguish fill the sky;
Convulsive powers the solid rocks divide,
While, o'er the heaving surge, the embodied spirits glide.

VI
Thrice welcome to my weary sight,
    Avenging ministers of wrath!
Ye heard, amid the realms of night,
    The spell, that wakes the sleep of death.
Where Hecla's flames the snows dissolve,
Or storms, the polar skies involve;
Where, o'er the tempest-beaten wreck,

ANNE BANNERMAN

    The raging winds and billows break
  On the sad earth, and in the stormy sea,
All, all shall shuddering own your potent agency.

VII

  To aid your toils, to scatter death,
    Swift, as the sheeted lightning's force,
  When the keen north-wind's freezing breath
    Spreads desolation in its course,
  My soul, within this icy sea,
  Fulfils her fearful destiny.
  Through time's long ages I shall wait
  To lead the victims to their fate;
With callous heart, to hidden rocks decoy,
And lure, in seraph-strains, unpitying, to destroy.

(1800)

17 THE SOLDIER

With swelling heart, I hear thy stifled sigh,
  Poor time-worn veteran! on thy hoary head
Beats the keen fury of the winter's sky,
  And slow thou mov'st, 'to beg thy bitter bread,'
While heaves impetuous thine indignant breast;
  O! when the vessel cut the Atlantic foam,
And bore thee, sick, and wounded, and oppressed,
  Then rushed thy fancy on the scene of home;
On all its guiltless pleasures;—her, who chased
  With looks of anxious tenderness, thy woes.
Eternal Heaven, that home—a dreary waste!
  And the cold grave, where thy fond hopes repose,
Were all that met thee on thy native soil,
And all thy country gave, for years of blood and toil.

(1800)

18 THE DARK LADIE

The knights returned from Holy Land,
Sir Guyon led the armed train;
And to his castle, on the sea,
He welcomed them again.

He welcomed them with soldier glee,
And sought to charm away their toil;
But none, on Guyon's clouded face,
Had ever seen a smile!

ANNE
BANNERMAN

And, as the hour of eve drew on,
That clouded face more dark became,
No burst of mirth could overpower
The shiverings of his frame;

And often to the bannered door,
His straining eyes, unbidden, turned;
Above, around they glanced wild,
But ever there returned.

At every pause, all breathless then,
And pale as death, he bent his ear,
Though not a sound the silence broke,
He seemed still to hear!

And when the feast was spread, and all
The guests, assembled, were at meat,
There passed them by, with measured step,
And took the upper seat,
A Ladie, clad in ghastly white,
And veiled to the feet:

She spoke not when she entered there;
She spoke not when the feast was done;
And every knight, in chill amaze,
Surveyed her one by one:

For through the foldings of her veil,
Her long black veil that swept the ground,
A light was seen to dart from eyes
That mortal never owned.

And then the knights on Guyon turned
Their fixed gaze, and shuddered now;
For smothered fury seemed to bring
The dew-drops on his brow.

But, from the Ladie in the veil,
Their eyes they could not long withdraw,
And when they tried to speak, that glare
Still kept them mute with awe!

Each wished to rouse his failing heart,
Yet looked and trembled all, the while;
All, till the midnight clock had tolled
Its summons from the southern aisle.

And when the last dull stroke had rung,
And left behind its deepening knell,

ANNE
BANNERMAN

The Ladie rose, and filled with wine,
Filled to the brim, the sparkling shell.

And to the alarmed guests she turned,
No breath was heard, no voice, no sound,
And in a tone, so deadly deep,
She pledged them all around,
That in their hearts, and through their limbs,
No pulses could be found.

And, when their senses back returned,
They gazed upon the steps of stone
On which the Dark Ladie had stood,
They gazed . . . but she was gone! . . .

Then Guyon rose, . . . and ah! to rest,
When every weary knight was fed,
After what they had seen and heard,
What wonder, slumber fled!

For, often as they turned to rest,
And sleep pressed down each heavy eye,
Before them, in her black veil wrapped,
They saw the Dark Ladie.

And then the voice, the tone, that stopped
Through all their limbs, the rushing blood;
The cup which she had filled with wine,
The steps on which she stood.

The sound, the tone, . . . no human voice
Could ever reach that echo deep;
And, ever as they turned to rest,
It roused them from sleep! . . .

The morning dawns . . . the knights are met,
And seated in the arched hall,
And some were loud, and some spoke low,
But Huart none at all!

'Dost not remember, well,' cries one,
'When wide the sacred banners flew,
And when, beneath the blessed Cross,
The infidels we slew.

'This same Sir Guyon, erst so brave,
In fight, who ever led the van,
Soon as the Sepulchre he saw,
Grew pale and trembled then?

ANNE BANNERMAN

'And as the kneeling knights adored,
And wept around that holy place,
O God! I've seen the big drops burst
For hours upon his face!

'And when I named the blessed name,
His face became as livid clay,
And, on his foamy lips, the sounds,
Unuttered, died away!'

'But O! that Ladie!' Huart cries, . . .
'That Ladie, with the long black veil,
This morn I heard! . . . I hear it still,
The lamentable tale!

'I hear the hoary-headed man,
I kept him till the morning dawn,
For five unbroken hours he talked,
With me they were as one!

'He told me he had lived long
Within this castle, on the sea;
But peace, O Heaven! he never had,
Since he saw the Dark Ladie!

''Twas chill,' he said, 'a hazy night,
Just as the light began to fail,
Sir Guyon came and brought with him
The Ladie in the veil:

'Yes! to this castle on the sea,
The wild surge dashing on its base,
He brought her in that frightful veil
That ever hides her face.

'And many a time,' he said, 'he tried
That ne'er-uncovered face to see:
At eve and morn, at noon and night;
But still it could not be!

'Till once! but O! that glaring eye,
It dried the life-blood, working here!
And when he turned to look again,
The Ladie was not near!

'But, sometimes, through her curtained tower,
A strange uncoloured light was seen,
And something, of unearthly hue,
Still passed on between:

ANNE BANNERMAN

'And then aloof its clasped hands
Were wrung, and tossed to and fro!
And sounds came forth, dull, deep, and wild,
And O! how deadly slow!

'He quaked to tell! . . . But, never more,
In quiet sleep, he rested long;
For still, on his alarmed ear,
That rousing echo rung!

'It glared for ever on his sight,
That fixed eye, so wildly keen!
Till life became a heavy load;
And long had heavy been.

'He told me that, at last, he heard
Some story, how this poor Ladie
Had left, alas! her husband's home
With this dread knight to flee:

'And how her sinking heart recoiled,
And how her throbbing bosom beat,
And how sensation almost left
Her cold convulsed feet:

'And how she clasped her little son,
Before she tore herself away;
And how she turned again to bless
The cradle where he lay.

'But where Sir Guyon took her then,
Ah! none could ever hear or know,
Or, why, beneath that long black veil,
Her wild eyes sparkle so.

'Or whence these deep unearthly tones,
That human bosom never owned;
Or why, it cannot be removed,
That folded veil that sweeps the ground?'

(1802)

FANNY HOLCROFT (1780–1844)

She was probably born in 1780, the daughter of Thomas Holcroft, actor, dramatist and radical and his third wife, whose given and maiden names are not known. They were married in 1778 and the wife died in 1790. Shortly after Fanny's birth, Thomas Holcroft abandoned his stage career and became deeply involved in radical politics. He met William Godwin in 1786 who later listed him as one of his 'four principal oral instructors'. In 1791 he assisted in the publication of Thomas Paine's *The rights of man* and in the following year joined the Society for Constitutional Information. In October 1794 he was indicted for high treason alongside Thomas Hardy, Horne Tooke, John Thelwall and other radicals but the proceedings against him were dropped. Like William Roscoe, he also had a passion for connoisseurship and collected paintings and books (which, like Roscoe, he was forced to sell when in financial difficulty). Holcroft's diary of 1798 also records Fanny's musical ability. She was often a 'principal performer' at Mozart and Haydn evenings. By this time, she had already begun to contribute to the *Monthly Magazine* and was later to assist her father by producing a number of translations for his *Theatrical record*, 2v. London 1805. She also wrote *Fortitude and frailty; a novel*, 4v. London 1817, containing a dedicatory poem to her father.

In January 1802 Fanny was briefly engaged by Lady Mountcashel as a governess to her daughters in Paris at a salary of £60 a year but was dismissed within three weeks. Most scholars assign the reasons for this to Lord Mountcashel's reaction to a denouncement of Thomas Holcroft as a spy which appeared in *The Times*, 16 January 1802. But this is based entirely on Holcroft's version of events. In a letter to Godwin, 17 February 1802, Holcroft states that 'Lady Mountcashel, after great civility, and placing my daughter at the pianoforte to play and sing, with praises, compliments, and every apparent satisfaction, put a letter into my hand at going away, to inform me that Lord Mountcashel, having been so repeatedly warned against me as a democrat tried for high treason, domestic peace required her to part with my daughter. I immediately sent for Fanny home' (Kegan Paul, ii.111). However, Lady Mountcashel's version of events cannot be so easily dismissed. In a letter to William Godwin, 21 February 1802, Lady Mountcashel described her 'disappointment at finding her a frivolous, romantic girl, with an uncultivated mind, a character devoid of delicacy, a total want of method, order and discretion; in short, with nothing to recommend her but a clumsy goodness of heart, a sweet temper, and her accomplishments, which consist of music, and some of the modern languages. Of all persons I have ever met with, she is the most unfit to be entrusted with the education of youth' (Kegan Paul, ii.114). Holcroft's version of events is partly supported by Lady Mountcashel's acknowledgement of her husband's hostility to Holcroft following the report in *The Times*. Lady Mountcashel's criticism of Fanny as a 'frivolous, romantic girl' is partly supported by the subject matter of her poems in the *Monthly Magazine* and much later. Charles Lamb noted this aspect of her character: 'Fanny expends herself in phrases that can only be justify'd by her romantic nature', letter to Charles Manning, 26 December 1815 (Marrs, iii.207).

Two reports of her marrying should probably be discounted. Peter Marshall, *William Godwin*, New Haven 1984, p.253, states that Fanny, 'who had just married', was employed by Lady Mountcashel as a governess but this is unlikely and is probably based on a misreading of Thomas Holcroft's letter to William Godwin of January 1802: 'You

FANNY HOLCROFT

enquired of S. concerning Fanny's marriage. The young man is not what his letters appeared to paint him. I forbear to say more, except that Fanny *behaves like an angel*, I give you this under my own hand, and as I can well perceive, feels no regret. She is strongly invited to assist Lady Mountcashel in the education of her daughters . . .' (Kegan Paul, ii.110). It is, of course, possible that she married but on balance, I feel the letter indicates that the marriage did not proceed. Further, she was always referred to as Fanny Holcroft in later years. The second report of a marriage is demonstrably false and based on a mistake by Thomas Moore. Eldridge Colby, *The life of Thomas Holcroft*, 2v. London 1925, i.liv, states that she married 'Carlyle's friend, Badhams'. However, the references by Thomas Moore to Fanny Holcroft are almost certainly wrong and refer to Louisa. 'Miss Holcroft' is referred to as a 'fine girl' (20 July 1820), 'a very nice girl, sang me a song or two to the harp' (6 August 1820), 'sang to Mrs Shelley and Miss Holcroft' (17 July 1824). Fanny Holcroft was certainly musical but was certainly not a girl by this time. The confusion seems to have arisen from a mistake by Moore himself. On 9 February 1830 he went to dinner at James Kenney's (Kenney had married Thomas Holcroft's widow, Louisa Mercier) and noted the presence of 'Mrs Badham [sic] (Fanny Holcroft that was) and her husband'. But it was Louisa (born 1806), who married John Badams in 1828 or 1829, and who would have been a girl in the early 1820s. Further, John Badams died in 1833 but Fanny Holcroft's death certificate does not record any connection. In 1809, she applied to the *Royal Literary Fund* for a grant to open a school. She died on 7 October 1844 at 40 Cumberland Street, Haggerstone [Shoreditch], the cause of death 'mania', with an illiterate Ann Elizabeth Todd of 19 Ship Street present at her death.

19 ANNABELLA

Lamenting o'er her orphan child,
   Young Annabella stood:
Her tresses loose, her action wild,
   Her eyes a briny flood.

Behold thy father slain! she cried,
   In frantic deep despair:
Cursed War divorced him from his bride,
   Each storm of Fate to dare.

Ah! why desert my faithful arms,
   To brave the conquering foe,
Invade my breast with dread alarms,
   And pierce this heart with woe?

Were roaring drums, and trumpets shrill,
   More grateful to thy ear
Than notes of love? that sweetly thrill,
   And hush to rest each fear!

FANNY
HOLCROFT

Could guiltless blood more thirst excite,
   Or riches bliss impart,
Than ev'ry fond and pure delight
   That dignifies the heart?

Oh! cursed, thrice cursed, be Glory's voice,
   That thunders war and rage;
That bids the soul of man rejoice
   To spare nor sex nor age!

And thou, sweet babe! once all my joy,
   But now my greatest woe!
Wilt thou the human race destroy,
   And earth with blood o'erflow?

Oh! rather would this widowed hand
   Cut short thy infant days,
Than thou shouldst bid the fiend-like brand
   Of War and Discord blaze!

Great God, receive my bursting soul!
   Release it from this breast!
No Mortal can by grief control,
   Or hush my sighs to rest!

Thus raved the beauteous weeping fair,
   While Frenzy seized her brain:
She dropped, the victim of Despair,
   Beside her Henry slain!

(1797)

20 THE PENITENT MOTHER

Repose, sweet babe! thy crying cease;
For thine's an age of truth and peace;
Kind love thy infant days shall rear,
Though love has planted daggers here.

Disgrace and grief benight my brow,
Fond victim of a perjured vow;
A vile seducer's guileful art
Betrayed my unsuspecting heart.

'Twas he destroyed my spotless fame,
But thou shalt long survive my shame;
For, when in death I sleep at rest,
The world will cease to wound the oppressed.

FANNY HOLCROFT

Then hush, sweet babe! thy cries give o'er,
Distract my tortured breast no more;
For love thy infant days shall rear,
And grant my hapless fate a tear.

(1797)

21 CONSCIENCE THE WORST OF TORTURES

'Twas night; mysterious silence reigned;
   Sleep waved his magic wand;
E'en prowling wolves, to mischief trained,
   Reposed, a harmless band.

High surging waves, and tempests bleak,
   Were hushed, awhile to rest;
Fierce Etna ceased in flames to break,
   Nor once disgorged her breast:

When, stretched on straw, the murderer lay,
   Terrific to behold!
His tottering frame spoke sad dismay,
   His eye convulsive rolled!

His chains he shook with frantic grief;
   Thrice smote his tortured breast:
Till fainting nature brought relief,
   And lulled his limbs to rest.

But fearful visions racked his brain;
   His transient slumbers broke:
Before him stood Montalto slain!
   He started, groaned, and woke.

Yet woke, alas, to maddening woe:
   The ghastly form pursued;
With bosom pierced, step sad and slow,
   His shroud with blood bedewed!

Its woe-fraught brow and haggard cheek
   Upraised the fiend despair:
A wild and foul-distracted shriek
   Dissolved it into air!

'Stay, stay,' he cried, 'thou damning shade!
   Revenge shall soon be thine.
No more my tardy death upbraid:
   Eternal death is mine!

FANNY HOLCROFT

'I'm called! The vengeful sword they raise!
   Racks, whips, and fury wait?
The pious brands of torture blaze,
   Ferocious man to sate!

'Yet sword and flames I'll dauntless brave:
   No groan shall racks extort;
If blood they thirst, blood let them have;
   Revenge too dearly bought!'

Thus raved the wretch, with anguish torn,
   Pursued by fell despair,
Till soon the sanguinary moon
   Bade him for death prepare.

With well-intentioned vengeance fraught,
   The fearful cohort meet:
Their mind to holy terror wrought;
   Their brow with ire replete.

Yet unappalled their victim stood,
   Death's threatening pangs defied;
'Montalto, lo! here's blood for blood!
   Behold; and quaff,' he cried.

Then dauntless met each fearful stroke,
   No pangs could force one groan;
His threatening eye defiance spoke,
   Till sense and life were flown.

(1797)

22 THE NEGRO

Transpierced with many a streaming wound,
   The Negro lay, invoking death:
His blood o'erflowed the reeking ground—
   He, gasping, drew his languid breath.

His sable cheek was ghastly, cold;
   Convulsive groans their prison broke:
His eyes in fearful horror rolled,
   While thus the wretch his anguish spoke:

'Accursed be the Christian race;
   Insatiate is their iron soul:
To hunt our sons—their favourite chase—
   They goad and lash without control.

FANNY HOLCROFT

'Torn from our frantic mother's breast,
  We bear our tyrant's galling chains;
Denied e'en death, that lulls to rest,
  The keenest woe, and fiercest pains.

'From sun to sun the Negro toils;
  No smiles approve his trusty care;
And, when the indignant mind recoils,
  His doom is whips, and black despair.

'Yet, Christians teach faith, hope, and love:
  Their God of mercy oft implore;
But can barbarians mercy prove,
  Or a benignant God adore?

'Hear then my groans, oh, Christian God!
  Thy curses hurl—but, no! forbear.
Let Christians wield Oppression's rod,
  Spread hatred, woe, and wild despair.

While I a nobler course pursue,
  Yes, let me die as I would live!
Yes, let me teach this Christian crew,
  The dying Negro can forgive.

And if, indeed, that power be thine,
  O Christian God! in mercy move
Thy people's hearts, by power divine,
  To justice, gentleness, and love.'

The sufferer ceased, death chilled his veins;
  His mangled limbs grew stiff and cold;
Yet whips nor racks inflict the pains
  Men feel who barter Man for Gold.

(1797)

23 THE CONDEMNED SAILOR

'Twas mine to watch the dreary night,
  The threatening storm to brave;
'Twas mine to view the morning light,
  'And hail myself a slave.'

But now sweet sleep shall not deny
  A respite to my grief:
'My former wrongs I now defy;'
  Oh death, thou bring'st relief!

I hail thy sad yet welcome shore,
   Where misery finds repose;
Where coward-boys shall strike no more
   Who struck his country's foes.

My indignant soul, by wrongs inflamed,
   Received a mortal wound:
A boy my veteran-locks defamed!
   I felled him to the ground.

Nor could the captain's wrathful eye
   The burst of passion quell:—
Tyrant, behold your minion lie;
   Thrust by this arm to hell!

Now bind these limbs; the scars efface,
   By honour proudly worn:
Nor chains, nor whips, can brand him base,
   Whose wrongs are nobly borne.

(1801)

FANNY HOLCROFT

24 THE DEBTOR

Oh, stranger! heed the famished debtor's prayer,
Let gentle pity snatch him from despair:
Though hardened guilt and folly revel here,
The guiltless oft shed many a bitter tear.

And many a wrong in silence they devour,
And feel the iron hand of ruthless power;
In vain my woes, my wants, cry loud for aid,
Since laws severe with rigour are obeyed.

What though for life he dooms the prisoner here,
Of health bereft, no ray of hope to cheer:
Still shall Horatio roll in wealth and state,
And senates still proclaim him good and great.

There lies my wife, on damp and sickly bed,
Her peace destroyed, her youth and courage fled;
With tearful eye she sees her child expire,
To all indifferent—death her sole desire.

Yet once what hopes, what bliss supreme we knew,
As mutual love and friendship stronger grew,
And cares parental purest rapture gave!
Now blasted, must they wither in the grave!

FANNY
HOLCROFT

But still my spirit to existence hangs,
Still would I live, though torn by cureless pangs;
No power, no pain, can stifle Nature's cry—
The hopeless wretch still fears, still loathes to die!

Then turn, kind stranger! heed the debtor's prayer,
Leave not, unmoved, this den of black despair;
All tongues exalt, all noble hearts revere
The hand that dries the starving debtor's tear!

(1802)

25 THE MADAGASCAR MOTHER
    The following is not a European Fiction; it is a real Madagascar Song, brought from that island by the Chevalier de Porni; a prose Translation of which may be seen in vol. I, p.551. of *Varieties of Literature*.

Why shrink'st thou, weak girl? Why this coward despair?
    Thy tears and thy struggles are vain:
Oppose me no more; of my curses beware!
    Thy terrors and grief I disdain.

The mother was dragging her daughter away
    To the white man, alas! to be sold.
'Oh spare me! (she cried) sure thou would'st not betray
    The child of thy bosom for gold?

'The pledge of thy love; I first taught thee to know
    A mother's affection and fears.
What crime has deserved thou should'st only bestow
    Dishonour and bondage and tears?

'I tenderly soothe every sorrow and care;
    To ease thee, unwearied I toil;
The fish of the stream by my wiles I ensnare;
    The meads of their flowers despoil.

'From the wintry blast I have sheltered thy head;
    Oft borne thee with zeal to the shade;
Thy slumbers have watched on the soft leafy bed;
    The mosquito oft chased from the glade.

'Who'll cherish thy age, when from thee I am torn?
    Gold ne'er buys affection like mine!
Thou'lt bow to the earth, while despairing I mourn,
    Not my sorrows or hardships, but thine.

'Then sell me not; save me from anguish and shame!
No child thou hast, mother, but me!
Oh! do not too rashly abjure the dear claim;
My bosom most trembles for thee.'

In vain she implored—wretched maid! she was sold;
To the ship, chained and frantic conveyed;
Her parent and country ne'er more to behold,
By a merciless mother betrayed.

(1803)

JANE ELIZABETH ROSCOE (later HORNBLOWER) (1797–1853)

She was born on 4 June 1797 in Liverpool, the youngest daughter of William Roscoe (1753–1831) and Jane (née Griffies) and baptised on 30 June 1799. Her father was a leading dissenting radical in Liverpool, who played an important role in the abolition of the slave-trade. He was also a leading connoisseur and book collector and a partner in the Liverpool Bank. With the end of war, the bank failed and he was declared bankrupt in 1816. His large collection of Italian paintings and antiquarian books was sold and the family was forced to give up Allerton Hall and moved to Lodge Lane, Liverpool. Her mother, the subject of many of William Roscoe's poems, died in 1824, and responsibility for looking after the now elderly and widowed father fell to Jane Elizabeth and her sister Mary Anne (1795–1845). (The eldest daughter, Elizabeth, born in 1783, had died in infancy.)

She contributed to *Poems for youth by a family circle*, 2v. London 1820–1821, and, as a result of its modest success, published anonymously *Poems. By one of the authors of Poems for youth by a family circle*, London 1820, which was reprinted the following year. The work has been attributed to her sister Mary Anne, but the internal evidence of subject matter and a ms note in a contemporary hand in the Liverpool City Library copy clearly indicate Jane Elizabeth Roscoe as the author. She also contributed a number of poems to the Liverpool-based Annuals, *Winter's Wreath*, *Remembrance* and *Juvenile Keepsake*, the last two being edited by her brother Thomas Roscoe (1791–1871). Her *Poems*, London 1843, contains verse dating back to 1829. She later contributed two anti-slavery sonnets to *The Liberty Bell* (the Boston-based anti-slavery annual to which Elizabeth Barrett Browning and Lady Byron also contributed): 'Sonnet. British West Indian emancipation', *The Liberty Bell*, Boston 1848, pp. 139–40, 'Sonnet. "Cast to the winds thy great and glorious scroll"', *The Liberty Bell*, Boston 1849, pp. 33–4. She married Francis Hornblower (1812–1853), a Unitarian minister, on 24 April 1838 at the Ancient Chapel, Toxteth Park. At some stage she may have worked as a District Visitor. Her husband died on 1 February 1853 and she died on 2 August 1853 at 125 Chatham Street, Liverpool, with Jane Ankers, possibly a servant, present at her death.

JANE ELIZABETH ROSCOE

26 SONNET

Though to my living eye be still denied
   The sight of Nature in her glorious mood,
   Amid her wilds of trackless solitude:
   —Yet in my dreaming soul the forms abide
Of grandeur and of beauty, and I brood
   O'er inexpressive thoughts; and spreading wide,
   Behold those scenes my fancy oft has wooed:
   But in my heart these visions fair I hide.
They mingle not with aught of this vain world;
   On shadowy wing alone I love to roam,
   For unto me their secret views unfurled
Are hope's young dwelling place and rapture's home.
   Alone I bow to Him who gave this light
   And formed my spirit for its radiant flight.

(1820)

27 THE VISIONARY

I have been lonely, even from a child;
Though bound with sweet ties to a happy home,
With all life's sacred charities around me;
I have been lonely—for my soul had thirst
The waters of this world could not assuage:
I found them bitter, and I had high dreams,
And strange imaginations—yea, I lived
Amid my own creations; and a world
Of many hopes and raptures was within me,
Such as I could not tell of; for I knew
Such feelings could not bear a sympathy;
They were too sacred to admit communion,
Too blessed to need it—to the fields and woods
Did my heart's fullness pour them; solitude.
Was the expansion of my secret visions,
When I could ask my soul to tell me all,
And many a bright and blessed reverie
Hath cheered my wanderings. I have heard sweet music
In my own thoughts; mysterious harmonies,
Felt, but not understood; vague, happy musings,
And shadowy sketches of my future fate,
In young and glowing colours. Are they faded?
—Years are gone by; and once again I commune
With my own spirit—it is passionless,
And silent now, its loveliest visions over;
And yet I do not shun this scrutiny.
Though I have fed my heart with perishing joys,

They have not been in vain; for those wild hopes,
And noble aims, and all those proud aspirings,
Gave me a loftier being. I have plunged
Within the maddening wave, unawed, to succour
An object of my love. I have stood calm
In danger's fiercest moment, with a trust
Above all mortal peril. I have wandered
O'er moors and mountains to assuage the woes
Of human kind. In all that could excite
I have been foremost:—then have woke and wept
To feel how little and how weak I was.—

JANE ELIZABETH ROSCOE

(1820)

28 LLANBERIS PASS

Where rocks tremendous frown on either side,
Casting an awful gloom, and starting forth
In wild projections, as with instant death
Threatening the venturous traveller, in a pass
Dark, dread, and desolate, alone I stood:
I gazed on nature's most terrific features,
And hailed them with a strange sublimity,
Such as those feel who have held high communion
With all her glorious forms;—and if I trembled,
It was with joy to read her mysteries—
The very danger filled me with a pleasure
And deep enthusiasm.—I had perilled
All for that burst of gloomy ecstasy
Which filled my spirit in that drear abyss.
It was no common feeling—and it told me
My soul had secret chords, which with a touch
Would waken into passion; for such scenes
Had been before in my imagination,
And were familiar to me. I had thirsted
For such a living vision, and rejoiced
In the dark city, when the brightening thought
That such things were came o'er me. It had been
A lofty consolation, 'mid the cares
And toils of my existence. Now I stood
Inhaling all the majesty of nature;
But was this all?—Was there no sudden impulse
Bore my soul upward, and impelled its gaze
Unto the Almighty Author?—Yes, my heart
With wonder and with gratitude was bounding,
And every throb was answering the appeal.
I saw a coming storm; there was a voice
Of thunder in the Heavens, which seemed to call

JANE
ELIZABETH
ROSCOE

For adoration; and the lightnings flashed
A sudden glory past me. On I hastened,
Awed by the jar of struggling elements:
When soon a gleam of beauty met my view.
Amid the mountain waste a little spot
Shone fair and verdant. The sun's parting ray
Still lingered on it, and I heard the tone
Of human voices, and astonished saw
A cottage hanging on the sloping brow
Of the deep precipice. What new emotions
It brought upon me!—human sympathies,
And rural pleasures, and domestic toils,
And all the hopes and cares of busy life.—
It vanished, and the solitary way
Still lay before me, and the darkening rocks
Became more intricate;—they too are vanished;
Yet in their grandeur often seem to rise:
And in my lone or melancholy hours
My memory muses on Llanberis Pass.

(1820)

29 SONNET

Pent in the city's darksome walls, I pine
   For the pure air of heaven, and mountain breeze;
   To hear the fresh winds sigh among the trees,
And gaze once more on nature's face divine,
Alas! in vain; for wearing pain is mine,
   Sickness and weariness:—sometimes I think,
   That, but for one dear being, on the brink,
I would not ask to linger—to confine
The heart that pants for freedom—to endure
   A tortured frame, with every blessing round—
   To dream of woods, and waters, and the sound
Of birds most musical—and feel how poor
The town's vain scenes, to one whose steps would be
On mountain wilds, 'mid nature's liberty.

(1843)

30 SONNET

Amidst the darkness of the ancient time,
   Did dreams of beauty linger—thought and grace
   Beamed forth serenely on the sculptured face;
Heroic deeds, the achievements of each clime,

Had their memorial, deathless and sublime,
  In the pure marble—now the virtuous few
  Reap not their fame—the noble deeds they do
Are all unknown—they perish in their prime.
Yet do they leave to this benighted earth
  A prouder gift than Grecian art bestowed,
  The burning thoughts that raise the soul to God,
The hopes that teach it of its heavenly birth,
And those immortal energies of mind
Which sanctify, and save, and bless mankind.

(1831, repr. 1843)

31 LIFE

The mystery of life—oh how it weighs
Upon the spirit's wings, when first youth dawns,
And aspirations beautiful and high
Fill the young heart with joy. The world's cold faith,
Like a dark cloud, comes interposed between
The heaven within, and God; and day by day,
Fades in the breast some fresh and glorious hope,
Nipped by its sceptic blight; that unbelief
Which senses crusted round with earthly things
Draw with their very breath—the poisonous faith
Of the world's customs and inglorious views,
Which, day by day, as deeper it imbibes
Wanders the soul from its diviner walk—
The stars are in eclipse—the heavens are dimmed,
Even God himself, on the eternal throne,
No more is conscious to the heart obscure;
Things palpable are all—and Mammon there
Sits as a sceptred king—and mortal glories,
With their vain, shadowy coruscations, shed
A visionary splendour. Darkened heart,
Where the sublime and true can enter not!
Where is the temple there for the Supreme,
The altar fit for God? He comes not there
Where earthly passions rage, where persecution
Lights her unholy fires, where avarice broods
Over his sordid dreams, where love deserves not
The glory of its name; poor selfish passion,
Which desolates the heart—He comes not there.
Yet this is life—this is the education
Which the world gives its votaries. Early death,
Which comes with shadowing peace upon his wings,
And folds the young, unstainèd heart to heaven,
Its visions bright, its dearest hopes unbroken,

JANE ELIZABETH ROSCOE

JANE
ELIZABETH
ROSCOE

Its aspirations yet upon their flight,
Unsoiled by the world's dust, why do we mourn thee?
Valuing the sweet breath of the dewy morn,
Less than the heat, and toil, and battling day.

(1843)

32 SONNET

Yes! there are sympathies fate cannot part,
   Of souls, and thoughts, that mingle with our own;
   Though earth and sea their barriers wide have thrown,
To sever us in being—yet our heart
Breathes the same hopes, the same aspiring knows,
   With all the pure and good whom we have met;
   Whose holy influence, lingering round us yet,
Burns at oppression, or at virtue glows.
Oh yes! our future being may disclose
   The impressions mind has left on kindred mind,
   Thoughts worthy heaven, all sacred and refined,
The angel-charm which friendship round us throws;
And then, beloved! it may be thine to see
The hope, strength, joy, which thou hast been to me.

(1830, repr. 1843)

33 SOLITARY IMPRISONMENT

Amid a gloom more terrible than darkness,
A cold, and still, and solitary gloom,
That with a feeble glimmering only makes
The wretchedness around just visible,
The friendless prisoner sits. He does not weep;
Nor from the depths of his dim solitude
Pour one complaining tone—the warm, blest fount
Of human tears is dry, the sympathies
That bound him to a world of hopes and fears,
And joys and sorrows, yes, the holy ties
Which made him *man* among his fellow-men,
Are broken by despair. He cannot weep.
With head bowed mournfully upon his breast,
And aimless eye, and arms hung lifeless down,
He sits in desperation. On his soul
There dawns no hope; there comes no blessed gleam
Of human kindness, rising like salvation
Amid the pangs of death. How can he raise
Unto the awful power above, those eyes

JANE
ELIZABETH
ROSCOE

Which never more must gaze on human kind?
How can he crave for mercy from the God
He has offended, when from fellow-beings,
Frail, passionate, and suffering, like himself,
He hath been cast forth thus? Upon his sin
He muses in distraction, till his anguish
Swells in wild agony, and 'mid the waves
Of fear, and shame, and terror, comes the doubt,
The overwhelming doubt, that reason will forsake him,
Amid the utter wreck of all beside.
Then starting from the cold earth, high he spreads
Despairing arms—and with pale, quivering lips,
And outstretched head, and eyes that seem to crave
The sight of human face, as the lost mariner
Looks to the shore in sinking, still he stands,
And mute as death, to listen for a voice!
The very wind that howls against his grating
Is music to him, and his hearth throbs quicker
To catch another, and a human sound!
No; the faint heavings of his own thin breath,
The slight convulsive movements of his heart,
Come chill upon him, and, with sickening ear,
He feels there is no other: the flushed cheek,
That had a moment warmed with mortal hope,
Fades to a damper paleness, and he sinks
Submissive on his stone; while his weak pulse
Flutters and falters, like a dying child's.
So day by day, and year by year, he sits,
The victim of his own and others' crimes;
A living monument! till, life itself
Become a lengthened curse, he trusts to die,
By spurning the scant food which only makes
That life a living death; he turns away
Disgusted from the offering; and though worn
Almost to frightfulness, a spectral form,
Rejects the proffered scrap, and calls on death,
As he would call a friend of youth, to save him!
O! wretched being! famine will not stay
To parley with despair; she urges him
Again, with double fierceness, to his food,
And the weak pulse revives, again to beat
The melancholy hours; and thus he drags
The remnant of his being: no one sees
Or pities *him*; his varying agony,
Shut from public view, disturbs no smile
Upon a happier cheek; no father craves
A blessing on his broken-hearted son;
No mother bends for him; no sister pours
Her young fond tears; no brother round the walls,

JANE
ELIZABETH
ROSCOE

That hold the playmate of his infancy,
Walks in his manlier sorrow, wistfully
To gaze upon his cell; the busy world,
With all the tumult and the stir of life,
Pursues its wonted course; on pleasure some,
And some on commerce and ambition bent,
And all on happiness; while each one loves
One little spot, in which his heart unfolds
With nature's holiest feelings,—one sweet spot,—
And calls it *home*. If there is sorrow there,
It runs through many bosoms, and a smile
Lights up in eyes around a kindred smile;
And if disease intrudes, the sufferer finds
Rest on the breast beloved. Outcast of all,
He sickens and *he* dies; and, having finished
The expiatory pangs, and drank his cup
Of mortal suffering, is denied a grave.
And this is mercy—this is human mercy!
O! truly did he read the heart's deep folds,
And the dark hues of its hypocrisy,
Who cried in bitterness, Alas! for man,
Whose tender mercies in themselves are cruel!

(1843)

34 VERSES

Do I not love at midnight to gaze forth
Upon the hallowed skies, and from their beauty
Drink solemn thoughts of purity and love,
Their sacred light conveying images
Of a more holy presence—even of Him,
All light, all purity? Do I not love
To send my thoughts beyond those crystal vaults,
Far into the deep heavens, to those calm homes
That wait the spirit, here beatified
By human griefs and sufferings? Are not sweet
The visions of their glory and repose,
That fall upon me softly? In such hour,
I feel my immortality—my heart
Answers the sacredness of all around—
The charm, the fascination of the scene,
And reads, delighted, evidence of God.
On seraph wings my thoughts have burst the bound
Of this low earth, and past those shining orbs,
Have traversed that wide ether, to the throne
Of Him, the living one—have seen the array
Of hosts angelic, who, in raptured state,

JANE ELIZABETH ROSCOE

Bend their blessed brows to hail him—have drank
Immortal music, tones divinely sweet,
Attuned to praise—have heard, in awed delight,
Voices I loved on earth as seraphim,
Hymning his goodness—ever, ever on,
In deeper, holier cadence—and, inspired
By sudden adoration, I have knelt
Beyond those radiant bands, at mortal's distance,
To the Incomprehensible, and burned
To be an angel too, and learn his will,
And do his high command, and traverse heaven
Upon the wings of an unwearied love!

Presumptuous musings—yet beheld perchance
With tenderness and pity, by the Power
Who breathed the aspirations in our breast
For all the bright and beautiful—for good
In every earthly form—and higher still
The boundless aspirations after Him,
The living thirst for the immortal waters,
Which not even faith supplies. My Heavenly Father!
I ask Thee not for more; still feed this fire;
'Mid the earth's darkening scenes, still guide me on,
And I will follow the Invisible,
Even with a child-like trust, nor ask for light,
Nor shrink from trial, but confiding give
This soul into thy keeping, and with smiles,
To burst these bonds, await thine angel, death.

(1843)

35 VERSES

I was within a home, where nature smiled,
In perfect loveliness—a range of hills,
As pure a blue as ever blessed the heaven,
Bounding the horizon—the autumnal fields
In rich profusion waving—every hedge
And little bank with brightest fragrance blooming—
In the dark lanes, shadowed with deepest green,
The wild flowers springing, fading, and renewing
From day to day their blossom, till the eye
Drank beauty carelessly, and the hand roved
From bud to bud, almost unconsciously,
So wildly fresh they grew; the hare-bell there
Upraised its little head of tender blue,
To the gale trembling; and the woodbine wreaths
Luxuriantly wound about the trees,

JANE ELIZABETH ROSCOE

With ivy intertwined, and forest shrubs;
The pale rose, there expanding, poured its slight
And rare perfume, and the dark crimson one
Blushed out its sweetness on the quiet air.
Our music was the warbling of a choir,
Whose little throats, of heaven-taught melody,
Are never out of tune: the only other
The artless strains of rustic gratitude,
Waked on the Sabbath morn, when simple hearts
Lift up their homage to the God who made them.

The home we dwelt in was in a seclusion
That did admit of none but nature's world;
The busy throngs of life were far away—
The rocks, the hills, the valleys, and the woods
Became our company—we haunted them,
And in return they breathed upon our souls
Their own blessed stillness, and the shade of peace.
But I was not alone; for there were hearts
That gazed and felt as I did—throbbed like mine,
At sights of grandeur and sublimity,
And worshipped nature in the self-same faith.
But they are severed now—in separate paths
Ordained to walk, and to each one assigned
Their own peculiar joys and pains, no more
Together to be shared—they met and parted,
As those who must have no continuance here.

(1843)

CAROLINE BOWLES (later SOUTHEY) (1786–1854)

She was born Caroline Anne Bowles at Lymington, Hampshire, on 7 October 1786, to Captain Charles Bowles of the East India Company and Anne (née Burrard). Her father appears to have retired shortly after her birth and purchased Buckland Cottage in Lymington. By 1816 both her parents had died and the financial dishonesty of a guardian meant that she would have lost Buckland Cottage. However, her father's adopted son intervened and provided her with an annuity of £150. She is said to have contracted smallpox in childhood and this may have contributed to her somewhat reclusive character. For the rest of her life she was to remain at the family cottage, rarely visiting London or mixing in literary circles. However, the financial difficulties induced her to attempt to live by her pen and she sent a long poem to Robert Southey. Much later Charlotte Brontë would also apply to Southey for advice and assistance. Both women were probably well aware of Southey's efforts to promote unknown and 'uneducated' poets, his close affinity to Cowper, and his kindness to Henry Kirke White. Eventually the poem was published anonymously as *Ellen Fitzarthur: a metrical tale, in five cantos*, London 1820. Friendship and correspondence with Southey ensued and they intended to collaborate on a work on Robin Hood which never materialised although a fragment survives. She went on to publish *The widow's tale: and other poems*, London 1822, *Solitary hours*, Edinburgh 1826, *Tales of the factories*, Edinburgh 1833, *The birthday: a poem . . . to which are added, occasional verses*, Edinburgh 1836, the change to an Edinburgh publisher being possibly the result of her numerous contributions to *Blackwood's Edinburgh Magazine* (under the signature C.). Although never a member of the London or Liverpool literary circles which did much to promote the Annuals, she frequently contributed prose and poetry to the *Literary Souvenir, Amulet, Winter's Wreath*, and several others in the period 1828–1836. On 4 June 1839 she married Robert Southey and moved to the Lake District, an act which entailed the loss of her annuity, only partially offset by Southey leaving her £2000 when he died in 1843. The marriage, although the result of a long friendship, proved difficult owing to Southey's rapid descent into senility. Following his death she returned to Buckland Cottage and received a crown pension of £200 in 1852. She died on 20 July 1854, the cause of death given as bronchitis from which she had been suffering for two years, and Elizabeth Browning was present at her death. She was buried at Lymington. *The poetical works*, Edinburgh 1867, is fairly complete and Edward Dowden edited *The correspondence of Robert Southey with Caroline Bowles*, Dublin 1881. The British Library holds 12v. of her manuscript poetical notebooks (Add. Mss. 47892, A–L) and other Mss.

36 THERE IS A TONGUE IN EVERY LEAF

There is a tongue in every leaf!
    A voice in every rill!
A voice that speaketh everywhere,
In flood and fire, through earth and air;
    A tongue that's never still!

'Tis the Great Spirit, wide diffused
    Through every thing we see,
That with our spirits communeth
Of things mysterious—Life and Death,
    Time and Eternity!

I see Him in the blazing sun,
    And in the thunder cloud;
I hear Him in the mighty roar
That rusheth through the forests hoar,
    When winds are piping loud.

I see Him, hear Him, *everywhere*,
    In *all things*—darkness, light,
Silence and sound; but, most of all,
When slumber's dusky curtains fall,
    At the dead hour of night.

CAROLINE
BOWLES

I *feel* Him in the silent dews,
    By grateful earth betrayed;
I feel Him in the gentle showers,
The soft south wind, the breath of flowers,
    The sunshine, and the shade.

And yet (ungrateful that I am!)
    I've turned in sullen mood
From all these things, whereof He said,
When the great whole was finished,
    That they were 'very good.'

My sadness on the loveliest things
    Fell like unwholesome dew—
The darkness that encompassed me,
The gloom I felt so palpably,
    Mine own dark spirit threw.

Yet He was patient—slow to wrath,
    Though every day provoked
By selfish, pining discontent,
Acceptance cold or negligent,
    And promises revoked.

And still the same rich feast was spread
    For my insensate heart—
Not always so—I woke again,
To join Creation's rapturous strain,
    'O Lord, how good Thou art!'

The clouds drew up, the shadows fled,
    The glorious sun broke out,
And love, and hope, and gratitude,
Dispelled that miserable mood
    Of darkness and of doubt.

(1823)

37 ON READING 'THE RECORDS OF WOMAN'

Is it twilight from some bright former day,
    Or Aurora of one to come,
That bids me thus feel when I hear thy lay,
    As if in my spirit's home?

Is it because thy measures wake
    All the sleepers in memory's cave?
Or is it because their flight they take
    With the winged ones beyond the grave?

CAROLINE
BOWLES

Is it because we are born to weep
   That thy page is blotted still?
Then why do our hearts so wildly leap
   At thy clarion's unearthly thrill?

Is it that each beat of the restless heart
   Finds an echo in thy tone,
As the hues of all deep, bright things have part
   In the rainbow's changeful zone.

'Tis because *thy* spirit hath soared with the strain,
   Yet the page has been wet with thy tear,
That thou lead'st us all in thy radiant train
   To thine own bright holier sphere!

(1829)

38 THE FATHER'S TALE
    Shall I not visit for these things, saith the Lord!   [Jeremiah, v.19]

Come near, my children! till the hour of prayer
   Close we, with serious talk, the Sabbath-day;
Come clustering round us—round your mother's chair
   And mine: Methinks I'd have you so alway,
But so it cannot be. Soon far and wide
In this world must your several paths divide.

But work ye to one end, and with one mind,
   Unto His glory, whose redeemed ye are,
Doing his pleasure—rendering to your kind
   As ye'd receive again. Though sundered far,
Your earthly portions, bright or overcast,
Doubt not ye shall all meet in Heaven at last.

And we—whose treasure and whose trust ye are,
   If faithful found at the great reckoning day,
Shall back receive ye, each a living star
   Wreathed in our crown of glory. Lo! the way
Is plain before us; let us but endure
Our time appointed, and the end is sure.

But oh! beloved ones—full many a snare
   And treacherous pitfall in your path doth lie;
Be constant still in watchfulness and prayer,
   Search out your secret hearts continually;
Lest, from the root of evil set therein,
Shoot up and flourish some triumphant sin.

CAROLINE BOWLES

At first 'a little one,'—and so excused—
   Or for a while in virtue's semblance dressed—
Till moral sense and feeling, self-abused,
   Are lulled at last to deep and deadly rest;
And the whole heart, corrupted to the core,
To work the Tempter's will, is given o'er.

Oh, my dear children! I have seen to-day,
   Have heard and seen what made my blood run cold.
There is a moral leprosy—I say
   A *plague* among us—yea, the love of gold;
And rank and foul idolators we see,
As e'er to ruthless Moloch bent the knee.

Ye've read (and shuddered) of those rites accursed,
   Of Jaggernaut, the Indian demon god,
Whose maddened votaries struggle to be first,
   When yearly his dread chariot comes abroad,
Headlong themselves or tender babes to dash
Before the horrid wheels, as on they crash.

Shuddering ye've read—but all in pity too
   For those poor fanatics have wept the while;
Those blinded ones, who 'know not what they do.'
   But here in England, in our *Christian* isle,
Baptized men, for love of cursed gain,
Heap Mammon's altar with their infant slain.

Marvel not, children! that ye see me so
   In spirit moved for poor humanity—
This morning, as is oft my wont, you know,
   Being awake, and stirring with the bee,
I took my way to visit that small mound
Ye wot of, in our parish burying-ground—

That low green grave, where your young sister lies,
   Whom late, with many tears, ye saw laid there—
Kiss off those drops from your fond mother's eyes—
   Children! ye see how dear to us ye are.
But God, who gave, required his own again—
We wept, and yielded up our little Jane.

But oh! with what an agony of prayer
   That *one* dear lamb selected from our fold
For his good pleasure, he the rest would spare;
   Even with like pleadings that may not be told,
This very morn, my precious ones! I prayed
By that green mound beneath the lime-tree's shade.

CAROLINE
BOWLES

While thus I stood, smote heavy on mine ear
   The funeral-bell; and, turning, I espied
An open grave, planked loosely over, near,
   That scarce a few short paces did divide
From that of mine own child; and it must be,
Methought, for one as early called as she.

Once—twice again (no more) that sullen sound
   Jarred with uneven stroke—and, at the call
Appeared, within the consecrated ground,
   No funeral pomp or mourners—plume and pall;
But minister and clerk—and, huddling nigh,
A squalid group—one wretched family.

Foremost, a man of wasted frame, and weak,
   But tall and bony—bowed, but not by years;
Grizzled his thick black locks—his sallow cheek
   Dug out, as if by long corroding tears;
But the deep sunken caves were parched and dry,
And glazed and meaningless his hollow eye.

With him came step for step, with shambling gait,
   A pale-faced boy, whose swollen and feeble knees
Bowed out and bent beneath his starveling weight;
   They two between them, slung with careless ease,
A little coffin, of the roughest boards
And rudest framing Parish help affords.

And close behind, with stupid looks agape,
   Two sickly, shivering girls, dragged shuffling on
A long-armed, withered creature, like an ape,
   From whose bleared eyeballs reason's light was gone;
The idiot gibbered in his senseless glee,
And the man turned—and cursed him bitterly.

Alas, my children! But the Judge of all
   Tries not the heart by superficial sign;
And when *we* think his thunderbolt must fall
   On some offender, oft the hand divine
Reserves its wrath the guiltier wretch to slay
Who led, or drove him from the righteous way.

Bareheaded, by the grave of mine own dead
   I stood, while his, that wretched Man's, was lowered
Into the narrow house. His shaggy head
   Sank on his breast; but when the earth was poured
Upon the coffin lid, there stirred in him
No visible change or tremor, face or limb.

CAROLINE BOWLES

And so he stood, while all was finished—
    The grave filled in—the daisied turf smoothed o'er;
Till one cried—'Father!' Then he raised his head
    With such a look!—I see it to this hour—
And turning, stamped down hard the new-laid sod,
Muttering with half-clenched teeth, 'One's gone—thank God!'

'One's gone!' I echoed, glancing where mine own
    Slept in *her* grave; 'and thou can'st tread *that spot*
So rudely—speak those words in such a tone!
    Art *thou* a father?' 'Would that I were not!'
Facing quick round his questioner to scan,
Made answer stern, that miserable Man.

Dark scowling from beneath his close-knit brow,
    His gloomy eye full fixed on mine, he said,
'Children may be good gifts to thee, and thou
    Mayst love them living, and lament them dead;
But mine are born to slavery and despair—
They're better off in Heaven or—anywhere!'

'Ye're of the Factories,' I began, but he
    Broke in with horrid laugh—'Aye, who can doubt
That same that sees us? Factory hands are we—
    Their mark's upon us—and it don't wear out.'
And dragging forward one poor girl—'Look there!'
He shouted out, and laid her shoulders bare,

Tearing the ragged shawl off—'*That's* fresh done!
    They sent her home scored black and blue last night,
To serve as mourning for the little one—
    We've no black rags.—And *that's* a goodly sight
For parents' eyes—that poor demented thing!
He was born straight and healthy—Duke or King

'Might have been proud of him; sharp-witted too—
    Aye, cutest of 'em all—till his time came
For the cursed Mill. They strapped him on to do
    Beyond his strength: He fell against a frame
Struck backward—Hurt his spine, the doctors say,
And grew deformed and foolish from that day.

'Sir! when *your* young ones are in bed, asleep,
    Mine must slave on—in dust, and steam, and flue:
You may with *yours* the Lord's day holy keep
    In his own house. 'Tis more than I can do,
(Brute as you think me,) from their rest that day,
Poor little wretches! to drag mine away.

                                                                    CAROLINE
                                                                    BOWLES

"Tis somewhere written in the Bible book,
    How that Christ loves young children, and for foes
Counts all who wrong them. Think ye, does *he* look
    In suchwise on our little ones, and those
Who rack their tender limbs, their sinews strain,
And coin out their young lives in cursed gain!

'There came a man to me but yesternight,
    Collecting pennies, towards setting free
Poor Negro slaves abroad! I laughed outright.
    Master! says I, no need to cross the sea
For your good work; on *this* side the salt waves,
No lack of Slavery, nor of *Infant Slaves*.

'Your pardon, sir!' he said, with softened tone
    Deep lowered; and touched his hat in act to go—
'But if I *have* forgot myself, you'll own
    Wrongs such as mine may make a man do so.
I've loved my children—God *he* knows how well—
But my heart's hardened—and my thoughts are hell.

'I've been myself, a wretched Factory boy—
    Untaught— uncared for—a poor foundling too;
I never felt the feeling *you* call joy,
    Nor leapt, nor laughed, as happy children do;
But I got on, and married like the rest
In reckless folly.—And I say 'tis best

'To die a sinless child, as mine lies there'—
    With aching pity, tenderly I strove
To soothe the wretched man in his despair:
    I talked to him of seeking strength above—
He shook his head—Of comfort found in prayer—
He groaned out, pointing to the grave, 'There! there!'

But we must seek him in his home distressed,
    Where ague-struck his helpless partner lies,
Nursing a wailing baby at her breast,
    That drains her life-blood with its scant supplies:
And we must try what Christian love can do,
For the sick soul, and sinking body too.

And oh, my children! fervent be our prayer,
    This night before we sleep, and day by day,
That from our country, this good land and fair!
    The moral plague-spots may be wiped away.
Ere from her heights, like guilty Tyre, she's hurled,
The wonder and opprobrium of a world.

(1833)

39 THE GRANDMOTHER'S TALE

Take heed that ye despise not one of these little ones. [St Matthew, xviii. 10]

'Up now, my little Margaret!
   Up! and we'll go together
With this warm shawl for Granny Jones;
I warrant me her poor old bones
   Ache sore this winter weather.

'Fold up your work. Impatient child!
   Not *so*—but smooth and neat.
Well, Margaret! well! 'tis almost done,
This task you thought an endless one;
And liberty by labour won
   Will now be doubly sweet.'

'But, dear Mamma, I can't bear work,
   Nor tasks, nor sitting still;
I often think how happier far
Than I poor cottage children are,
   Who do just what they will.'

'Rash child! pray God forgive that thought,
   In ignorance expressed;
You little know what they endure
Too oft, those children of the poor,
   Whose lot you think so blessed.

'But come, 'tis almost half past twelve,
   And we've no time to lose:
Bid Susan wrap you up to-day
In all your warmest things; and stay,
   Put on your thickest shoes.

'Now for it then—But what a swing
   Was that you gave the gate!
Hop! step! and jump! Now do for *once*,
Though you *do long* to be a dunce,
   Walk by my side sedate—

'Yes—for two minutes—and she's off!
   Chasing a withered leaf—
My child! must that light happy heart
One day sustain its painful part
   Or mortal care and grief?'

'What's that at Granny Jones's door?
   A man and cart—and see!
They're lifting something out. Oh, dear!

CAROLINE
BOWLES

'Tis some one very sick, I fear;
   A child—whose can it be?'

'Why, what's the matter, Granny Jones,
   You're making such ado?
Nay, *you* can't lift that poor sick thing.
Whose is it? wherefore do they bring
   The helpless charge to you?'

'Oh, lady! 'tis my daughter's child:
   My poor dead Mary's own.
Four helpless little ones she left
Of every earthly stay bereft
   In this hard world alone.

'Their father gone, and past all work
   A poor old creature I—
The parish kept them for a while,
Then sent them many a weary mile,
   To some great Factory.

'My mind misgave me when they sent
   My pretty lambs away;
But I was helpless, poor, and old,
And should be grateful, I was told,
   That so well off were they.

'Sure of kind usage, wholesome food,
   And raiment of the best;
And easy work, and chastening mild,
Unharmful to a tender child,
   And time for play and rest.

'And oh! what most I had at heart—
   My babes, they promised me,
Should still be kept on Sabbath-days
Constant to church, and from bad ways,
   And evil company.

'The eldest, Bell and Jean, were twins,
   And they were nine years old;
Jemmy was eight, and this poor lamb,
My little loving Miriam,
   But only six, just told.

'Well! well! they took 'em all away—
   Six years agone 'twill be
Come next Shrove Tuesday; and since then
They've still kept on, those cruel men!
   Falsely deceiving me;

CAROLINE BOWLES

'Telling me still from time to time,
    When I for tidings prayed,
That all my precious ones were well,
Even after Jem and Isabel
    Were in the churchyard laid.

'Dear heart! to think what cruel wrongs
    Those pretty creatures bore!
I know all now; for neighbour Prince
Has been to that bad place, and since
    Has told me, o'er and o'er,

'How in those dreadful Factories
    The young small things they keep
At work all day, and half the night,
Aye, hours and hours by candle-light;
    And if they drop asleep,

'Or wink, or flag, they're strapped and wealed,
    And forced to keep on—on—
Till wellnigh sight and sense they lose:
Oh, Christ! that Christian men should use
    The babes thou lovest so!

'Can those poor Blacks they tell about
    Be treated half so bad,
Whose taskmasters are called accursed?—
And yet I have not told the worst—
Well, lady! Isabel went first,
    And then the little lad.

'No wonder they fell sick and died—
    The very breath they drew
With dust and steam was thick and rank;
So they (the tenderest) first sank,
    And there remained but two,

'Miriam and Jeanie—a stout lass
    Was she—our bonny Jean!
And held out bravely, till one day,
('Twas but a moment's work they say,
    Scarcely a moment's pain,)

'By some great shaft her arm was caught—
    Only *one* scream she gave,
And the wheel whirled her round and round,
They told me, with a crunching sound—
    Oh! to my very grave

CAROLINE
BOWLES

'*That* sound, and Jeanie's dying scream,
   Will go with me.—Dear heart!
Sweet little lady! do you cry
At hearing my sad history?
   I've told it but in part.

'Think, little Miss! for a young child
   How hard it must have been—
A child like you, as I may say,
To be kept in the live-long day,
Aye—sixteen mortal hours!—no play,
   And scarce a rest between—

'And scarce for meals a scant half hour,
   Nor always that—oh! no—
When trade is stirring, they must ply
Their tasks all meal-time, hurriedly
Snatching their morsel cold and dry
   While pacing to and fro.

'And then, poor babes! they drop asleep
   Without a prayer at night—
Worn fairly out—by scores to lie,
Huddled like brutes in one close sty,
Till waked, by wakeful misery,
   Before the earliest light.

'The inside of God's holy house
   Those young ones never see.
Not theirs the sin; but oh! that thought
When neighbour Prince the tidings brought,
   Was worst of all to me.

'But still my little Miriam lived,
   "Though going fast," he said;
"Still drove to work—and so will be
Till the last minute, dame!" says he;
   "Aye, till she drops down dead"—

'Oh! that was more than I could bear;
   So crawling painfully,
I reached the Parish board, and prayed
They'd fetch me back my little maid,
   To die at home with me.

'I prayed them on my bended knees,
   But all in vain—till one
('Twas Farmer Williams) took my part,
And said, (God bless his dear kind heart!)

CAROLINE BOWLES

"We'll have her home, dame! in my cart,
  By Tuesday's set of sun."

'He kept his word. God bless him for it!
  My child's come home to die.
Look, Lady! where so pale she's laid—
Dropped off asleep—my merry maid,
Whose rosy cheeks, the folks all said,
  It did one good to see.

'Look! how her little knees are bowed,
  And wasted every limb!
Well, here at least my lamb may rest,
Till taken to her Saviour's breast,
  To dwell in Heaven with Him.

'Hark! how she's moaning in her sleep,
  And starts, and wakes—See! see!'
'Was that the bell? Oh, dear! oh, dear!'
'Hush! hush, my babe! no bell you hear—
You'll never, never more go near
  That dreadful Factory.'

'She's fast again. Well, Granny! now
  We must be gone. Poor thing!
I'll send you down some strengthening food,
And cordials that may do her good,
  And Margaret here shall bring—

'What! my wild Margaret sobbing still?
  Ah! now, dear child, you know
And feel how wrong and foolishly,
In wilful mood you spoke to me
  Not quite an hour ago.

'*Now* do you envy?'—'Oh, Mamma!'
  'Well, well, my child! I see
You feel the lesson of this day;
To-night, before your slumbers, pray
  It may engraven be

'On that young heart; that *gratefully*
  Your lot you may compare
With that of thousands of your kind,
To whom the All-wise Unerring Mind
Hath for their portion here assigned
  Privation, pain, and care.

'And now, good Granny! fare ye well—
We'll bring you down to-morrow
Warm flannels, and a little wine,
For that poor babe. The hand Divine
Alone can ease your sorrow.'

(1833)

FELICIA DOROTHEA HEMANS (née BROWNE) (1793–1835)

She was born on 25 September 1793 at 118 Duke Street, Liverpool, the daughter of George Browne, a merchant, and Felicity (née Wagner). In 1800 financial difficulties resulted in the family moving to Gwrych, near Abergele, North Wales. She was educated at home by her mother and acquired a knowledge of French, German and Italian, to which she later added Spanish and Portuguese. She showed precocious talent and published early: *Poems*, Liverpool 1808, and *England and Spain; or, valour and patriotism*, London 1808. Shelley attempted to enter into correspondence with her at this time but her family intervened and prevailed upon his friends to stop him writing. Her next publication, *The domestic affections*, London 1812, displays many of the themes and images which would continue to obsess her for the rest of her life and on which she would endlessly improvise: the sanctity of the family home as the place of nurturing, security and refuge yet also the powerful site of human drama as family voices and 'departed spirits' (those who have left the home through age, death or travel) compete, a reality of two voices, one present and one recalled; the ocean as the site of power where humans are powerless and also as the serene burial ground of travellers. These polarities operate with astonishing frequency in her work and sometimes degenerate into paradox—Hemans, as her contemporaries thought, was the epitome of feminine passions and femininity, yet she was also obsessed by war. The pleasures of home are a constant motif undercut by obsessions of exile and travel. She was similarly obsessed by the symbolism of the sea yet was always troubled by it. As she one wrote, 'Did you ever observe how strangely sounds and images of waters—rushing torrents, and troubled ocean waves, are mingled with the visionary distresses of dreams and delirium? To me there is no more perfect emblem of peace than that expressed by the scriptural phrase, "there shall be no more sea".' *The works* (1839), i.86. These paradoxes find a strange echo in her life. In 1812 she married Captain Alfred Hemans, an army officer, and they had five children. They separated in 1818 and he went to live in Italy while she remained in Wales with the children, an irony which Hemans, for whom the freedom of the south and the figure of Corinne were central concerns, cannot have missed. During this period she published *The restoration of the works of art to Italy*, Oxford 1816, *Modern Greece*, London 1817, *Translations from Camoens, and other poets, with original poetry*, Oxford 1818, *Tales, and historic scenes*, London 1819, *The Sceptic*, London 1820, and *Dartmoor*, London 1821, none of which is particularly distinguished. Her most important verse is contained in *The forest sanctuary; and other poems*, London 1825, *Records of woman: with other poems*, Edinburgh and London 1828, and *Songs of the affections, with*

FELICIA DOROTHEA HEMANS

poems, Edinburgh and London 1830. She was also a prolific contributor to many of the annuals, the *New Monthly Magazine* and *Blackwood's*. After her death, David Moir edited *Poetical remains*, Edinburgh and London 1836, and her sister, Harriet Hughes, published a collected edition, *The works of Mrs Hemans: with a memoir of her life*, 7v. Edinburgh 1839.

Her mother, with whom she had always lived apart from the period when she was married, died in 1827 and the following year she moved to Wavertree, near Liverpool. In 1831 she moved to Dublin where her brother was commissioner of police. She died on 16 May 1835 and was buried in St Anne's Church, Dublin. Her friend Maria Jane Jewsbury gave a portrait of her as 'Egeria' in *The three histories*, London 1830.

40 BRING FLOWERS

Bring flowers, young flowers, for the festal board,
To wreathe the cup ere the wine is poured;
Bring flowers! they are springing in wood and vale,
Their breath floats out on the southern gale,
And the touch of the sunbeam hath waked the rose,
To deck the hall where the bright wine flows.

Bring flowers to strew in the conqueror's path—
He hath shaken thrones with his stormy wrath!
He comes with the spoils of nations back,
The vines lie crushed in his chariot's track,
The turf looks red where he won the day—
Bring flowers to die in the conqueror's way!

Bring flowers to the captive's lonely cell,
They have tales of the joyous woods to tell;
Of the free blue streams, and the glowing sky,
And the bright world shut from his languid eye;
They will bear him a thought of the sunny hours,
And a dream of his youth—bring him flowers, wild flowers!

Bring flowers, fresh flowers, for the bride to wear!
They were born to blush in her shining hair.
She is leaving the home of her childhood's mirth,
She hath bid farewell to her father's hearth,
Her place is now by another's side—
Bring flowers for the locks of the fair young bride!

Bring flowers, pale flowers, o'er the bier to shed,
A crown for the brow of the early dead!
For this through its leaves hath the white-rose burst,
For this in the woods was the violet nursed.
Though they smile in vain for what once was ours,
They are love's last gift—bring ye flowers, pale flowers!

Bring flowers to the shrine where we kneel in prayer,
They are nature's offerings, their place is *there*!
They speak of hope to the fainting heart,
With a voice of promise they come and part,
They sleep in dust through the wintry hours,
They break forth in glory—bring flowers, bright flowers.

FELICIA DOROTHEA HEMANS

(1825)

41 THE AMERICAN FOREST-GIRL

Wildly and mournfully the Indian drum
   On the deep hush of moonlight forests broke:—
'Sing us a death-song, for thine hour is come.'
   So the red Warriors to their Captive spoke.
Still, and amidst those dusky forms alone,
   A youth, a fair-haired youth, of England stood,
Like a king's son; though from his cheek had flown
   The mantling crimson of the island-blood,
And his pressed lips looked marble. Fiercely bright,
And high around him, blazed the fires of night;
Rocking beneath the cedars to and fro
As the wind passed, and with a fitful glow
Lighting the victim's face:—but who could tell
Of what within his secret heart befell,
Known but to Heaven that hour?—Perchance a thought
Of his far home, then so intensely wrought
That its full image, pictured to his eye
On the dark ground of mortal agony,
Rose clear as day!—And he might *see* the band
Of his young sisters wandering hand in hand
Where the laburnums drooped; or happy binding
The jasmine, up the door's low pillars winding;
Or, as day faded on their gentle mirth,
Gathering, with braided hair, around the hearth
Where sat their mother;—and that mother's face
Its grave sweet smile yet wearing in the place
Where so it ever smiled!—Perchance the prayer
Learned at her knee came back on his despair;
The blessing from her voice, the very tone
Of her '*Good-night*' might breathe from boyhood gone!
—He started and looked up:—thick cypress boughs,
   Full of strange sound, waved o'er him, darkly red
In the broad stormy firelight; savage brows,
   With tall plumes crested and wild hues o'erspread,
Girt him like feverish phantoms; and pale stars
Looked through the branches as though dungeon-bars,
Shedding no hope!—He knew, he felt his doom.—

FELICIA DOROTHEA HEMANS

Oh! what a tale to shadow with its gloom
That happy hall in England!—Idle fear!
Would the winds tell it?—who might dream or hear
The secret of the forests? To the stake
   They bound him; and that proud young Soldier strove
His father's spirit in his breast to wake,
   Trusting to die in silence!—He, the love
Of many hearts!—the fondly-reared—the fair,
Gladdening all eyes to see!—And fettered there
He stood beside his death-pyre, and the brand
Flamed up to light it, in the chieftain's hand!
—He thought upon his God. Hush! hark!—a cry
Breaks on the stern and dread solemnity!
A step hath pierced the ring! Who dares intrude
On the dark Hunters in their vengeful mood?
A Girl—a young slight Girl!—a fawn-like child
Of green savannahs and the leafy wild,
Springing unmarked till then, as some lone flower,
Happy because the sunshine in its dower;
Yet one that knew how early tears are shed,
For *hers* had mourned a playmate brother dead.

She had sat gazing on the victim long,
Until the pity of her soul grew strong;
And, by its passion's deepening fervour swayed,
Even to the stake she rushed, and gently laid
His bright head on her bosom, and around
His form her slender arms to shield it wound
Like close Liannes; then raised her glittering eye,
And clear-toned voice that said—'He shall not die!'

—'He shall not die!'—the gloomy forest thrilled
   To that sweet sound. A sudden wonder fell
On the fierce throng; and heart and hand were stilled—
   Struck down, as by the whisper of a spell.
They gazed—their dark souls bowed before the maid,
She of the dancing step in wood and glade!
And as her cheek flushed through its olive hue,
As her black tresses to the night-wind flew,
Something o'ermastered them from that young mien—
Something of Heaven, in silence felt and seen;
And seeming, to their child-like faith, a token
That the Great Spirit by her voice had spoken.

They loosed the bonds that held their Captive's breath;
From his pale lips they took the cup of Death;
They quenched the brand beneath the cypress tree—
'Away,' they cried, 'young Stranger! thou art free.'

(1826)

42 CORINNE AT THE CAPITOL

FELICIA
DOROTHEA
HEMANS

Les femmes doivent penser qu'il est dans cette carrière bien peu de sorte qui puissent valoir la plus obscure vue d'une femme aimée et d'une mère heureuse. [Madame de Stael]

I
Daughter of the Italian heaven!
Thou, to whom its fires are given,
Joyously thy car hath rolled
Where the conqueror's passed of old;
And the festal sun that shone
O'er three hundred triumphs gone,
Makes thy day of glory bright
With a shower of golden light.

II
Now thou tread'st the ascending road
Freedom's foot so proudly trod;
While, from tombs of heroes borne,
From the dust of empire shorn,
Flowers upon thy graceful head,
Chaplets of all hues are shed,
In a soft and rosy rain,
Touched with many a gem-like stain.

III
Thou hast gained the summit now!
Music hails thee from below;—
Music, whose rich notes might stir
Ashes of the sepulchre;—
Shaking with victorious notes
All the bright air as it floats.
Well may Woman's heart beat high
Unto that proud harmony!

IV
Now afar it rolls—it dies,
And thy voice is heard to rise
With a low and lovely tone,
In its thrilling powers alone;
And thy lyre's deep, silvering string,
Touched as by a breeze's wing,
Murmurs tremblingly at first,
Ere the tide of rapture burst.

V
All the spirit of thy sky
Now hath lit thy large dark eye,—
And thy cheek a flush hath caught

FELICIA
DOROTHEA
HEMANS

From the joy of kindled thought;—
And the burning words of song
From thy lips flow fast and strong,
With a rushing stream's delight
In the freedom of its might.

VI

Radiant daughter of the sun!
Now thy living wreath is won.
Crowned of Rome!—oh! art thou
Happy in the glorious lot?—
Happier, happier far, than thou
With the laurel on thy brow,
She that makes the humblest hearth
Lovely but to one on earth!

(1827)

43 THE GRAVE OF A POETESS

Ne me plaignez pas—si vous saviez combien de peines ce tombeau m'a epargnées!

I stood beside thy lowly grave;—
  Spring-odours breathed around,
And music in the river-wave
  Passed with a lulling sound.

All happy things that love the sun
  In the bright air glanced by,
And a glad murmur seemed to run
  Through the soft azure sky.

Fresh leaves were on the ivy bough
  That fringed the ruins near;
Young voices were abroad—but thou
  Their sweetness couldst not hear.

And mournful grew my heart for thee,
  Thou in whose woman's mind
The ray that brightens earth and sea,
  The light of song was shrined.

Mournful, that thou wert slumbering low,
  With a dread curtain drawn
Between thee and the golden glow
  Of this world's vernal dawn!

Parted from all the song and bloom
  Thou wouldst have loved so well,

FELICIA
DOROTHEA
HEMANS

To thee the sunshine round thy tomb
   Was but a broken spell.

The bird, the insect on the wing,
   In their bright reckless play,
Might feel the flush and life of Spring,
   —And thou wert passed away!

—But then, e'en then, a nobler thought
   O'er my vain sadness came;
The immortal spirit woke and wrought
   Within my thrilling frame.

Surely on lovelier things, I said,
   Thou must have looked ere now,
Than all that round our pathway shed
   Odours and hues below!

The shadows of the Tomb are here,
   Yet beautiful is Earth!
What seest thou then where no dim fear,
   No haunting dream hath birth?

Here a vain love to passing flowers
   Thou gavest—but where thou art,
The sway is not with changeful hours,
   There love and death must part!

Thou hast left sorrow in thy song,
   A voice not loud, but deep;
The glorious bowers of Earth among,
   How often didst thou weep!

Where couldst thou fix on mortal ground
   Thy tender thoughts and high?
—Now peace the Woman's heart hath found,
   And joy the Poet's eye!

(1827)

44 WOMAN ON THE FIELD OF BATTLE

   ————— Where hath not woman stood,
Strong in affection's might?—A reed, upborne,
By an o'ermastering current!——

Gentle and lovely Form!
   What didst thou here,
When the fierce battle-storm
   Bore down the spear?

FELICIA DOROTHEA HEMANS

Banner and shivered crest
    Beside thee strown,
Tell, that amidst the best,
    Thy work was done.

Yet strangely, sadly fair,
    O'er the wild scene,
Gleams through its golden hair
    That brow serene.

Low lies the stately head,
    Earth-bound the free;—
How gave those haughty Dead
    A place to thee?

Slumberer! thine early bier
    Friends should have crowned,
Many a flower and tear
    Shedding around.

Soft voices, clear and young,
    Mingling their swell,
Should o'er thy dust have sung
    Earth's last farewell.

Sisters, about the grave
    Of thy repose,
Should have bid violets wave,
    With the white rose.

Now must the trumpet's note,
    Savage and shrill,
For requiem o'er thee float,
    Thou fair and still!

And the swift charger sweep
    In full career,
Trampling thy place of sleep—
    Why cam'st thou here?

Why?—Ask the true heart why
    Woman hath been
Ever, where brave men die,
    Unshrinking seen?

Unto this harvest-ground
    Proud reapers came—
Some for that stirring sound,
    A Warrior's name:

FELICIA
DOROTHEA
HEMANS

Some for the stormy play,
   And joy of strife;
And some to fling away
   A weary life.

But thou, pale Sleeper! thou
   With the slight frame,
And the rich locks, whose glow
   Death cannot tame:

Only one thought, one power,
   Thee could have led;
So through the tempest's hour
   To lift thy head!

Only the true, the strong,
   The love, whose trust
Woman's deep soul too long
   Pours on the dust.

(1827)

45 WOMAN AND FAME

Happy—happier far than thou,
With the laurel on thy brow;
She that makes the humblest hearth,
Lovely but to one on earth.

Thou hast a charmed cup, O Fame!
   A draught that mantles high,
And seems to lift this earthly frame
   Above mortality.
Away! to me—a woman—bring
Sweet waters from affection's spring.

Thou hast green laurel-leaves that twine
   Into so proud a wreath;
For that resplendent gift of thine,
   Heroes have smiled in death.
Give *me* from some kind hand a flower,
The record of one happy hour!

Thou hast a voice, whose thrilling tone
   Can bid each life-pulse beat,
As when a trumpet's note hath blown,
   Calling the brave to meet:
But mine, let mine—a woman's breast,
By words of home-born love be blessed.

FELICIA
DOROTHEA
HEMANS

A hollow sound is in thy song,
   A mockery in thine eye,
To the sick heart that doth but long
   For aid, for sympathy;
For kindly looks to cheer it on,
For tender accents that are gone.

Fame, Fame! thou canst not be the stay
   Unto the drooping reed,
The cool fresh fountain, in the day
   Of the soul's feverish need;
Where must the lone one turn or flee?—
Not unto thee, oh! not to thee!

(1828)

46 ARABELLA STUART

'The Last Arabella,' as she has been frequently entitled, was descended from Margaret, eldest daughter of Henry VII, and consequently allied by birth to Elizabeth, as well as James I. This affinity to the throne proved the misfortune of her life, as the jealousies which it constantly excited in her royal relatives, who were anxious to prevent her marrying, shut her out from the enjoyment of that domestic happiness which her heart appears to have so fervently desired. By a secret, but early discovered union with William Seymour, son of Lord Beauchamp, she alarmed the cabinet of James, and the wedded lovers were immediately placed in separate confinement. From this they found means to concert a romantic plan of escape; and having won over a female attendant, by whose assistance she was disguised in male attire, Arabella, though faint from recent sickness and suffering, stole out in the night, and at last reached an appointed spot, where a boat and servants were waiting. She embarked; and, at break of day, a French vessel, engaged to receive her, was discovered and gained. As Seymour, however, had not yet arrived, she was desirous that the vessel should lie at anchor for him; but this wish was overruled by her companions, who, contrary to her entreaties, hoisted sail, 'which,' says D'Israeli, 'occasioned so fatal a termination to this romantic adventure. Seymour, indeed, had escaped from the Tower; —he reached the wharf, and found his confidential man waiting with a boat, and arrived at Lee. The time passed; the waves were rising; Arabella was not there; but in the distance he descried a vessel. Hiring a fisherman to take him on board, he discovered, to his grief, on hailing it, that it was not the French ship charged with his Arabella; in despair and confusion he found another ship from Newcastle, which for a large sum altered its course, and landed him in Flanders.'—Arabella, mean-

FELICIA
DOROTHEA
HEMANS

time, whilst imploring her attendants to linger, and earnestly looking out for the expected boat of her husband, was overtaken in Calais Roads by a vessel in the King's service, and brought back to a captivity, under the suffering of which her mind and constitution gradually sank.—'What passed in that dreadful imprisonment, cannot perhaps be recovered for authentic history,—but enough is known; that her mind grew impaired, that she finally lost her reason, and, if the duration of her imprisonment was short, that it was only terminated by her death. Some effusions, often begun and never ended, written and erased, incoherent and rational, yet remain among her papers.'—D'Israeli's *Curiosities of Literature*.—The following poem, meant as some record of her fate, and the imagined fluctuations of her thoughts and feelings, is supposed to commence during the time of her first imprisonment, whilst her mind was yet buoyed up by the consciousness of Seymour's affection, and the cherished hope of eventual deliverance.

> And is not love in vain,
> Torture enough without a living tomb? [Byron]

> Fermossi al fin il cor che balzò tanto. [Pindemonte]

I

'Twas but a dream!—I saw the stag leap free,
  Under the boughs where early birds were singing,
I stood, o'ershadowed by the greenwood tree,
  And heard, it seemed, a sudden bugle ringing
Far through a royal forest: then the fawn
Shot, like a gleam of light, from grassy lawn
To secret covert; and the smooth turf shook,
And lilies quivered by the glade's lone brook,
And young leaves trembled, as, in fleet career,
A princely band, with horn, and hound, and spear,
Like a rich masque swept forth. I saw the dance
Of their white plumes, that bore a silvery glance
Into the deep wood's heart; and all passed by,
Save one—I met the smile of *one* clear eye,
Flashing out joy to mine.—Yes, *thou* wert there,
Seymour! a soft wind blew the clustering hair
Back from thy gallant brow, and thou didst rein
Thy courser, turning from that gorgeous train,
And fling, methought, thy hunting-spear away,
And, lightly graceful in thy green array,
Bound to my side; and we, that met and parted,
  Ever in dread of some dark watchful power,
Won back to childhood's trust, and, fearless-hearted,
  Blent the glad fulness of our thoughts that hour,
Even like the mingling of sweet streams, beneath

FELICIA DOROTHEA HEMANS

Dim woven leaves, and midst the floating breath
Of hidden forest flowers.

II

'Tis past!—I wake,
A captive, and alone, and far from thee,
My love and friend! Yet fostering, for thy sake,
A quenchless hope of happiness to be;
And feeling still my woman's spirit strong,
In the deep faith which lifts from earthly wrong,
A heavenward glance. I know, I know our love
Shall yet call gentle angels from above,
By its undying fervour; and prevail,
Sending a breath, as of the spring's first gale,
Through hearts now cold; and, raising its bright face,
With a free gush of sunny tears erase
The characters of anguish; in this trust,
I bear, I strive, I bow not to the dust,
That I may bring thee back no faded form,
No bosom-chilled and blighted by the storm,
But all my youth's first treasures, when we meet,
Making past sorrow, by communion, sweet.

III

And thou too art in bonds!—yet droop thou not,
Oh, my beloved!—there is *one* hopeless lot,
But one, and that not ours. Beside the dead
There sits the grief that mantles up its head,
Loathing the laughter and proud pomp of light,
When darkness, from the vainly-doting sight,
Covers its beautiful! If thou wert gone
  To the grave bosom, with thy radiant brow,—
If thy deep-thrilling voice, with that low tone
Of earnest tenderness, which now, ev'n now,
Seems floating through my soul, were music taken
For ever from this world,—oh! thus forsaken,
Could I bear on?—thou liv'st, thou liv'st, thou'rt mine!
With this glad thought I make my heart a shrine,
And by the lamp which quenchless there shall burn,
Sit, a lone watcher for the day's return.

IV

And lo! the joy that cometh with the morning,
  Brightly victorious o'er the hours of care!
I have not watched in vain, serenely scorning
  The wild and busy whispers of despair!
Thou hast sent tidings, as of heaven.—I wait
  The hour, the sign, for blessed flight to thee.
Oh! for the skylark's wing that seeks its mate

FELICIA
DOROTHEA
HEMANS

As a star shoots!—but on the breezy sea
We shall meet soon.—To think of such an hour!
Will not my heart, o'erburdened by its bliss,
Faint and give way within me, as a flower
Borne down and perishing by noontide's kiss?
Yet shall I *fear* that lot?—the perfect rest,
The full deep joy of dying on thy breast,
After long-suffering won? So rich a close
Too seldom crowns with peace affection's woes.

V

Sunset!—I tell each moment—from the skies
The last red splendour floats along my wall,
Like a king's banner!—Now it melts, it dies!
I see one star—I hear—'twas not the call,
The expected voice; my quick heart throbbed too soon.
I must keep vigil till yon rising moon
Shower down less golden light. Beneath her beam
Through my lone lattice poured, I sit and dream
Of summer-lands afar, where holy love,
Under the vine, or in the citron-grove,
May breathe from terror.
　　　　　　　Now the night grows deep,
And silent as its clouds, and full of sleep.
I hear my veins beat.—Hark! a bell's slow chime.
My heart strikes with it.—Yet again—'tis time!
A step!—a voice!—or but a rising breeze?
Hark!—haste!—I come, to meet thee on the seas.

* * * * * * * *

VI

Now never more, oh! never, in the worth
Of its pure cause, let sorrowing love on earth
Trust fondly—never more!—the hope is crushed
That lit my life, the voice within me hushed
That spoke sweet oracles; and I return
To lay my youth, as in a burial-urn,
Where sunshine may not find it.—All is lost!
No tempest met our barks—as billow tossed;
Yet were they severed, even as we must be,
That so have loved, so striven our hearts to free
From their close-coiling fate! In vain—in vain!
The dark links meet, and clasp themselves again,
And press out life.—Upon the deck I stood,
And a white sail came gliding o'er the flood,
Like some proud bird of ocean; then mine eye
Strained out, one moment earlier to descry
The form it ached for, and the bark's career

FELICIA DOROTHEA HEMANS

Seemed slow to that fond yearning: It drew near,
Fraught with our foes!—What boots it to recall
The strife, the tears? Once more a prison-wall
Shuts the green hills and woodlands from my sight,
And joyous glance of waters to the light,
And thee, my Seymour, thee!

                I will not sink!
Thou, *thou* hast rent the heavy chain that bound thee;
And this shall be my strength—the joy to think
   That thou mayst wander with heaven's breath around thee,
And all the laughing sky! This thought shall yet
Shine o'er my heart, a radiant amulet,
Guarding it from despair. Thy bonds are broken,
And unto me, I know, thy true love's token
Shall one day be deliverance, though the years
Lie dim between, o'erhung with mists of tears.

VII

My friend, my friend! where art thou? Day by day,
Gliding, like some dark mournful stream, away,
My silent youth flows from me. Spring, the while,
   Comes and rains beauty on the kindling boughs
Round hall and hamlet; Summer, with her smile,
   Fills the green forest;—young hearts breathe their vows;
Brothers long parted meet; fair children rise
Round the glad board; Hope laughs from loving eyes:
All this is in the world!—These joys lie sown,
The dew of every path—On *one* alone
Their freshness may not fall—the stricken deer,
Dying of thirst with all the waters near.

VIII

Ye are from dingle and fresh glade, ye flowers!
   By some kind hand to cheer my dungeon sent;
O'er you the oak shed down the summer showers,
   And the lark's nest was where your bright cups bent,
Quivering to breeze and rain-drop, like the sheen
Of twilight stars. On you Heaven's eye hath been,
Through the leaves, pouring its dark sultry blue
Into your glowing hearts; the bee to you
Hath murmured, and the rill.—My soul grows faint
With passionate yearning, as its quick dreams paint
Your haunts by dell and stream,—the green, the free,
The full of all sweet sound,—the shut from me!

IX

There went a swift bird singing past my cell—
   O Love and Freedom! ye are lovely things!

With you the peasant on the hills may dwell,
    And by the streams; but I—the blood of kings,
A proud, unmingling river, through my veins
Flows in lone brightness,—and its gifts are chains!
Kings!—I had silent visions of deep bliss,
Leaving their thrones for distant, and for this
I am cast under their triumphal car,
An insect to be crushed.—Oh! Heaven is far,—
Earth pitiless!

Dost thou forget me, Seymour? I am proved
So long, so sternly! Seymour, my beloved!
There are such tales of holy marvels done
By strong affection, of deliverance won
Through its prevailing power! Are these things told
Till the young weep with rapture, and the old
Wonder, yet dare not doubt,—and thou, oh! thou,
    Dost thou forget me in my hope's decay?—
Thou canst not!—through the silent night, even now,
    I, that need prayer so much, awake and pray
Still first for thee.—Oh! gentle, gentle friend!
How shall I bear this anguish to the end?

Aid!—comes there yet no aid?—the voice of blood
Passes Heaven's gate, ev'n ere the crimson flood
Sinks through the greensward!—is there not a cry
From the wrong heart, of power, through agony,
To pierce the clouds? Hear, Mercy! hear me! None
That bleed and weep beneath the smiling sun,
Have heavier cause!—yet hear!—my soul grows dark—
Who hears the last shriek from the sinking bark,
On the mid seas, and with the storm alone,
And bearing to the abyss, unseen, unknown,
Its freight of human hearts?—the o'ermastering wave!
Who shall tell how it rushed—and none to save?

Thou hast forsaken me! I feel, I know,
There would be rescue if this were not so.
Thou'rt at the chase, thou'rt at the festive board,
Thou'rt where the red wine free and high is poured,
Thou'rt where the dancers meet!—a magic glass
Is set within my soul, and proud shapes pass,
Flushing it o'er with pomp from bower and hall;—
I see·one shadow, stateliest there of all,—
Thine!—What dost *thou* amidst the bright and fair,
Whispering light words, and mocking my despair?
It is not well of thee!—my love was more
Than fiery song may breathe, deep thought explore,
And there thou smilest, while my heart is dying,

FELICIA
DOROTHEA
HEMANS

FELICIA DOROTHEA HEMANS

With all its blighted hopes around it lying;
Even thou, on whom they hung their last green leaf—
Yet smile, smile on! too bright art thou for grief!

Death!—what, is death a locked and treasured thing,
Guarded by swords of fire? a hidden spring,
A fable fruit, that I should thus endure,
As if the world within me held no cure?
Wherefore not spread free wings—Heaven, Heaven! control
These thoughts—they rush—I look into my soul
As down a gulf, and tremble at the array
Of fierce forms crowding it! Give strengths to pray,
So shall their dark host pass.

                    The storm is stilled.
  Father in Heaven! Thou, only thou, canst sound
The heart's great deep, with floods of anguish filled,
  For human line too fearfully profound.
Therefore, forgive, my Father! if Thy child,
Rocked on its heaving darkness, hath grown wild,
And sinned in her despair! It well may be,
That Thou wouldst lead my spirit back to Thee,
By the crushed hope too long on this world poured,
The stricken love which hath perchance adored
A mortal in Thy place! Now let me strive
With Thy strong arm no more! Forgive, forgive!
Take me to peace!

                 And peace at last is nigh.
  A sign is on my brow, a token sent
The o'erwearied dust, from home: no breeze flits by,
  But calls me with a strange sweet whisper, blent
Of many mysteries.

                 Hark! the warning tone
Deepens—its word is *Death*. Alone, alone,
And sad in youth, but chastened; I depart,
Bowing to heaven. Yet, yet my woman's heart
Shall wake a spirit and a power to bless,
Ev'n in this hour's o'ershadowing fearfulness,
Thee, its first love!—oh! tender still, and true!
Be it forgotten if mine anguish threw
Drops from its bitter fountain on thy name,
Though but a moment.

                 Now, with fainting frame
With soul just lingering on the flight begun,
To bind for thee its last dim thoughts in one,
I bless thee! Peace be on thy noble head,

FELICIA
DOROTHEA
HEMANS

Years of bright fame, when I am with the dead!
I bid this prayer survive me, and retain
Its might, again to bless thee, and again!
Thou hast been gathered into my dark fate
Too much; too long, for my sake, desolate
Hath been thine exiled youth; but now take back,
From dying hands, thy freedom, and re-track
(After a few kind tears for her whose days
Went out in dreams of thee) the sunny ways
Of hope, and find thou happiness! Yet send,
Even then, in silent hours a thought, dear friend!
Down to my voiceless chamber; for thy love
Hath been to me all gifts of earth above,
Though bought with burning tears! It is the sting
Of death to leave that vainly-precious thing
In this cold world! What were it then, if thou,
With thy fond eyes, were gazing on me now?
Too keen a pang!—Farewell! and yet once more,
Farewell!—the passion of long years I pour
Into that word: thou hearest not,—but the woe
And fervour of its tones may one day flow
To thy heart's holy place; there let them dwell—
We shall o'ersweep the grave to meet—Farewell!

(1828)

47 THE SPELLS OF HOME

> There blend the ties that strengthen
>   Our hearts in hours of grief,
> The silver links that lengthen
>   Joy's visits when most brief.   [Bernard Barton]

By the soft green light in the woody glade,
On the banks of moss where thy childhood played;
By the household trees through which thine eye
First looked in love to the summer-sky;
By the dewy gleam, by the very breath
Of the primrose tufts in the grass beneath,
Upon thy heart there is laid a spell,
Holy and precious—oh! guard it well!
By the sleepy ripple of the stream,
Which hath lulled thee into many a dream;
By the shiver of the ivy-leaves
To the wind of morn at thy casement-eaves,
By the bees' deep murmur in the limes,
By the music of the Sabbath-chimes,
By every sound of thy native shade,
Stronger and dearer the spell is made.

FELICIA DOROTHEA HEMANS

By the gathering round the winter hearth,
When twilight called unto household mirth;
By the fairy tale or the legend old
In that ring of happy faces told;
By the quiet hour when hearts unite
In the parting prayer and the kind 'Good-night;'
By the smiling eye and the loving tone,
Over thy life has the spell been thrown.

And bless that gift!—it hath gentle might,
A guardian power and a guiding light.
It hath led the freeman forth to stand
In the mountain-battles of his land;
It hath brought the wanderer o'er the seas
To die on the hills of his own fresh breeze;
And back to the gates of his father's hall,
It hath led the weeping prodigal.

Yes! when thy heart in its pride would stray
From the pure first loves of its youth away;
When the sullying breath of the world would come
O'er the flowers it brought from its childhood's home;
Think thou again of the woody glade,
And the sound by the rustling ivy made,
Think of the tree at thy father's door,
And the kindly spell shall have power once more!

(1828)

48 THE BEINGS OF THE MIND

> The Beings of the Mind are not of clay;
>   Essentially immortal, they create
> And multiply in us a brighter ray,
>   And more beloved existence; that which Fate
> Prohibits to dull life, in this our state
>   Of mortal bondage, by these spirits supplied
> First exiles, then replaces what we hate;
>   Watering the heart whose early flowers have died,
> And with a fresher growth replenishing the void. [*Childe Harold*]

Come to me with your triumphs and your woes,
   Ye forms to life by glorious poets brought!
I sit alone with flowers and vernal boughs,
   In the deep shadow of a voiceless thought;
Midst the glad music of the spring alone,
And sorrowful for visions that are gone.

Come to me! make your thrilling whispers heard,
   Ye, by those masters of the soul endowed
With life and love, and many a burning word,

That bursts from grief, like lightning from a cloud,
And smites the heart, till all its chords reply,
As leaves make answer when the wind sweeps by.

Come to me! visit my dim haunt!—the sound
　Of hidden springs is in the grass beneath,
The stock-dove's note above, and all around
　The poesy that with the violet's breath
Floats through the air, in rich and sudden streams,
Mingling, like music, with the soul's deep dreams.

Friends, friends!—for such to my lone heart ye are,—
　Unchanging ones! from whose immortal eyes
The glory melts not as a waning star,
　And the sweet kindness never, never dies,
Bright Children of the Bard! o'er this green dell
Pass once again, and light it with your spell.

Imogen, fair Fidele! meekly blending
　In patient grief, 'a smiling with a sigh,'
And thou, Cordelia! faithful daughter, tending
　That sire, an outcast to the bitter sky,
Thou of the soft low voice!—thou art not gone!
Still breathes for me its faint and flute-like tone.

And come to me! sing me thy willow-strain,
　Sweet Desdemona! with the sad surprise
In thy beseeching glance, where still, though vain,
　Undimmed, unquenchable affection lies—
Come, bowing thy young head to wrong and scorn,
As a frail hyacinth by showers o'erborne.

And thou too, fair Ophelia! flowers are here,
　That well might win thy footsteps to the spot—
Pale cowslips, meet for maiden's early bier,
　And pansies for sad thought—but needed not.
Come with they wreaths, and all the love and light
　In that wild eye still tremulously bright!

And Juliet, vision of the South! enshrining
　All gifts that unto its rich Heaven belong.
The glow, the sweetness, in its rose combining,
　The soul its nightingales pour forth in song;
Thou, making death deep joy—but couldst thou die?
No! thy young love hath immortality!

From Earth's bright faces fades the light of morn,
　From Earth's glad voices drops the joyous tone;
But ye, the Children of the Soul, were born

FELICIA
DOROTHEA
HEMANS

    Deathless, and for undying love alone;
And oh! ye Beautiful! 'tis well, how well,
In the soul's world with you, where change is not, to dwell!

(1828)

49 THE LAND OF DREAMS

> And dreams, in their development, have breath,
> And tears, and tortures, and the touch of joy;
> They leave a weight upon our waking thoughts,
> They make us what we were not—what they will.
> And shake us with the vision that's gone by.   [Byron]

O Spirit-Land! thou land of dreams!
A world thou art of mysterious gleams,
Of startling voices, and sounds at strife—,
A world of the dead in the hues of life.

Like a wizard's magic glass thou art,
When the wary shadows float by and part;
Visions of aspects now loved, now strange,
Glimmering and mingling in ceaseless change.

Thou art like a City of the Past,
With its gorgeous halls into fragments cast,
Amidst whose ruins there glide and play,
Familiar forms of the world's to-day.

Thou art like the depths where the seas have birth,
Rich with the wealth that is lost from earth—
All the blighted flowers of our days gone by,
And the buried gems in thy bosom lie.

Yes! thou art like those dim sea-caves,
A realm of treasures, a realm of graves!
And the shapes, through thy mysteries that come and go,
Are of Beauty and Terror, of Power and Woe.

But for *me*, O thou picture-land of sleep!
Thou art all one world of affections deep—
And wrung from my heart is each flushing dye,
That sweeps o'er thy chambers of imagery.

And thy bowers are fair—even as Eden fair!
All the beloved of my soul are there!
The forms, my spirit most pines to see,
The eyes, whose love hath been life to me.

They are there—and each blessed voice I hear,   FELICIA
Kindly, and joyous, and silvery clear;   DOROTHEA
But under-tones are in each, that say—   HEMANS
'It is but a dream, it will melt away!'

I walk with sweet friends in the sunset's glow,
I listen to music of long ago;
But one thought, like an omen, breathes faint through the lay—
'It is but a dream, it will melt away!'

I sit by the hearth of my early days,
All the home-faces are met by the blaze—
And the eyes of the mother shine soft, yet say—
'It is but a dream, it will melt away!'

And away, like a flower's passing breath, 'tis gone,
And I wake more sadly, more deeply lone!
Oh! a haunted heart is a weight to bear—
Bright faces, kind voices!—where are ye, where?

Shadow not forth, O thou land of dreams!
The past as it fled by my own blue streams—
Make not my spirit within me burn,
For the scenes and the hours that may ne'er return.

Call out from the *future* thy visions bright,
From the world o'er the grave take thy solemn light,
And oh! with the Loved, when no more I see,
Show me my home, as it yet may be.

As it yet may be in some purer sphere,
No cloud, no parting, no sleepless fear;
So my soul may bear on through the long, long day,
Till I go where the beautiful melts not away.

(1828)

50 THE WINGS OF THE DOVE
    Oh! that I had the wings of a dove, that I might flee away and be at rest!

  Oh! for thy wings, thou dove!
Now sailing by with sunshine on thy breast;
  That borne like thee above,
I too might flee away, and be at rest!

  Where wilt thou fold those plumes,
Bird of the forest-shadows, holiest bird?
  In what rich leafy glooms,
By the sweet voice of hidden water stirred!

FELICIA DOROTHEA HEMANS

    Over what blessed home,
What roof with dark, deep summer-foliage crowned,
    O fair as Ocean's foam!
Shall thy bright bosom shed a gleam around?

    Or seek'st thou some old shrine
Of nymph or saint, no more by Votary wooed,
    Though still, as if divine,
Breathing a spirit o'er the solitude?

    Yet wherefore ask thy way?
Blessed, ever blessed, whate'er its aim, thou art!
    Unto the greenwood spray
Bearing no dark remembrance at thy heart!

    No echoes that will blend
A sadness with the rustlings of the grove;
    No memory of a friend
Far off, or dead, or changed to thee, thou Dove!

    Oh! to some cool recess
Take, take me with thee on the summer-wind!
    Leaving the weariness,
And all the fever of this life behind:

    The aching and the void
Within the heart whereunto none reply,
    The early hopes destroyed—
Bird! bear me with thee through the sunny sky.

    —Wild wish, and longing vain,
And brief upspringing to be glad and free!
    Go to thy woodland reign!
My soul is bound and held—I may not flee.

    For even by all the fears
And thoughts that haunt my dreams—untold, unknown,
    And by the woman's tears
Poured from mine eyes in silence and alone;

    Had I thy wings, thou Dove!
High 'midst the gorgeous isles of cloud to soar,
    Soon the strong cords of love
Would draw me earthwards—homewards—yet once more!

(1828)

51 THE TWO HOMES

FELICIA DOROTHEA HEMANS

> Oh! if the soul immortal be,
> Is not its love immortal too?

Seest thou my home?—'Tis where yon woods are waving
In their dark richness, to the sunny air;
Where yon blue stream, a thousand flower-banks laving;
Leads down the hills a vein of light—'tis there!

Midst these green haunts how many a spring lies gleaming,
Fringed with the violet, coloured with the skies,
My boyhood's haunt, through days of summer dreaming,
Under young leaves that shook with melodies!

My home!—the spirit of its love is breathing
In every wind that plays across my track,
From its white walls the very tendrils wreathing
Seem with soft links to draw the wanderer back.

There am I loved—there prayed for!—there my mother
Sits by the hearth with meekly thoughtful eye,
There my young sisters watch to greet their brother;
Soon their glad footsteps down the path will fly!

There, in sweet strains of kindred music blending,
All the home-voices meet at day's decline;
One are those tones, as from one heart descending—
—There laughs *my* home. Sad stranger! where is thine?

—Ask'st thou of *mine*?—In solemn peace 'tis lying,
Far o'er the deserts and the tombs away;
'Tis where *I* too am loved, with love undying,
And fond hearts wait my step—But where are they?

Ask where the earth's departed have their dwelling,
Ask of the clouds, the stars, the trackless air!—
I know it not—yet trust the whisper, telling
My lonely heart, that love unchanged is there.

And what is home, and where, but with the loving?
Happy *thou* art, that so canst gaze on thine!
My spirit feels but, in its weary roving,
That with the dead, where'er they be, is mine.

Go to thy home, rejoicing son and brother!
Bear in fresh gladness to the household scene!
For me, too, watch the sister and the mother,
I will believe—but dark seas roll between.

(1829)

FELICIA DOROTHEA HEMANS

52 THE DREAMING CHILD

> Alas! what kind of grief should thy years know?
> Thy brow and cheek are smooth as waters are
> When no breath troubles them.   [Beaumont & Fletcher]

And is there sadness in thy dream, my Boy?—
What should the cloud be made of?—blessed child!
Thy spirit, borne upon a breeze of joy,
All day hath ranged through sunshine, clear yet mild;

And now thou tremblest!—Wherefore?—in *thy* soul
There lies no Past, no Future. Thou hast heard
The sound of presage from the distance roll,
Thy breast bears traces of no arrowy word:

From thee no Love hath gone: thy mind's young eye
Hath looked not into Death's, and thence become
A questioner of mute Eternity,
A weary searched for a viewless home:

Nor hath thy sense been quickened into pain,
By feverish watching for some step beloved;—
Free are thy thoughts, an ever-changeful train,
Glancing like dewdrops, and as lightly moved.

Yet now, on billows of strange Passion tossed,
How art thou wildered in the cave of Sleep!
My gentle child! midst what dim phantoms lost,
Thus in mysterious anguish dost thou weep?

Awake! they sadden me—those early tears,
First gushings of the strong dark River's flow,
That *must* o'ersweep thy soul with coming years—
The unfathomable flood of human woe!

Awful to watch, ev'n rolling through a dream,
Forcing wild spray-drops but from Childhood's eyes!—
Wake, wake! as yet thy life's transparent stream
Should wear the tide of none but summer skies.

Come from the shadow of those realms unknown,
Where now thy thoughts dismayed and darkling rove,
Come to the kindly region all thine own,
The Home still bright for thee with guardian Love!

Happy, fair child! that yet a Mother's voice
Can win thee back from visionary strife!—
Oh! shall *my* Soul, thus wakened to rejoice,
Start from the dream-like Wilderness of Life?

(1829)

53 THE DREAMER

FELICIA DOROTHEA HEMANS

> There is no such thing as *forgetting* possible to the mind; a thousand accidents may, and will, interpose a veil between our present consciousness, and the secret inscription on the mind; but alike, whether veiled or unveiled, the inscription remains for ever. [*English Opium-Eater*]

> Thou hast been called, O, Sleep, the friend of wo,
> But 'tis the *happy* who have called thee so. [Southey]

Peace to thy dreams!—thou art slumbering now,
The moonlight's calm is upon thy brow;
All the deep love that o'erflows thy breast,
Like the scent of a flower in its folded bell,
When eve through the woodlands hath sighed farewell.

Peace!—the sad memories that through the day,
With a weight on thy lonely bosom lay,
The sudden thoughts of the changed and dead,
That bowed thee, as winds bow the willow's head,
The yearnings for faces and voices gone—
All are forgotten!—Sleep on, sleep on!

Are they forgotten?—It is not so!
Slumber divides not the heart from its woe.
E'en now o'er thine aspect swift changes pass,
Like lights and shades over wavy grass:
Tremblest thou, Dreamer!—O love and grief!
Ye have storms that shake e'en the closed-up leaf!

On thy parted lips there's a quivering thrill,
As on a lyre ere its chords are still;
On the long silk lashes that fringe thine eye,
There's a large tear gathering heavily;
A rain from the clouds of thy spirit pressed—
Sorrowful Dreamer! this is not rest!

It is Thought at work amidst buried hours,
It is Love keeping vigil o'er perished flowers.—
Oh! we bear within us mysterious things,
Of Memory and Anguish, unfathomed springs,
And Passion, those gulfs of the heart to fill,
With bitter waves, which it ne'er may still.

Well might we pause ere we gave them sway,
Flinging the peace of our couch away!
Well might we look on our souls in fear,
They find no fount of oblivion here!
They forget not, the mantle of sleep beneath—
How know we if under the wings of death?

(1829)

FELICIA DOROTHEA HEMANS

54 TO THE MOUNTAIN WINDS

> ———How divine
> The liberty, for frail, for mortal man,
> To roam at large among unpeopled glens,
> And mountainous retirements, only trod
> By devious footsteps!—Regions consecrate
> To oldest time!—And, reckless of the storm
> That keeps the raven quiet in his nest,
> Be as a presence or a motion—One
> Among the many there.   [Wordsworth]

Mountain winds! oh! whither do ye call me?
   Vainly, vainly would my steps pursue!
Chains of care to lower earth enthral me,
   Wherefore thus my weary spirit woo?

Oh! the strife of this divided being!
   Is there peace where ye are borne on high?
Could we soar to your proud eyries fleeing,
   In our hearts would haunting memories die?

Those wild places are not as a dwelling
   Whence the footsteps of the loved are gone!
Never from those rocky halls came swelling
   Voice of kindness in familiar tone!

Surely music of oblivion sweepeth
   In the pathway of your wanderings free;
And the torrent, wildly as it leapeth,
   Sings of no lost home amidst its glee.

There the rushing of the falcon's pinion,
   Is not from some hidden pang to fly;
All things breathe of power and stern dominion—
   Not of hearts that in vain yearnings die.

Mountain winds! oh! is it only
   Where man's trace hath been, that so we pine?
Bear me up, to grow in thought less lonely,
   Even at nature's deepest, loneliest shrine?

Wild, and mighty, and mysterious singers!
   At whose tone my heart within me burns;
Bear me where the last red sunbeam lingers,
   Where the waters have their secret urns!

There to commune with a loftier spirit
   Than the troubling shadows of regret;
There the wings of freedom to inherit,
   Where the enduring and the winged are met.

Hush, proud voices! gentle be your falling!
    Woman's lot thus chainless may not be;
Hush! the heart your trumpet sounds are calling,
    Darkly still may grow—but never free!

FELICIA
DOROTHEA
HEMANS

(1830)

55 THE RETURN TO POETRY

Once more the eternal melodies from far,
Woo me like songs of home: once more discerning
Through fitful clouds the pure majestic star,
Above the poet's world serenely burning,
Thither my soul, fresh-winged by love, is turning,
—As o'er the waves the wood-bird seeks her nest,
For those green heights of dewy stillness yearning,
Whence glorious minds o'erlook the earth's unrest.—
—Now be the spirit of Heaven's truth my guide
Through the bright land!—that no brief gladness, found
In passing bloom, rich odour, or sweet sound,
May lure my footsteps from their aim aside:
Their true, high quest—to seek, if ne'er to gain,
The inmost, purest shrine of that august domain.

(1834)

56 INTELLECTUAL POWERS

O Thought! O Memory! gems for ever heaping
    High in the illumined chambers of the mind;
And thou, divine Imagination! keeping
    Thy lamp's lone star mid shadowy hosts enshrined;
How, in one moment, rent and disentwined
    At fever's fiery touch apart they fall,
Your glorious combinations!—broken all.
As the sand-pillars by the desert's wind
Scattered to whirling dust!—O soon uncrowned!
Well may your parting swift, your strange return,
    Subdue the soul to lowliness profound,
Guiding its chastened vision to discern
    How by meek faith heaven's portals must be past
Ere it can hold your gifts inalienably fast.

(1835)

57 REMEMBRANCES OF NATURE

O Nature! thou didst rear me for thine own,
    With they free singing birds and mountain brooks,

FELICIA
DOROTHEA
HEMANS

Feeding my thoughts in primrose-haunted nooks
With fairy phantasies and wood-dreams lone.
And thou didst teach me every wandering tone
Drawn from the many whispering trees and waves,
And guide my step to founts and starry caves,
And where bright mosses wove thee a rich throne
'Midst the green hills: and now that, far estranged
From all sweet sounds and odours of thy breath,
Fading I lie, within my heart unchanged
So glows the love of thee, that not for death
Seems that pure passion's fervour—but ordained
To meet on brighter shores thy majesty unstained.

(1835)

MARIANNE PROWSE (née JEFFERY) (1798–1850)

She was born Mary Ann on 11 January 1798 at Teignmouth, Devon, the eldest daughter of William and Sarah Jeffery. Her sister, Sarah Frances, was born on 7 December 1799. She was christened on 11 February 1798.

On their visit to Teignmouth in December 1817, George and Tom Keats took lodgings at 20 The Strand, and became acquainted with Mrs Jeffery and her daughters. The family extended various kindnesses to Tom Keats when he was ill and George Keats engaged in some mild flirtations with the daughters, 'steady, quiet Marianne and laughing thoughtless Sarah'. John Keats joined the brothers in March 1818. Marianne continued to write to Keats after his departure but none of these letters seem to have survived. She may well have been the 'P. Fenbank' who sent Keats a sonnet ('Star of high promise!—not to this dark age') and £25 in November 1819 from Teignmouth. Various other passages in her *Poems*, London 1830, are thought to draw from and refer to Keats.

She married Isaac Sparke Prowse, a wine-merchant, on 21 June 1829 at Kenton, Devon. An only child, William Jeffery Prowse, was born on 6 May 1836 in Torquay and later became a writer of comic verse. When her husband died in 1844 the son was brought up by an uncle, John Sparke Prowse, a shipbroker and notary public at Greenwich. She died on 13 January 1850 at Park Place, Torquay, the cause of death 'debility', with an illiterate Mary Parsons, of 8 Braddons Rows, Torquay, present at her death.

58 NATURE

I would that I might wander far away,
   Into some quiet valley's green recess,
Where not a sound should stir the peaceful day,
   Save forest melodies, whose wild excess,
Blown by the pausing winds, might gently sway
   My soul from her dark thinkings, and repress
Cares, which have worn away my happiness.

It were a pleasant place think to stray alone   MARIANNE
   'Mid palace trees, whose thick boughs intertwined   PROWSE
Make softened twilight of the gorgeous noon;
   Or, haply, 'neath some aged oak reclined,
Gather its fairy goblets; or far-gone
   In a rich dream of poesy, unwind
   Rare spells to disenthral the prisoned mind.

To live alone with Nature; to unfold
   Her teeming mysteries; to rove at will
Through her untrodden haunts: at will behold
   Her varied forms of beauty—lake and hill,
And purple vintage, and the living gold
   Of her full harvests; or at midnight still
   Mark the bright stars their radiant course fulfil.

Eternal Nature! I have ever vowed
   My worship unto thee; thy changeful moods
Of summer loveliness and wintry cloud,
   The majesty of thy deep solitudes,
My soul has loved: then, while the toiling crowd
   Bow unto Fortune for her fancied goods,
   Give me the silence of thy pathless woods.

(1829, repr. 1830)

59 HOME

Source of our first affections; sacred Home!
Of human loves the earliest and most pure;
How do thy hallowed sympathies endure,
Outliving all beside! yea, though we roam
With the great ocean like a world outspread
Between; or though long years have numbered
Their weary lapse, since thy most treasured spot
Died on our tearful gaze—back springs the soul,
Back over time and space:—oceans may roll,
And years stretch on—still art thou unforgot.

The heart's *last* sanctuary:—back to thee
The sorrow-stricken and the lonely flee;
Thine are the pleasant memories that float
Like notes of the wind-harp—wakening a train
Of former thought, with each imperfect strain;
Fond, dreamy recollections; every note
Wafting some long escaped melody—
As sounds that steal upon the ear, and die,
When summer twilight blends the earth and sky.

(1830)

60 ON VISITING A CATARACT

We stood at eve where the flashing waves,
Rushed down from their mountain home;
On the dizzy brink of the time worn caves,
In a haze of silvery foam.

Ever on—ever on—how the haughty flood
Came forth like a king in his pride;
While we, as entranced, on the margin stood,
Nor thought of the world beside.

But our hands were clasped, and our voices blent,
With the tumbling torrent's roar,
Like the notes of some fabled instrument,
Along an enchanted shore.

Yet at length we sighed as we earnest viewed
That ceaseless flood go by;
In each heart a dreary thought would intrude,
That we saw our own destiny.

Yes, we felt as we marked that restless stream,
Speed on to his ocean bed;
That thus it must be with each youthful dream,
Which our souls had cherished.

And more sad—for the stores of that mighty spring,
Ever flow, yet are still supplied;
While nought a return of the joys can bring,
Which are lost in oblivion's tide.

(1830)

61 TO * * * * *

To thee upon the waters! a green wealth
    A 'summer luxury' of leaves and flowers,
    Is all around me: bright perfumed showers
Of sunny blossoms strew the ground; 'tis health
To look upon such beauty: with kind stealth
    Would I convey to thee the charmed powers
    Of all the chiefest things in these fair bowers,
    To fall like blessings on thy sultry hours.

Dost thou not feel their freshness? there is sped
    A gentle spirit with my offerings;
    Welcome him wanderer, for lo! he brings
From thine own land, odours the rose hath shed

On cooling dew-drops newly gathered;
   And as he shakes them from his twinkling wings
   Upon thy brow, they shall recall past things,
The days of youth and their imaginings.

Long years have passed by, and thou hast seen
   The glory and magnificence of kings:
   And where the vast South-ocean darkly flings
His world of waters like a mighty screen
Shrouding the unknown pole—thy path has been—
   Yet is there not amid thy wanderings
   A recollection of far dearer things.
A thought of home to which thy spirit clings?

Thy land, thine own dear land! dost thou not pine
   For her green valleys, for her mossy caves,
   Round which the silver-voiced streamlet laves
The sun-struck flowers to freshness—how divine
Would be to thee to mark the wild flower twine
   Its fairy fingers round the oak that braves
   The wintry storms that flee from him like slaves,
Thou—who art in the wilderness of waves.

(1830)

62 WRITTEN DURING A STORM AT NIGHT

Hark to the mingled voices of the storm!
The elements have met in fearful wrath,
And the earth trembles at the awful strife.
How the red lightnings flash, and spread, and glare,
Athwart the black magnificence of heaven,
As if to fright old darkness from his throne—
While the deep thunder lifts his mighty voice,
The war-note of the skies—and the fierce winds
Are lashing the vexed ocean into rage—
There is a grandeur in this midnight storm,
And the raised passions, loathing the dull round
Of common life, yield to the excitement wild,
And blend themselves with the roused elements.
But 'tis a fearful sympathy! each blast
Bears on his savage wing, the dying groans
Of fathers, husbands, and the shriller wail
Of woman's agony! the feeling heart
Sickens at length of its inhuman joy,
And in this dire commotion pitying thoughts
Rob the drear scene of its strange power to charm,
And calm the feverous rapture of the brain.

MARIANNE PROWSE

There's grandeur in the tempest—but to me
There is intenser feeling—more of awe,
When night comes on in calmest majesty—
Still,—as the hush of death—no sound—no stir—
Moveless and quiet, as creation slept,
And old primeval silence reigned again—
In that most holy stillness, I delight
To be awake, and meditate, and muse
On thoughts beyond the bounds of dull mortality.
The pomp of other days goes slowly by—
The gorgeousness, the glory, and the bloom,
That ages have rolled over—the proud train
Of all that once was mightiest—sounding names
Of desolating heroes, whose stern sway
Made this green earth a sepulchre, that they
Might wear a diadem! but Time is just—
The oppressor and the oppressed are equal names—
The grave-worm hath his share, the earth hath hers—
And History, that universal cheat,
With its false glory, and its hollow praise,
Just points us to the truth, that all the past
Is vanity—What may the future be?—
The past gives answer—but the daring soul
Looks fearless onward, and essays to pierce
The gracious cloud that veils Futurity.
With steadfast gaze, and unappalled, she views
Destruction seize on all created things,
And from the general wreck new worlds arise
Teeming with life and happiness—nor here
Pauses the immortal mind, but upward soars
To the great Cause of Being, there to rest
As in her source and centre—there to find
All feelings lost in boundless adoration.

(1830)

63 THE DESOLATE

Dost question of my fate? I was of those
The dreamers of the world, who fondly deem
Their lot to come shall be unclouded bliss:
It was a bitter 'wakening, when I stood
Amid the cold realities of life,
And found no sympathy, though my heart bled;
And, feelings which were given me as a curse,
Worked on my brain, till madness like a sleep
Restoring o'erwrought nature, hid from me
The wretched present, and regretted past.
I said my youth was glorious; but, first one,

MARIANNE PROWSE

And then another of my young hopes died,
And tears were paid their obsequies, yet still
The current of my soul flowed fresh and free—
Still could I dream of happiness to come,
Still store futurity with every joy—
Would I had died before the fond belief
Had faded quite away—Oh! better far
To leave this prison-world ere it can taint
The bosom with its sorrow or its sin;
When kind regret can mix with our last sighs,
And dear humanities so strongly move,
That half with human feelings—half divine,
The spirit pauses in its long farewell.
Oh! better thus, than wait till death becomes
Wooed with a love unnatural—till all
The beauty and the bloom of the fair earth,
Are spread before the sated eye in vain—
And not one hope clings to the wearied heart,
Nor hovers one faint blessing on the lips,
To be preserved in the living shrine
Of weeping tenderness—such is my fate,
Friendship—and love—and kindred—all but names
Telling of shadows that have floated by
And mocked my eager grasp!

* * * * * *

The light of hope was round me, ever spreading
Bright exhalations like the beamy north;
So wondrous dazzling, that my ardent soul
Was cheated by the glory—on I went
In the bright track, nor cast a thought behind—
The weariness, the misery, and gloom
Of former days, past from me as a dream,
The arch of promise glittering in my view,
Forward I sprang—when lo! the meteor blaze
Was quenched at once—the rainbow tints decayed,
And all was dark again!—what need I tell
How dizzily my senses reeled—how fierce
The struggle of my soul became, thus left
Amid the heavy darkness of despair!
Madly I raved, and told my frantic grief
To the wild winds, that with a demon art
Mocked at my frenzy, as the echo came,
And with its hateful voice, gave back the name
That burned upon my lips, and brain, and heart—
      I had become all thought—I could not lose
Perception for an hour—by night—by day—
A fearful tongue was whispering in my ear,
'Death! Death!' and yet I could not, dared not die.

MARIANNE PROWSE

This torture had its date; and then there came
A blending of all feelings—love, and hate,
And scorn, and laughter that had nought of mirth
Held for awhile their influence,—how I mocked
At fate, and with exultance loud, defied
The power of destiny—and this held long,
Till reason was overthrown, and powerless sank
In the unequal conflict—
                              Twas at length,
When years of infant weakness were o'erpast,
I came again into the world; the fire
Of my impetuous passions quenched for ever.
Lonely and self-subdued, I saw the stir,
The pleasures, and the perils of the world,
And felt that I had no part in human things:
My heart was early withered—Hast thou youth,
On thine own mountains seen some towering pine
Stricken by the red lightning? it may stand
Long as its fellows of the hill, but comes
No more the graceful foliage of its prime
To clothe its scathed limbs: and oh how like
Has been my fate to a young blasted pine!
No spring-time thoughts shall e'er reclothe my soul
With its lost verdure.—
                              Dost marvel *now*
That I grew aged in my youth? Go read
The history of many a faded cheek,
And rayless eye—and think that each hath proved
Some of the feelings that have wasted me,
And thou shalt wonder when thy task is done,
That they have not more potency to change
The raven locks to silver—and to freeze
The warm and glowing stream in the young veins
With their first touch, nor leave for after years
A miserable wreck, from whence the soul
Hath long, long since departed.

(1830)

LETITIA ELIZABETH LANDON (later MACLEAN) (1802–1838)
She was born on 14 August 1802 at 25 Hans Place, Chelsea, the eldest of three children to John Landon, an army agent, and Catherine Jane Bishop. At the age of five, she attended Miss Rowden's school at 22 Hans Place, Chelsea where Lady Caroline Lamb and Mary Russell Mitford had earlier been students. During the course of the Napoleonic wars, John Landon prospered and the family moved to Trevor Park in East Barnet. Her education was then supervised by her cousin, Elizabeth, and she had access to a library where she read English classics, foreign literature, travel accounts and adventure narratives. With the end of the war,

John Landon's business sharply declined and the family moved back to London, settling in 1816 at Old Brompton. One of their neighbours was William Jerdan, then editor of the *Literary Gazette*. On being shown some of her poems, he encouraged her and she began to contribute to the *Literary Gazette* from March 1820. The following year she published *The fate of Adelaide, a Swiss romantic tale; and other poems*, London 1821. Shortly after this, she began to contribute 'Poetic Sketches' to the *Literary Gazette*, under the signature L. E. L., which, as Bulwer-Lytton later recalled, excited great interest and curiosity among young men. Her next works, *The improvisatrice; and other poems*, London 1824, and *The troubadour; catalogue of pictures, and historical sketches*, London 1825, were immediate successes, and both were reprinted several times. She also began to contribute regularly to the Annuals, most notably, *Forget-me-not, Literary Souvenir, Amulet, Keepsake, Fisher's Drawing-Room Scrapbook* (which she edited from 1832 to 1838), and the *Heath's Book of Beauty*. She contributed more verse than any other poet to such magazines. She later published *The golden violet, with its tales of romance and chivalry*, London 1827, *The Venetian bracelet, the lost pleiad, a history of the lyre*, London 1829, and *The vow of the peacock*, London 1835. She also published two novels, *Romance and reality*, 3v. London 1831, and *Ethel Churchill*, 3v. London 1837. Her friend Emma Roberts edited a posthumous collection, *The zenana, and minor poems*, London 1839, and Laman Blanchard edited her *Life and literary remains*, 2v. London 1841. W. B. Scott's edition of *The poetical works*, London 1873, is a serious attempt to collect the vast array of her fugitive pieces.

She exhibited a dangerous mixture of romanticism, thoughtlessness and indiscretion, and this led to various rumours about her. These rumours probably resulted in John Foster breaking off his engagement to her and in June 1838 she impulsively married George Maclean, the Governor of Cape Coast Castle, on the African Gold Coast. She travelled to the Gold Coast with him but died barely four months later in mysterious circumstances on 15 October 1838. Murder has sometimes been suspected (the evidence is slight) but suicide was widely accepted at the time although accidental death was also advanced.

LETITIA ELIZABETH LANDON

64 CORINNA

She stood alone; but on her every eye
Dwelt in mute ravishment; her long black hair
Flew loose upon the gale, but half confined
By the light veil and wreathes of braided rose,
Shading her bosom's matchless ivory,
And fell upon the lyre, like hyacinths
Twined fancifully round; a pensive shade
Was on the brightness of her deep blue eyes,
Where the sweet tenderness of woman's glance
Softened the minstrel's fire that sparkled there.—
The song arose; it was just such a strain
The soft Erato wakes, when she would sing
Of loveliness, and love by sorrow shaded;
Her voice (the Siren's is not sweeter, when

LETITIA ELIZABETH LANDON

She breathes her music to calm moonlight seas,)
Was fraught with tender feelings, and called forth
An answering harmony within the heart;
And even when it ceased, the listener's ear,
Thrilled with its wild and witching melody.
She stood, like some fair creature of the skies,
In mild unconscious beauty, and her eyes
Sunk to their timid station on the ground:
Her cheek was delicately pale; but when
They placed the laurel crown upon her brow,
Her face was mantled by a burning blush,
Bright, beautiful, like summer's glowing eve,
Such as young Psyche wore, when Love first taught
His own sweet language.

(1821)

65 THE ENCHANTED ISLAND

And there the island lay, the waves around
Had never known a storm; for the north wind
Was charmed from coming, and the only airs
That blew brought sunshine on their azure wings,
Or tones of music from the sparry caves,
Where the sea-maids make lutes of the pink conch.
These were sea breezes,—those that swept the land
Brought other gifts,—sighs from blue violets,
Or from June's sweet Sultana, the bright rose,
Stole odours. On the silver mirror's face
Was but a single ripple that was made
By a flamingo's beak, whose scarlet wings
Shone like a meteor on the stream: around,
Upon the golden sands, were coral plants,
And shells of many colours, and sea weeds,
Whose foliage caught and chained the Nautilus,
Where lay they as at anchor. On each side
Were grottoes, like fair porticoes with steps
Of the green marble; and a lovely light,
Like the far radiance of a thousand lamps,
Half-shine, half-shadow, or the glorious track
Of a departing star but faintly seen
In the dim distance, through those caverns shone,
And played o'er the tall trees which seemed to hide
Gardens where hyacinths rang their soft bells
To call the bees from the anemone,
Jealous of their bright rivals' golden wealth.
—Amid those arches floated starry shapes,
Just indistinct enough to make the eye

Dream of surpassing beauty; but in front,
Borne on a car of pearl, and drawn by swans,
There lay a lovely figure,—she was queen
Of the Enchanted Island, which was raised
From ocean's bosom but to pleasure her:
And spirits, from the stars, and from the sea,
The beautiful mortal had them for her slaves.

    She was the daughter of a king, and loved
By a young Ocean Spirit from her birth,—
He hovered o'er her in her infancy,
And bade the rose grow near her, that her cheek
Might catch its colour,—lighted up her dreams
With fairy wonders, and made harmony
The element in which she moved; at last,
When that she turned away from earthly love,
Enamoured of her visions, he became
Visible with his radiant wings, and bore
His bride to the fair island.

LETITIA
ELIZABETH
LANDON

(1825)

66 STANZAS ON THE DEATH OF MRS HEMANS

    The rose—the glorious rose is gone.   [*Lays of Many Lands*]

Bring flowers to crown the cup and lute,—
    Bring flowers,—the bride is near;
Bring flowers to soothe the captive's cell,
    Bring flowers to strew the bier!
Bring flowers! thus said the lovely song;
    And shall they not be brought
To her who linked the offering
    With feeling and with thought?

Bring flowers,—the perfumed and the pure,—
    Those with the morning dew,
A sigh in every fragrant leaf,
    A tear on every hue.
So pure, so sweet thy life has been,
    So filling earth and air
With odours and with loveliness,
    Till common scenes grew fair.

Thy song around our daily path
    Flung beauty born of dreams,
That shadows on the actual world
    The spirit's sunny gleams.

LETITIA ELIZABETH LANDON

Mysterious influence, that to earth
    Brings down the heaven above,
And fills the universal heart
    With universal love.

Such gifts were thine,—as from the block,
    The unformed and the cold,
The sculptor calls to breathing life
    Some shape of perfect mould,
So thou from common thoughts and things
    Didst call a charmed song,
Which on a sweet and swelling tide
    Bore the full soul along.

And thou from far and foreign lands
    Didst bring back many a tone,
And giving such new music still,
    A music of thine own.
A lofty strain of generous thoughts,
    And yet subdued and sweet,—
An angel's song, who sings of earth,
    Whose cares are at his feet.

And yet thy song is sorrowful,
    Its beauty is not bloom;
The hopes of which it breathes, are hopes
    That look beyond the tomb.
Thy song is sorrowful as winds
    That wander o'er the plain,
And ask for summer's vanished flowers,
    And ask for them in vain.

Ah! dearly purchased is the gift,
    The gift of song like thine;
A fated doom is hers who stands
    The priestess of the shrine.
The crowd—they only see the crown,
    They only hear the hymn;—
They mark not that the cheek is pale,
    And that the eye is dim.

Wound to a pitch too exquisite,
    The soul's fine chords are wrung;
With misery and melody
    They are too highly strung.
The heart is made too sensitive
    Life's daily pain to bear;
It beats in music, but it beats
    Beneath a deep despair.

LETITIA
ELIZABETH
LANDON

It never meets the love it paints,
   The love for which it pines;
Too much of Heaven is in the faith
   That such a heart enshrines.
The meteor wreath the poet wears
   Must make a lonely lot;
It dazzles, only to divide
   From those who wear it not.

Didst thou not tremble at thy fame,
   And loathe its bitter prize,
While what to others triumph seemed,
   To thee was sacrifice?
Oh, Flower brought from Paradise
   To this cold world of ours,
Shadows of beauty such as thine
   Recall thy native bowers.

Let others thank thee—'twas for them
   Thy soft leaves thou didst wreathe;
The red rose wastes itself in sighs
   Whose sweetness others breathe!
And they have thanked thee—many a lip
   Has asked of thine for words,
When thoughts, life's finer thoughts, have touched
   The spirit's inmost chords.

How many loved and honoured thee
   Who only knew thy name;
Which o'er the weary working world
   Like starry music came!
With what still hours of calm delight
   Thy songs and image blend;
I cannot choose but think thou wert
   An old familiar friend.

The charm that dwelt in songs of thine
   My inmost spirit moved;
And yet I feel as thou hadst been
   Not half enough beloved.
They say that thou wert faint, and worn
   With suffering and with care;
What music must have filled the soul
   That had so much to spare!

Oh, weary One! since thou art laid
   Within thy mother's breast—
The green, the quiet mother-earth—
   Thrice blessed be thy rest!

LETITIA ELIZABETH LANDON

Thy heart is left within our hearts,
    Although life's pang is o'er;
But the quick tears are in my eyes,
    And I can write no more.

(1835)

67 [FRAGMENT]

The altar, 'tis of death! for there are laid
The sacrifice of all youth's sweetest hopes.
It is a dreadful thing for woman's lip
To swear the heart away; yet know that heart
Annuls the vow while speaking, and shrinks back
From the dark future that it dares not face.
The service read above the open grave
Is far less terrible than that which seals
The vow that binds the victim, not the will:
For in the grave is rest.

(1837)

68 [FRAGMENT]

Oh, what a waste of feeling and of thought
Have been the imprints on my roll of life!
What worthless hours! to what use have I turned
The golden gifts which are my hope and pride!
My power of song, unto how base a use
Has it been put! with its pure ore I made
An idol, living only on the breath
Of idol worshippers. Alas! that ever
Praise should have been what praise has been to me—
The opiate of the mind!

(1837)

69 THE POLAR STAR

    This star sinks below the horizon in certain latitudes. I watched it sink lower and lower every night, till at last it disappeared.

A star has left the kindling sky—
    A lovely northern light—
How many planets are on high,
    But that has left the night.

LETITIA
ELIZABETH
LANDON

I miss its bright familiar face,
   It was a friend to me,
Associate with my native place,
   And those beyond the sea.

It rose upon our English sky,
   Shone o'er our English land,
And brought back many a loving eye.
   And many a gentle hand,

It seemed to answer to my thought,
   It called the past to mind,
And with its welcome presence brought
   All I had left behind.

The voyage it lights no longer, ends
   Soon on a foreign shore;
How can I but recall the friends,
   Who I may see no more?

Fresh from the pain it was to part—
   How could I bear the pain?
Yet strong the omen in my heart
   That says—We meet again.

Meet with a deeper, dearer love,
   For absence shows the worth
Of all from which we then remove,
   Friends, home, and native earth.

Thou lovely polar star, mine eyes
   Still turned the first on thee,
Till I have felt a sad surprise
   That none looked up with me.

But thou hast sunk below the wave,
   Thy radiant place unknown;
I seem to stand beside a grave,
   And stand by it alone.

Farewell!—ah, would to me were given
   A power upon thy light,
What words upon our English heaven
   Thy loving rays should write!

Kind messages of love and hope
   Upon thy rays should be;
Thy shining orbit would have scope
   Scarcely enough for me.

LETITIA ELIZABETH LANDON

Oh, fancy vain as it is fond,
   And little needed too,
My friends! I need not look beyond
   My heart to look for you!

(Wr. 1838, pub. 1839)

CATHERINE GRACE GODWIN (née GARNETT) (1798–1845)
She was born in Glasgow on 25 December 1798, the second daughter of Dr Thomas Garnett and Catherine Grace (née Cleveland). Her father was an eminent chemist and the first holder of the Chair of Chemistry at the Royal Institution. Her mother died at her birth in 1798, her father in 1802. A subscription was raised for the publication of his Royal Institution Lectures for the benefit of the orphaned daughters who were subsequently brought up by a friend of their mother, Miss Worboys, at Barbon, near Kirby Lonsdale in Westmorland, where Catherine Grace Godwin was to remain for the rest of her life and where she became acquainted with Wordsworth and Southey. She dedicated 'The wanderer's legacy' (1828) to Wordsworth and he replied with an important letter on the Spenserian stanza. She married Thomas Godwin, formerly of the East India Company, on 11 August 1824 at Old Church, St Pancras, London, and they returned to Barbon. Her sister died in a fire in Pistoia, Italy, in 1832, shortly after her marriage, and this seems to have curtailed Catherine Grace's literary activity. In the summer of 1844, she embarked on a continental tour with her husband, visiting Switzerland and Germany. She contributed to the Annals, *Blackwood's* and *Literary Gazette* and published *The night before the bridal, a Spanish tale. Sappho a dramatic sketch, and other poems*, London 1824, *The wanderer's legacy; a collection of poems on various subjects*, London 1829, *The reproving angel. A vision*, [London] 1835. After her death her poetry was collected in *The poetical works . . . Ed. with a sketch of her life by A. Cleveland Wigan*, London 1854. She died at Barbon on 5 May 1845, no cause of death given, with a Grace Lupton present. Her husband died in July 1852. They were buried at Firbank.

70 **TO FELICIA HEMANS**
    Bright names will hallow song.

Hadst thou, beneath the cloudless skies
   Of old heroic lands,
Poured forth thy thrilling melodies
   Amidst assembled bands,
Unnumbered harps had waked for thee
Triumphant peals of jubilee.

And they had voted thee a crown,
   A laurel chaplet green;
And hailed thee in thy blest renown

CATHERINE GRACE GODWIN

The Lyre's transcendant queen;
And borne thee through their ancient ways,
The idol of a nation's gaze.

Such were thy meed: but holier far,
   All gentle as thou art,
To thee, than crown or triumph's car,
   The homage of the heart:
So shalt thou reign, like summer's smile,
The gladness of thy native isle.

Thou of a hundred lays!—on thee,
   As on the inspired of old,
A voice, a power, a ministry,
   Things glorious to unfold,
Hath fallen, earth's depths to thee unsealing,
And Heaven in harmonies revealing.

The south-wind came on viewless wings
   From bowers of fragrance rare,
And sighing o'er thy harp's bright strings,
   Left all its sweetness there:
The sun-set gleams to each soft tone
Bequeathed a splendour all their own.

And, varied as the iris-hues,
   Thy graceful numbers blend:
Now like the summer's sparkling dews
   In radiance they descend;
Now pensive as the cypress-glooms
That rest on oriental tombs.

Anon, a solemn cadence floats
   O'er twilight landscapes dim,
Grand as the organ's rolling notes,
   Sweet as a choral hymn,
Borne fitfully upon the gale
From some lone chapel of the dale.

Enchantress! in thy fervid songs
   Fame, joy, grief's piercing sound,
All, all that to the heart belongs,
   Have general echoes found:
Thine too are the impassioned spells
That lie in earth's wild, sad farewells.

All gentle, and all holy themes,
   Truth, hope, faith's martyr name,
Touched by the spirit's golden dreams,

CATHERINE
GRACE
GODWIN

    Have found immortal fame:
Even death, the stern one, doth appear,
Hymned by thy harp, less dark and drear.

Oh! thou a splendent chain hast wrought
    Of life's endearing ties,
Strong human love, and many a thought
    Of home's fond memories:
And richer still thy verse hath shrined
The mysteries deep of woman's mind.

Woman, the true, the ill-requited!
    From whose meek spirit flows
A purer incense crushed and blighted,
    Like to the wounded rose—
Oh beautiful and meet her praise
Sounds in a gifted sister's lays!

Methought, as o'er me blandly stole
    The witchery of the strain,
Since thou hadst breathed my inmost soul,
    I ne'er would sing again:
Yet, ere its voice of song be mute,
Thy name shall sanctify my lute.

(1830)

71 THE LADY JANE GREY IN HER STUDY

Before I went into Germany (says Roger Ascham the learned preceptor of Queen Elizabeth) I came to Broadgate in Leicestershire to take my leave of the noble lady Jane Grey to whom I was exceeding much beholding. Her parents the duke and duchess, with all the household, gentlemen and gentlewomen, were hunting in the park. I found her in her chamber reading *Phaedon Platonis*, in Greek, and that with as much delight as some gentlemen would read a merry tale in Boccace. After salutation and duty done, with some other talk, I asked her why she should lose so much pastime in the park? Smiling, she answered me, 'I wist all their sport in the park is but a shadow of the pleasure I find in Plato'.

It was a chamber faire, with arras dight,
    And carvings old of princely heraldries,
And from the windows came a gorgeous light,
    Through panes distained with rich motley dyes,
    Like iris-hues that spanne capricious skies;
And these, in many a bright reflected gleame,
    On floore and ceiling, met the gazer's eyes;
So that the cell a faëry haunt did seeme,
Or grot of naïad coy beneath the crystal streame.

CATHERINE
GRACE
GODWIN

And from those quaint and archèd casements farre
   The ken did wander o'er a beauteous scene
Of copse and glade, where erst in sylvan warre
     Diana might have led her traine, I weene;
     And bowers yclad in summer's mantle greene,
Were there displayed, and brook and dimpled meer,
   Glancing the broad and ancient woods betweene,
Where the proud swan her graceful course did steer,
Or paused herself to view glassed in its surface clear.

About that room most lavishly were spread
   All things that showed the tablet of her mind,
Who dwelt therein; as rare flowers ever shed
     Their own sweete essence round them, till the wind
     Comes with its prying touche those sweetes to find.
Some female toys, a lute that might engage
     A lonesome hour to gentlest thoughts resigned,
Did silent rest upon the antique page,
Stamped with the wisdom high of Graecia's golden age.

But as the pearl entirely doth excel
   In worth, in lustre, and in loveliness,
The goodly structure of its shrouding shell;
     So she, the goddess of that fane, no less
     Inclined all tongues her glory to confess.
Not that she sought, by splendour of attire,
     To win the acclaim of flattering wantonness;
Her pure soul nursed alone the great desire
To catch the living tones of Truth's celestial lyre.

Her ivory hand upon the open book
   Was softly laid, the while her fair clear browe
Beamed with a pensive, yet a radiant looke,
     And her cheeke, crimsoned with a transient glowe,
     Like that the sun in parting love doth throwe
Athwart the western heavens. Her dove-like eye,
     Which e'en then all the martyred sainte did show,
Filled with the light of mind's infinity
Gazed upward through earth's glooms on immortality.

Entranced she sate, albeit the merry sonnde
   Of whoop, and halloo, and of horn, soe shrill,
Blent with the baying of the unleashed honnde,
     Came echoed back from grove and neighbouring hill,
     Bespeaking how the chace went blithely still.
That sweete faire ladye found it fuller joy
     To thrid the mazes Plato's subtle skill
Erst wove stray thought most blandly to decoy.
The which to her meeke mind brought peace without alloy.

(1836)

MARY ANN BROWNE (later GRAY) (1812–1845)

She was born on 24 September 1812 at The Thicket, near Maidenhead, Berkshire, the eldest of three children. Her mother, Mary Ann Simmons, came from Liverpool, with which the family probably retained a connection. Mary Ann Browne displayed an early talent for poetry, and as a child invented her own alphabet. In or around 1816 the family moved to a larger house, The Elms, Maidenhead, probably because of the need to accommodate the growing family. Her sister Martha Simmons Browne was born on 25 September 1813 and shared the same birthday as Felicia Hemans. This, together with moves to Liverpool and Ireland, gave rise to rumours that Mary Ann was Felicia Hemans' sister.

She began contributing to the Reading-based *Berkshire Chronicle* in 1826. The following year she published *Mont Blanc, and other poems*, London 1827, which probably drew her to the attention of Mary Russell Mitford who lived nearby at Three Mile Cross, and a long friendship ensued up to her death. The poem also attracted the attention of Letitia Landon. In the same year she appears to have had a pamphlet privately printed, *The widow* (1827), but did not distribute it and no copies appear to have survived. This was soon followed by *Ada, and other poems*, London 1828, which went through three editions in the same year, and by *Repentance and other poems*, London 1829. In September 1828, Coleridge wrote to Hanshall, wishing to make her acquaintance: 'I shall be proud in my old age, to meet a young lady who promises so fairly to adorn the era of my literary successors.' She spent the summer and autumn of 1828 at Swansea, after which the family moved to Worton Lodge in Isleworth, near London. Now much closer to London literary society, she met William Jerdan, became friends with his daughters, and began contributing to the Annuals. She also became friends with John Martin, the painter, and attended literary evenings at Dr Borthwick Gilchrist's, the orientalist. She also met Letitia Landon around this time, probably through Jerdan—by 1830 both Browne and Landon were early contributors to the *Literary Gazette*. The two appear to have become good friends and Landon visited her at Worton Lodge. The effect of such early fame and the introduction to London society seems to have provoked ambivalent feelings. On the one hand, Mary Russell Mitford, who had known her since she was fourteen, recalled how she was 'praised to the skies one day, utterly neglected the next—taken, as if a woman, into London society, and then thrown back upon a family circle in a provincial town, her health and spirits suffered'. However, in her own autobiography, written in 1840, which appears not to have survived, Browne described her experience on returning to the family home in rather different terms: 'I never felt such a palpable revolution of thought and feeling as took place on my journey here. Between Brentford and Isleworth, London seemed a dizzy dream. I was like a bird of the air restored from captivity to my native element.' In reality, the two positions are reconcilable. Most of the women poets of the period were from provincial towns or cities outside London, and the conflict between 'fame' and 'home' is powerfully present in other women poets, most notably Hemans, Landon and Jewsbury, but to a greater or lesser extent operates in many others. In the summer of 1831, the family moved to Bootle, on the outskirts of Liverpool, but finally settled at Soho Street, in Liverpool itself. The move was intended to further the 'commercial education' of the son, Thomas Briarly Browne, who later went to Trinity College Dublin and entered the church. During her time in Liverpool, she worked as a District Visitor (an early type of social worker who visited the sick and dying, orphanages and prisons) and continued to write verse in the midst of her 'distressing duties', publishing *The coronal; original poems, sacred and miscellaneous*, London and Liverpool 1833, *The birthday gift*, London and Liverpool 1834, and *Ignatia, and other poems*, London and Liverpool 1838. At this time she began to study German seriously and produced a number of translations of German poetry. She also became well acquainted with the Liverpool literary society surrounding the Annuals and knew the Chorleys and Howitts. She also met Maria Jane Jewsbury. She began to contribute to the *Dublin University Magazine* in June 1839 and became a regular contributor when she went to live in Dublin where her brother was studying. In 1840 she wrote an autobiography and published *Sacred poetry*, London 1840. In 1842 she married the Revd James Gray, nephew of James Hogg, the 'Ettrick Shepherd', and they moved to Sunday's Wells, on the outskirts of Cork. (She had earlier visited Cork in 1833 and her exact connection with the area is not known.) Her final publication appeared in Dublin, *Sketches from the antique: and other poems*, 1844. In early 1845 she gave birth to a son, but died of a heart attack on 28 January 1845 and was buried at St Paul's Church, Cork.

72 A WORLD WITHOUT WATER

> Yesternight I prayed aloud,
>   In anguish and in agony;
> Upstarting from the fiendish crowd
>   Of shapes and thoughts that tortured me.   [Coleridge]

I had a dream in the dead of night;
  A dream of agony;
I thought the world stood in affright,
Beneath the hot and parching light
  Of an unclouded sky:
I thought there had fallen no cooling rain
For months upon the feverish plain,
  And that all the springs were dry:

And I was standing on a hill,
  And looking all around:
I know not how it was; but still
  Strength in my limbs was found,
As if with a spell of threefold life,
  My destinies were bound.

Beneath me was a far-spread heath,
  Where once had risen a spring,
Looking as bright as a silver wreath
  In its graceful wandering:
But now the sultry glance of the sun,
  And the glare of the dark blue sky,
Had checked its course,—no more to run
  In light waves wandering by.

MARY ANN BROWNE

And farther on was a stately wood,
    With its tall trees rising high.
But now like autumn wrecks they stood
    Beneath a summer sky:
And every leaf, though dead, did keep
    Its station in mockery;
For there was not one breath to sweep
    The leaves from each perishing tree;
And there they hung dead, motionless;
    They hung there day by day,
As though Death were too busy with other things
    To sweep their corpses away.

Oh, terrible it was to think
    Of human creatures then!
How they did seek in vain to drink
    In every vale and glen;
And how the scorched foot did shrink
    As it touched the slippery plain:
And some had gathered beneath the trees
    In hope of finding shade;
But alas! there was not a single breeze
    Astir in any glade!

The cities were forsaken,
    For their marble wells were spent;
And their walls gave back the scorching glare
    Of that hot firmament:
But the corpses of those who died were strewn
    In the street, as dead leaves lay,
And dry they withered—and withered alone,
    They felt no foul decay!

Night came. The fiery Sun sank down,
    And the people's hope grew strong:
It was a night without a moon,
It was a night in the depth of June,
    And there swept a wind along;
'Twas *almost cool*: and then they thought
Some blessed dew it would have brought.

Vain was the hope!—there was no cloud
    In the clear dark blue Heaven;
But, bright and beautiful, the crowd
    Of stars looked through the even.
And women sat them down to weep
    Over their hopeless pain:
And men had visions dark and deep,
    Clouding the dizzy brain:

And children sobbed themselves to sleep,
   And never woke again.

The morning rose—not as it comes
   Softly 'midst roses and dew—
Not with those cool and fresh perfumes
   That the weariest heart renew,
—But the Sun sprang up, as if eager to see
   What next his power could do!

A mother held her child to her breast
   And kissed it tenderly,
And then she saw her infant smile;
   What could that soft smile be?
A tear had sprung with a sudden start,
   To her hot feverish eye;
It had fallen upon that faint child's lip
   That was so parched and dry.

I looked upon the mighty Sea;
   Oh, what a sight it was!
All its waves were gone save two or three,
   That lay like burning glass,
Within the caves of those deep rocks
   Where no human foot could pass.

And in the very midst, a ship
   Lay in the slime and sand;
With all its sailors perishing
   Even in sight of land;
Oh! water had been a welcome sight
   To that pale dying band!

Oh, what a sight was the bed of the Sea!
   The bed where he had slept,
Or tossed and tumbled restlessly,
   And all his treasures kept
For ages: he was gone; and all
   His rocky pillows shown,
With their clustering shells, and sea-weed pall,
   And the rich gems round them thrown.

And the monsters of the deep lay dead,
   With many a human form,
That there had found a quiet bed
   Away from the raging storm;
And the fishes, sodden in the sun,
   Were strewn by thousands round;
And a myriad things, long lost and won,
   Were there, unsought for, found.

MARY ANN BROWNE

MARY ANN
BROWNE

I turned away from earth and sea,
    And looked on the burning sky,
But no drop fell, like an angel's tear—
    The founts of Heaven were dry:
The birds had perished every one;
    Not a cloud was in the air,
And desolate seemed the very Sun,
    He looked so lonely there!

And I began to feel the pang—
    The agony of thirst;
I had a scorching swelling pain,
    As if my heart would burst.
My tongue seemed parched; I tried to speak—
    The spell that instant broke;
And, starting at my own wild shriek,
    In mercy I awoke.

(1832)

73 ROCKS

Herbless and crownless, with your foreheads bare
    Unto the blast, your bald heads reared towards Heaven,
    Unheeding winds and tempests, round you driven—
Your bosoms scorning every floweret fair,
Ye stand a fearless band!—yet often, when
    The storm is past, and summer suns are bright,
    Or in the quiet of a moonlit night,
Ye look most beautiful—and only then,
    Though ever grand. Oh! ye are like to those
Who for their faith in elder times were slain,
Scorning alike this low world's joy or pain,
    And Fame's green laurel, or soft Pleasure's rose;
And only deigning to receive a crown
Of light—and that from Heaven's own realms sent down!

(1832)

74 THE SONG OF THE ELEMENTS

FIRST VOICE—EARTH

I sit amidst the universe,
    As I've sat for ages gone,
And though God hath bound me with a curse,
    I am bathed in the light of the sun;
And I bear within my bosom the pride
    Of many a kingly throne,—

MARY ANN
BROWNE

There the diamond and ruby are scattered wide,
    And the changeless rocks are my zone;
And the mighty forest springs from my breast,
    And the mountain doth upward dart,
And though the clouds are on its crest,
    Its root is in my heart.
I am the mother of all things
    That have filled me since life began;
The nursing mother of founts and springs,
    The own true mother of man:
His limbs are formed from my finest clay,
    And let him die by earth or sea,
He must perish and pass away,
    And come again to me.
Oh, man is strong in his power and might,
    But I, his mother am more strong;
He is mine by a parent's right—
    Sisters! take up the song!

All the Elements

We four dwell all apart, yet, still
    We are bound by a viewless chain,
The thrones, that God hath given, we fill
    Each with a separate reign.
Contending oft, like the kings of earth,
    Triumphant for an hour;
Yet the fallen rising again, in the birth,
    Of its own unvanquished power.

Second Voice—Air

I lap the earth as with a robe,
    And I bind it like a rim,
And the clouds that shadow o'er the globe
    Upon my bosom swim.
And in the summer eve I play
    O'er earth like a sportive child;
And in the winter night I sway
    The world, with a tempest wild:
I dash on the rocks the helpless seas,
    Like wine from a reveller's cup,
And the proud earth cannot hold her trees,
    If I will to root them up.
And then I come in the autumn morn,
    With a fresh and stirring voice,
And I shake in the valley the golden corn,
    And the dying flowers rejoice:
I creep into the withering rose,
    And lull it as if to sleep,
Then up I start from that false repose,

And its leaves to the cold earth sweep.
Man must breathe me, or he dies
　　The minion of my power,
I have supplied with the breath of sighs
　　His heart from his earliest hour:
And, like an unseen enemy,
　　I battle with the strong;
Such might as this is claimed by me,—
　　Sisters! take up the song!

All the Elements

We four dwell all apart, yet, still
　　We are bound by a viewless chain,
The thrones, that God hath given, we fill
　　Each with a separate reign.
Contending oft, like the kings of earth,
　　Triumphant for an hour;
Yet the fallen rising again, in the birth,
　　Of its own unvanquished power.

Third Voice—Fire

I live in the light of the blazing sun,
　　And in the shining stars;
And restless o'er the world I run,
　　And nought my glory mars.
Silently, creep I through the earth,
　　'Midst many a precious stone,
And till the volcano gives me birth,
　　My being is unknown;
And in the tempest's glooming cloud,
　　I hide my burning wing,
And wait till the wind gives summons loud,
　　And then from my tent I spring!—
Like a conqueror from the ambush I come,
　　With a fatal glimmering spear,
And with a quick and sudden doom,
　　Earth's mightiest things I sear.
I can strike a man dead, if 'tis my will,
　　As a leaf falls from the tree,
'Tis I who makes his heart's pulse thrill,
　　He lives not without me.
Oh, man is a wondrous creature! our aid
　　Must make him stand or fall,
A thing of elements, and made
　　Dependant on them all!
He prides himself in the pomp and power,
　　That do to us belong;—
We laugh at him in his proudest hour;
　　Sisters! take up the song!

MARY ANN BROWNE

ALL THE ELEMENTS
We four dwell all apart, yet, still
  We are bound by a viewless chain,
The thrones, that God hath given, we fill
  Each with a separate reign.
Contending oft, like the kings of earth,
  Triumphant for an hour;
Yet the fallen rising again, in the birth,
  Of its own unvanquished power.

FOURTH VOICE—WATER
I burst from the earth, but for my birth
  I claim God's will alone,
Who made me queen of a realm serene,
  And placed me on my throne;
My throne of sunken rocks and caves,
  Where the crimson coral dwells,
Where I may let my weary waves
  Sleep on the pearly shells;
And in vast rocks sometimes I'm pent,
  Like a soul for some dark crime:
Till the prison at last is broken and rent,
  And comes my rejoicing time.
And I float sometimes in a quiet river,
  Under the cloud's passing shade,
And its broad breast doth in sunlight quiver,
  In loveliness arrayed;
And, down in my depths, I let the light
  Of the quiet blue sky dwell,
And the images of stars at night
  Are seen in my lovely cell.
Sometimes in the north I lie,
  Congealed, like a mighty isle,
Cold and unmoved 'neath the wintry sky,
  Unwon by the light's faint smile.
And then at last there shines a day
  Sunnily on my home,
And the icy bars to my path give way,
  And thundering out I come!
And rush upon the fated bark,
  With my waves in unprisoned glee,
And we whirl it down to the caverns dark,
  That are treasure rooms for me!
In the desert vast, where the caravan
  Is drooping for lack of shade,
Oh, how lordly, haughty man,
  Is my dependant made!—
As much as when in his fragile ship
  My waves did round him throng.

MARY ANN BROWNE

He dies if I do not bathe his lip.
Sisters! take up the song!

ALL THE ELEMENTS

We four dwell all apart, yet, still
   We are bound by a viewless chain,
The thrones, that God hath given, we fill
   Each with a separate reign.
Contending oft, like the kings of earth,
   Triumphant for an hour;
Yet the fallen rising again, in the birth,
   Of its own unvanquished power.

(1832)

75 A VISION OF POWER

The visions that beset the couch,
   Oh, who shall say from whence they come?
What watchful spirit's magic touch
      Paints them in light or gloom?

Last night, a dream came o'er my soul,
   A strange, a wild, a doubtful dream,
Most like the heavy clouds that roll,
      Lit by the lightning's gleam.

It was for such a dream, indeed,
   A night most fit—intensely dark,
Still, noiseless—I, who waked to read,
      No rustling leaf could mark.

And all was dark, and all asleep,
   Save my own soul, and in the skies
The stars, pure burning stars, to keep
      Still watch, like seraphs' eyes.

I slept, I know not how it was—
   Ye never can the moment tell,
When from the waking world ye pass
      To worlds invisible.

I slept, and in my sleep I dreamed
   I was again a very child,
A babe, on whom life's blessing streamed,
      Happy and undefiled.

MARY ANN BROWNE

Yet restless in my happiness,
   For even then I felt a power,
A mighty power, to ban or bless,
      Unfolding every hour.

('Twas strange that in my dream I thought
   I watched a mind upon its throne,
And marked how every impulse wrought,
      And yet it was my own.)

I felt this power I could extend
   O'er the small sphere wherein I dwelt,
I found my playmates it would bend,
      Or to my purpose melt.

Moons, years went by, before its name
   Was in my heart revealed and shrined,
Then did I feel from Heaven it came—
      The mighty power of Mind.

And then came youth, the link between
   Childhood and womanhood; again
I seemed of those around the queen,
      And bound them in my chain.

And still I had a thirst for more,
   A craving and insatiate pride;
Strong hearts were laid my heart before,
      Yet 't was unsatisfied.

I longed for fame—I longed to be
   More than a women e'er had been;
To have a burning destiny,
      As lightning bright and keen.

I looked on nature with an eye
   That saw her boundless loveliness;
I drew from earth, and sea, and sky,
      And in rich thoughts did dress

Sweet images; and then I took
   A harp, and touched it, and on themes
Where others had not dared to look
      I formed a thousand dreams.

And with an ever-varying song,
   Sweet, wild, or solemn, I subdued,
And held in bonds, as nature strong,
      The listening multitude.

MARY ANN BROWNE

I had my wish,—in every clime
    My strains were echoed, and were sung,
Let them be tender, or sublime,
        In every nation's tongue.

My heart throbbed high, my young brain whirled,
    'T was dizzy with its flashes bright,
That o'er the wondering crowd were hurled,
        Like lightnings through the night.

Time passed away—my songs had bowed
    The souls of men, and nought was gained,
Save the false incense of the crowd,
        And half their praises feigned.

Because they dared not but admire
    The idol of the passing day,—
Alas—my spirit had a fire
        That could not pass away.

It craved for more,—a fame like mine
    To other minstrels might be given,
And I might fall from my proud shrine,
        As falls a star from Heaven.

I looked upon the deeds of men,
    I studied look, and tone, and word,
And traced them back to heart and brain,
        As by a secret chord.

I learnt what feelings most pervade
    The hearts of all, and how my skill
Might best be used, my power be made
        To bend them to my will.

At last I spoke. The thunder cloud
    Bursts o'er the woods, and every tree,
With all its leaves, stands still and bowed,—
        And so were men by me.

I spake before the face of day,
    I stood beneath my native sky,
And, flinging woman's fears away,
        I spake of liberty,

Of slavish fear, of bonds of men,
    Of justice, and of human laws;
And oh, how thrilled my feverish brain,
        When burst the loud applause!

MARY ANN
BROWNE

My dream grew vague,—I know not how
    Through many changing states I passed,
And still I found the nations bow
        Unto my spirit vast.

And years went on. In that one dream,
    How many years seemed rolling by!
At length unclouded shone the beam
        Of my great destiny.

I ruled all knowledge, wisdom, worth,
    I ruled the pen, the sword, the shrine;
And all the sovereignty of Earth,
        In one wide range, was mine!

My throne was fixed in pomp and state,
    My edicts o'er the land I hurled,
And high in boundless power I sate,
        The empress of the world.

And there was nothing left to win;
    Dominion o'er the earth I bore—
Yet was the restless fire within
        Still craving on for more!

Aye, it was torture—burning hell,
    To think that all that could be gained,
All that seemed unattainable,
        Already was attained!

And now to be alone, alone—
    A being placed above my kind,
A helpless idol on my throne,
        With nought to feed my mind;

No sweet affection, no pure stream,
    Where I might turn aside and drink!
Oh, even in my baseless dream,
        How my chilled heart did shrink!

I looked on many a subject's hearth,
    And envied bliss I was denied;
The children's laugh of careless mirth,
        By love so sanctified;

The buoyant steps, that seemed to rove
    The freer for affliction's ties;
The glistening light of happy love,
        In woman's gentle eyes.

MARY ANN
BROWNE

I flung me down in agony—
    The scorching of my throbbing brain
Was such a truthful misery,
        I feel even now the pain;

I flung me down in agony—
    My soul within me was on fire,
To think that I must fall and die,
        And *here* be nothing higher.

'Oh,' said I, in that wretched hour,
    'That I in my first dream had died,
With all my fresh, strong, inward power
        Just bursting forth in pride!'

And then I felt my heart so swell
    With its great anguish, as I spoke,
That from its chords it forced the spell,
        And my strange vision broke.

I never *was* ambition's slave;
    Sometimes I've wished the poet's wreath
Might blossom o'er my lowly grave,
        Whilst I lay cold beneath;

But would not win with such wild pain
    The whole world's majesty and might;
Nor, even in a dream, again
        Feel what I felt last night.

(1834)

76 FRAGMENTARY VERSES
    A change came o'er the spirit of my dream. [Byron]

I dreamed I was alone on earth. Methought
    I was a being separate and apart
From all the world besides; that never wrought
    A spirit, like the spirit in my heart,
With all its thirsty aspirations, all
    Its ceaseless yearnings, its insatiate fever,
Its vigorous struggles with its earthly thrall,
    Its visions of delight—vain self-deceiver!
It had deep thoughts that found no uttered tone,
No voice might speak them—I was all alone.

Alone, alone for years, even in the dawn
    Of mind and thought, when the young heart, desiring

MARY ANN
BROWNE

Draughts from the glorious well of knowledge drawn,
  Was quick and hasty in its wide requiring.
Who answered me? who knew each ardent longing?
  Who cared to unlock the spring by which I stood?
Who saw and numbered all the visions thronging
  Within my soul, a newly opened flood?
They heard my eager questions, strange and free,—
  With cold, uncaring words they answered me.

Trees, flowers, stars, sunsets! how I turned to these,
  For there were mysteries veiled within their power;
How I have listened for the awakening breeze,
  Yearning to hear a voice in the deep hour
Of night, shaped from its tones; some clear revealing
  Of unattained knowledge, some bright tale
Of the soul's history, or the birth of feeling,
  Some drawing back of the impervious veil!
In vain! dim gleams, that quivered and decayed,
And came no more, that feverish watch repaid.

Forms flitted by my couch, and in my dreams,
  My day-dreams, they were mingled; radiant eyes,
Fitfully bright, like stars on mountain streams,
  And clasping hands and hearts, with sympathies
Linked to mine own, bright visions, all undimmed
  With earthly fear or sorrow; yet beneath
The gulf was fathomless, o'er which they skimmed
  Like passing barks, a gulf where Life and Death
Mysteriously were mingling, with all things
  Too vast for mortal mind's imaginings.

Hopelessly did I wonder, hopeless nursed
  The aching wish in freer air to move;
Then in my heart arose another thirst,
  A longing for some answering human love:
How should I seek it but through sympathy?
  And *this* I fancied, and my heart adored
Dreams, idols, phantasies, for none to me
  Gave back the affection, whose full tide I poured,
In its undying brightness, with its trust
And passion.—Where? Upon the barren dust.

Some marvelled at the feelings, too intense
  To be returned by them; some turned away,
And laughed to scorn the passionate vehemence
  That would have shattered hearts of common clay
With its outbursting; some reflected back
  A portion of its light,—as the cold moon
The burning sunshine; yet the onward track

Of my wild spirit followed not, and soon
Wearied and left me. No—there was not one
Found who could *love* like me.—I was alone!

* * * * *

But thou! oh thou who minglest in my soul,
    Like a deep river with the ocean! Thou,
Through whose strong heart the thoughts, like torrents, roll,
    Yet who unto all gentle dreams canst bow!
Thou, who hast eyes *that see as mine*, that drink
    The glory of the starlight, and behold
The inner world of beauty, that would shrink
    From the dull spirits of the coarse and cold—
Am I alone? No—the deep gulf is past—
My heart hath found its home, its like, at last.

The deep, clear music of the Poet's heart,
    Flowing in inner currents, soft and bland;
The vivid dreams, that thence to being start,
    Of these I speak, and thou canst understand.
Why should I care for others? Thou to me
    Art the One Being—all I have on earth;
Life's other forms are dreams and phantasy,—
    Unreal shapes, whose smiles and frowns are worth
Not half so much as the dim clouds that lour,
Mingled with sunshine, in a summer shower.

All other loves were but idolatry,
    The helpless pouring forth of the soul's spring;—
This is the free, glad gift, without a sigh
    O'er the heart's weakness,—a fond offering
To a true sovereign; oh, the hoarded wealth
    Of truth and faith I have to give thee yet!
Thoughts thought, dreams dreamed, affections nursed
        by stealth,—
    These shall be thine, all thine; and no regret
Shall mingle more with the impassioned tone
Of my heart's chords.—I am no more alone!

(1838)

77 THE EMBROIDERESS AT MIDNIGHT

She plies her needle till the lamp
    Is waxing pale and dim;
She hears the watchman's heavy tramp,
    And she must watch like him—
Her hands are dry, her forehead damp,
    Her dark eyes faintly swim.

MARY ANN
BROWNE

Look on her work!—here blossom flowers,
    The lily and the rose,
Bright as the gems of summer hours,
    But not to die like those;
Here, fadeless as in Eden's bowers,
    For ever they repose.

Once, maiden, thou wast fresh and fair,
    As those sweet flowers of thine;
Now, shut from sunny light and air,
    How canst thou choose but pine?
Neglected flows thy raven hair,
    Like the uncultured vine.

Think how her trembling hand will clasp
    The treasure it will hold,
With that which seems a greedy grasp—
    Yet not for love of gold:
That look—that sigh's relieving gasp,
    Its deeper springs unfold.

Think how her hasty feet will roam
    The market and the street,
To purchase for her humble home
    The food and clothing meet,
And with what gladness she will come
    Back to this poor retreat!

Poor maiden! if the fair ones who
    Thy graceful 'broidery buy,
Only *one-half* thy struggles knew,
    And filial piety,
Methinks some drop of pity's dew
    Would gem the proudest eye!

It is not *here* its full reward
    Thy gentle heart will prove;
Here ever must thy lot be hard,
    But there is One above
Who sees, and will not disregard,
    Thy consecrated love.

Look on her work!—no common mind
    Arranged that glowing group—
Wild wreaths the stately roses bind,
    Sweet bells above them droop—
Ye almost *see* the sportive wind
    Parting the graceful troop!

MARY ANN
BROWNE

Look on her work!—but look the more
   On her unwearied heart,
And put aside the chamber-door
   That doth the daughter part
From that dear mother, who before
   Taught her this cunning art.

She sleeps—that mother, sick and pale—
   She sleeps—and little deems
That she, who doth her features veil
   All day, in flitting gleams
Of anxious hope, this hour doth hail,
   But not for happy dreams.

God bless her in her lone employ,
   And fill those earnest eyes
With visions of the coming joy,
   Waiting her sacrifice,
When they, who give her this employ,
   Pay her its stinted price!

(1843)

MARIA ABDY (née SMITH) (1797–1867)

She was born on 25 February 1797 in London, the daughter and only child of Richard Smith, a solicitor in the City of London, and Maria (née Smith). She was a niece of Horace and James Smith. Her early years were spent in the area of Russell Square and she displayed a precocious talent for literature. She married John Channing Abdy, rector of St John's, Southwark in 1821, and he encouraged her first contributions to the *New Monthly Magazine* (under the signature 'M.A.'). She went on to contribute to the *Metropolitan*, under the editorship of Thomas Camp-bell, and many of the Annuals, particularly *Forget-Me-Not, Friendship's Offering, Keepsake* and several others. She gathered many of her periodical and fugitive contributions in a series of privately printed collections, *Poetry*, London 1834, *Poetry. Second series*, London 1838, *Poetry. Third series*, London 1842, *Poetry. Fourth Series*, London 1846, *Poetry. Fifth series*, London 1850, *Poetry. Sixth series*, London 1854, *Poetry. Seventh series*, London 1858, and *Poetry. Eighth series*, London 1862.

An only son, Albert Channing Abdy, was christened on 3 July 1829 at St John Horsleydown, Bermondsey. Her husband died in 1845 but this did not prevent the son going to Worcester College Oxford, as had his father, and he later took orders and at the time of her death was living in Streatham. She died on 19 July 1867 at 7 Upper Marine Terrace, Margate, the cause of death 'decay of nature', with a T. Smith Rowe, M.D., of 1 Cecil Street, Margate, present at her death. According to her will, made in 1865, she was described as 'formerly of Harley Street, Cavendish Square [London], late of 18 German Place, Brighton. Her estate, the greater part of which (including her books and papers) went to her son, was valued at under £10,000, and included a generous provision of £100 in cash and a £500 annuity for her servant. She was buried at St Peter's Churchyard, Isle of Thanet.

78 THE ENCHANTED GROUND

'Lady, danger hovers round:
Turn from the Enchanted Ground;
Though the scene be fair and bright,
Though it smile with flowers and light,
Evil spirits wander there,
Glancing, warbling, to ensnare;
Shun the sight, avoid the sound—
Fly from the Enchanted Ground!'

'Little can thy counsel sage,
Warning friend, my fears engage;
Dread enchantments but prevail
In the wondrous fairy-tale;
Sorcery no spell can bind
O'er the firm, enlightened mind;
Joys in yonder hall abound:
Say not 'tis Enchanted Ground.'

'Lady, list to Wisdom's call:
Enter not yon splendid hall;
There unnumbered lamps are shining,
Gems are sparkling, roses twining,
Harps resound in sportive measure,
Voices breathe the songs of pleasure;
Yet delusion reigns around:
Trust me, 'tis Enchanted Ground.

'Shouldst thou visit once the dome,
Changed will seem thy peaceful home;
Images of radiant guise
Still will float before thine eyes;
Dazzling forms and siren lays
Haunt thee in thy household ways;
And thy heart be ever found
Lingering on Enchanted Ground.

'See! in trembling doubt she waits,
Gazing on the glittering gates;
Now the silvery bells are ringing,
Now the minstrel band are singing,
Now the wanderer they accost,
Welcoming the bright, the lost—

MARIA ABDY

She has passed the fatal bound,
She has reached Enchanted Ground.

"Tis my mournful solace still
One last duty to fulfil:
Heaven accept for her my prayer—
Guard her with thy watchful care;
Teach her heart to own thy power;
And, at Life's last solemn hour,
Let not one like her be found
Slumbering on Enchanted Ground!'

(1833)

79 THE POETESS

    Not idly did the Muses' choir select
    The barren laurel for their ornament:
    Cold, destitute of odour as of fruit,
    It weighs upon the brow to which it promised
    Full compensation for each sacrifice.   [Grillparzer's Sappho]

I saw her in her youth's bright dawn; her eye
Smiled like the sunshine of a summer sky;
Her cheek of rose, and lip of deeper glow,
Seemed yet unsullied by one tear of woe:
She loved to cull the spring's first flowers, and wear
The blossoms in her curls of ebon hair;
Or range the ocean cliffs, and search their cells,
For vivid sea-weed, and for glittering shells;
And strangers might have deemed her simple pleasures
Were sought alone in Nature's boundless treasures:
But hers was not a common soul or mind:
Remote from crowds, sequestered from mankind,
In her lone walks, she early learned to choose
A loved companion in the silent Muse;
With her would soar on Fancy's eagle wings,
Till lost in bright and vast imaginings!

A few short years elapsed—I saw her then,
A lovely meteor in the paths of men:
She smiled amid the sound of mirth and song,
The idol of a gay and glittering throng;
Yet, though with eager gaze her form I viewed,
Rich in the ripened bloom of womanhood,
Methought the votive crowd's assiduous duty
Surpassed the homage paid alone to Beauty:
I learned the cause—her high and gifted lays
Had won the public ear, the public praise;
Cold critics even on her brow had set

MARIA ABDY

The trophy of Fame's golden violet;
And princes hung delighted on her strains;
And statesmen there forgot their toils and pains;
And beauties left for them the halls of gladness;
And warriors wept o'er their delicious sadness.
Yet, though triumphant joy was in her face,
It had not lost its sweet and bashful grace;
And when the crowd who rapture felt or feigned
Spoke of the unfading laurels she had gained,
She brightly blushed, and trembling turned aside,
And woman's shame prevailed o'er woman's pride.

I saw her ere another year had past—
But oh! how altered since I met her last!
Her tale was short—she loved in evil hour—
Loved with that wild, intense, absorbing power,
Felt by the soul of minstrel fire alone,
And to all others foreign and unknown.
Her love was fixed on one of common mould,
Graceful and gay, but selfish, vain, and cold;
He could not prize that passion, raised, refined,
Nay, with dull envy he beheld the mind,
Whose ardent energy, and high wrought tone,
Seemed to reproach the weakness of his own.
He scorned her heart.—Around her early tomb,
Fair maidens came with wreaths of vernal bloom,
And sorrowing youths, with laurels, bright and green,
And wailing numbers, sought the woeful scene,
And wept the pride and darling of the age,
The lovelier Sappho of a purer page;
But he, the frozen one, for whom she died,
Turned from her grave, and wooed a heartless bride.

Daughter of Mind!—how oft is this thy fate
To dwell in lonely brightness desolate;
To win the homage of a servile train,
Yet lose the only heart thou sigh'st to gain!
Man through the paths of minstrelsy may stray,
Nor heed the perils of the thorny way:
But Woman, whose devoted, tender feelings,
Acquire new force from Fancy's wild revealings,
Will steep in tears her laurels of renown,
Unless Love blends with them his myrtle crown;
And Love beholds her on her dizzy height
Robed in resplendent ways of dazzling light,
And seeks some humbler maid in lowly bower,
To soothe and solace with his smiling power.
Hear this, ye cold of heart, and envy not
The barren splendour of her cheerless lot.

Nor covet the bright wreaths her song secures,
And murmur that such glories are not yours!
Oh! think, while owning all that most you prize,
Dear social intercourse, domestic ties,
How hard her lot, from all such joys confined,
The sovereign of a desert waste of mind:
When her gay strains the voice of praise are waking,
Know that the heart which breathes them may be breaking;
And when her lyre a lay of sorrow pours,
And the cold world admires, applauds, adores,
Think that around that lyre the cypress clings,
And, like the swan, her own sad dirge she sings!

(1834)

80 LINES WRITTEN ON THE DEATH OF MRS HEMANS

Yes, she has left us. She, whose gifted lays
So nobly earned a nation's love and praise,
Entranced the high and lofty ones of earth—
And shed a radiance o'er the peasant's hearth,
She from the world is taken. Her sweet lute
Hangs on the willow desolate and mute;
And while we half unconsciously repeat
Strains we have learned as household words to greet,
How mournful is the thought, that she can pour
Songs of such touching melody no more!

Oh! what a range of mind was here, how bright
Her pages seemed with Inspiration's light;
And yet, though skilled in dazzle and o'erwhelm,
Queen of Imagination's fairy realm,
Her highest excellence appeared to be
In the calm region of reality.
In Nature's wondrous workings lay her art,
From that exhaustless mine, the human heart,
She brought her gems. 'Twas hers, with gentle skill
The slumbering feelings to arouse and thrill
With colours not more beautiful than true
The modest virtues of her sex she drew.
'Records of Woman.' At that name arise
Fair shapes of truth and goodness to our eyes:
Not the gay phantoms seen in Fancy's trance,
Not the bright paragons of old romance,
Nor yet the wonders of a later age,
The heroines of Reason's formal page,
Full of cold, calculating, worldly sense,
And self-elate in moral excellence!

No—at Religion's pure and sacred flame
Her torch she kindled—'twas her wish and aim
That in her female portraits we should see
The blest effects of humble piety,
Proving that, in this world of sin and strife,
None could fulfil the charities of life,
Or bear its trials, save the path they trod
Were hallowed by the guiding grace of God.

And well her spirit in her life was shown,
No character more lovely than her own
Fell from her gifted pen—though numbers breathed
Her name, though laurel bands her brow enwreathed,
She sought not in the world's vain scenes to roam,
Her duties were her joys, her sphere was home:
And Memory still a pensive pleasure blends
With the affliction of her weeping friends,
When they recall the meek calm lowliness
With which she bore the blaze of her success:
But trials soon as well as triumphs came,
Sickness subdued her weak and languid frame,
Then was she patient, tranquil, and resigned,
Religion soothed and fortified her mind;
She knew that for the blessed Saviour's sake,
In whom she trusted, she should sleep to wake
In glory, and she yielded up her breath,
Feeling she won eternity by death.

Oh! may her holy principles impress
The soul of each surviving poetess;
No trivial charge is to her care consigned,
Who gives to public view her stores of mind:
Even though her sum of treasures may be small,
Good can be worked, if Heaven permit, by all:
She who a single talent holds in store,
By patient zeal may make that little more;
And though but few, alas! can boast the powers
Of her now lost, the gift may still be ours
Humbly to imitate her better part,
And strive to elevate each reader's heart
To themes of purer and of holier birth
Than the low pleasures and vain pomps of earth.
Never may Woman's lays their service lend
Vice to encourage, soften, or defend,
Nor may we in our own conceit be wise,
Weaving frail webs of mere moralities:
No, may we ever on His grace reflect,
To whom we owe our cherished intellect,
Deem that such powers in trust to us were given

MARIA ABDY

To serve and glorify our Lord in heaven,
And place, amid the highest joys of fame,
Our best distinction in a Christian name.

(1835)

81 THE DESERTED WIFE TO HER SISTER

Sister, a rapid year has fled,
   Since, gay in girlhood's pride,
Forth from my father's house I sped,
   A glad triumphant bride;
I thought not then of ills to come,
   Nor dreamed the time was nigh,
When I must seek my early home,
   To suffer and to die.

The tears I shed to leave it then,
   Were like the summer showers,
That, stealing o'er the thirsty glen,
   Revive the drooping flowers;
But now they fall in bitter grief,
   Like winter's driving rain,
Crushing the frail and blighted leaf
   That ne'er can smile again.

An ear; sweet sister, pure as thine,
   I may not ask to hear
The wrongs, the insults that were mine
   Through that degrading year:
Suffice it, that deserted, spurned
   By him who claimed my truth,
To the loved home I trembling turned
   That sheltered me in youth.

Nor—though unbidden may intrude
   The sad regretful tear—
Doubt of my fervent gratitude
   For all my blessings here;
The ark received in her distress
   The poor desponding dove,—
I met a father's kind caress,
   A mother's gentle love.

And thou, sweet sister!—words are vain
   Thy tender faith to show;
Thou can'st forsake the mirthful train,
   To soothe my daily woe:

Nor do thy cares in darkness cease;
   Ever, with noiseless tread,
Thou com'st to whisper sounds of peace
   Around my sleepless bed.

Soon shall thy task of love be o'er;
   And when thy thraldom ends,
Thou may'st rejoin, in smiles once more,
   Thy kindred and thy friends;
Yet, sister, hear my words of truth,
   In life's last sad decline,
Fain would I guard thy trusting youth
   From miseries like mine.

I mourned my lover's erring life—
   I knew him light—profane—
Yet deemed the fond, devoted wife
   His changeless faith might gain;
Of intellect and beauty proud,
   I little feared to see
A trivial and delusive crowd
   Preferred to love and me.

Untaught of God, unused to prayer,
   I yet aspired to win
A victim from the subtle snare
   Of soul-destroying sin.
Thou know'st the rest—oh, sister, shun
   The rashness I deplore!
Nor deem thou canst be loved by one
   Who loves not virtue more.

Still o'er the wanderer watchful prove,
   Still pray his sins may cease;
But, sister, give him not thy love,
   Nor trust him with thy peace;—
No—bid him humbly kneel and weep
   To One who rules the sod;
He cannot faith with woman keep,
   Who holds no faith with God.

(183?)

82 THE RAILWAY TUNNEL

Borne by the wondrous power of steam
   With startling speed through regions dreary,
Some panic-struck and fearful seem,
   Some languid, spiritless, and weary;

MARIA ABDY

For me, I willingly forsake
   The upper world, its glare and riot,
And love awhile my course to take
   Through ways of subterranean quiet.

While earth's deep caverns I explore,
   Thought leads me on its magic pinions,
To trace the time when Pluto bore
   A bride to share his dark dominions;
Just so, methinks, might Proserpine
   Gaze on the gathering shades that bound her,
Just so behold the torches shine
   At fitful intervals around her.

Nor have I need to apprehend
   That listless tedium may steal o'er me,
Knowing the darkness soon shall end,
   And life's fair scenes smile forth before me;
Then from the light and leafy spray,
   Shall gay and warbling birds be singing,
Then, fostered by the warmth of day,
   Sweet flowers shall in my way be springing.

I marvel much that mortals view
   With so much terror and dejection,
The paths of life they journey through
   Beneath a safe and wise direction;
Even in the darkest, saddest way,
   Some comfort surely may be near us,
Hope oft may dart a flashing ray,
   And pleasant thoughts compose and cheer us.

It is not healthful to the mind,
   Always to dwell in scenes of glitter;
None but the world's vain pupils find
   Secluded stillness dull and bitter:
The cheerful spirit then prepares
   Its feast of intellect and reason,
And, with contented gladness, bears
   The shade of its allotted season.

To those who own a heavenly guide,
   Distrust must always be a stranger;
His mercy ever is supplied
   In darkness, solitude, and danger;
When dreary gloom our road invades,
   He bids our hearts to thrill in lightness,
And guides us through the deepest shades,
   To greet the day's unclouded brightness.

(1843)

THE DRESSMAKER

MARIA ABDY

Dark midnight o'er the stately city throws
A still and silent mantle of repose;
Hushed are the sounds of day; pale stars arise,
Gemming with faint, soft gleam the vaulted skies;
And we might deem that all were wrapped in sleep,
Save those who wake to suffer and to weep,
Did not the rich, full tones of music float
On the calm air, and the clear, lingering note
Of woman's voice, by science made more sweet,
Steal on the ear. The gay and wealthy meet
To-night in yon proud mansion. Pass we now
Within the splendid hall: bright tapers glow
On every side, shedding a golden ray
That seems to tint the scene with mimic day:
Crowds, joyous crowds, glide through the gilded rooms,
And sparkling gems, rich robes, and waving plumes
Shine gaily forth. Exotics, sweet and rare,
Diffuse their fragrance o'er the balmy air;
And breathing pictures greet the raptured eye,
And bright and gorgeous mirrors multiply
The groups around. Maids beautiful and young,
There blush and smile, yet, 'mid the dazzling throng,
One fairer than the rest, enchants the glance;
Nor doth she, like a damsel of romance,
Appear 'when unadorned, adorned the most';
None can attire more rare and studied boast,
None are more skilfully and aptly graced
By the blent aid of fashion and of taste.
The shadowy web seems light as woven air,
That coyly screens her arms and bosom fair;
Soft, silver draperies cast a chastened light
O'er the pure robe of fair and spotless white,
That clings caressingly her form around,
Then falls in rich abundance to the ground;
Half veiling, half disclosing to the eye,
A shape of matchless grace and symmetry.
But she, thus decked by nature and by art,
Has thoughts of dearer triumph in her heart.
Amid that crowd, a youth of noble name
Hath long in anxious homage sought to claim
Her smiles, and poured those flatteries in her ear
Which youths delight to breathe, and maids to hear.
Now through the gay, admiring crowd he breaks;
Now by her side, in soft, low tones he speaks
Of love long felt, of feeling, true and fond,
Of the pure joys of wedlock's sacred bond.
She hears him; and, amid that glittering scene,

MARIA ABDY

She feels as though, arrayed in russet sheen,
She listened to a village lover's vows,
Beneath the white and fragrant hawthorn boughs.
She sighs consent. Anon, the guests depart;
And she among the rest, with throbbing heart,
And cheeks that still retain their vivid bloom,
Reaches in silent happiness her home;
Then to her mother's chamber softly steals,
And her glad tale of prosperous love reveals.
The worldly matron smiles in joyous pride:
'I felt this night must bring success,' she cried,
'Such charms, so skilfully improved by art,
Might well subdue the coldest lover's heart;
Go, dearest, dream awhile of coming bliss.'
The gentle girl returns her mother's kiss,
Then seeks her couch, too blessed at first to sleep,
Till gradually, in rest composed and deep
She sinks, and lies beneath morn's smiling light,
Wrapped in soft visions of the previous night.

And 'mid that proud assemblage, glad and gay,
Who praised the maiden in her fair array,
Say, was there one who deigned to cast a thought
On her whose hand the graceful garment wrought?
How doth *she* pass the midnight hour? Perchance,
From some far gallery, she bends a glance
On that bright girl, and feels elate at heart,
Deeming she bears in her success a part;
Perchance, the tranquil evening she may spend
In social converse with a valued friend;
Perchance, ere now, her blooming cheek has pressed
Her pillow, and she lies in peaceful rest.
Not so, not so. Ye who can bear to see
Her drear and joyless dwelling, come with me!

—Tis midnight; and within a narrow room,
Where one faint taper glimmers through the gloom,
A pale, sad girl her needle swiftly plies,
While sleep seems struggling in her heavy eyes,
Revealing by their dim and clouded light,
The vigils kept through many a weary night.
Once she was glad; her spirit was elate
With buoyant hope; and, 'mid the halls of state,
Where dwell the high-born daughters of the land,
Decked by the labours of her active hand,
None were more fair and gay. Now lingering toil
Hath done its work; fled is her former smile;
Her cheek is wan, her eye hath lost its ray;
The haggard look of premature decay

Blights her young charms; she feels the sickening chill
Of sorrow, yet pursues her labours still.
Morn breaks: the soft and quivering sunbeam falls
In wakening radiance on the humble walls
Of her lone room. Fain would she lay aside
The toil whereby she ministers to pride;
Fain from her weary task awhile repair
To breathe the freshness of the early air;
She pauses: she recalls her cottage home,
Where the rich roses in their dewy bloom
Clung round the lattice. On the breezy hill
She seems to roam, and breathe the fragrance still
Of the wild thyme. Doth she not fondly look
On the warm sunbeams dancing on the brook?
Does she not gather cowslips in the dell,
And hear the lark's glad song? No, no: the spell
Of memory fades away: she gazes round:
The gay and glittering shreds that strew the ground,
The robe half finished, that appears to ask
Her aiding hand, remind her of her task:
Dispel the phantoms of bright, buried years,
And rouse her to a world of toil and tears.

—Time flies. The course of wealthy love runs smooth;
And the fair maiden and the noble youth
Who, in the hall of gay and festal glee,
First breathed their vows of mutual constancy,
Now stand together in God's sacred fane,
Those vows to ratify. A brilliant train
Of friends and kindred wait their presence there;
And bridesmaids with white roses in their hair,
And clad in tasteful raiment, stand beside
The playmate of their youth, the gentle bride,
Watching, in smiling earnestness, to see
If the rich veil be flowing gracefully,
And the fair ringlets quaintly fall beneath
The crowning blossoms of the bridal wreath.
Oh! worldly Pomp! where dost thou enter not,
Since, even in this pure and holy spot,
Such thoughts intrude? How few are thinking now
Of the deep meaning of that solemn vow,
Binding these young, true lovers heart to heart
In ties that death, and death alone, can part.
None gaze upon the bride in doubt or fear,
None pour soft words of counsel in her ear;
Their speech is of her charms, and of the dress
Which adds new lustre to her loveliness.
Who wrought the garment? She who toiled before
In the sad task, say, must *she* evermore

MARIA ABDY

Fresh offerings to the feet of beauty bring?
But none regard her lot. The joy-bells ring;
Musicians pour their practised strains around;
And the proud mother hears the mingled sound,
Pronouncing, while her heart with triumph swells,
No music tuneful as those marriage bells!

    The sunny morning hours have passed away;
Tis now a later period of the day;
The bells that spoke the nuptials of the fair,
Now float not gaily on the breezy air.
The bell speaks still, but calls not to rejoice;
Hark to the heavy sound! Its solemn voice
Doth not of scenes of joy and gladness tell;
'Tis the deep breathing of the funeral knell.
A few sad friends in tears and silence come,
Attending to her last and quiet home
The pale, fair sufferer. Wearied with her woes,
At length within the grave she finds repose.
Poor, helpless victim of the rich and great!
Worse than Egyptian bondage was thy fate.
How didst thou sacrifice by slow degrees
Thy bloom, thy health, thy leisure, and thy ease!
Even the pure Sabbath's still and peaceful calm,
Giving to wounded hearts a healing balm,
Rejoiced thee not! The sweet and sacred chimes
Mocked thy dull ear: they told of happier times,
When thou with friends and neighbours would'st repair
Through the cool valley to the house of prayer,
Seeking God's presence. Languid and oppressed,
The Sabbath ceased to be a day of rest
To thy worn frame; yet thou, in patient love,
Could'st meekly lift thine orisons above;
And feel, through life's slow, desolate decline,
That soon the grave's still Sabbath would be thine.
I grieve to trace the progress of thy pain;
Yet wilt thou not have toiled and died in vain,
If thy brief history tend to mitigate
Existing woes; to lessen and abate
The sum of human suffering. I appeal
To those whose hearts are ever prompt to feel,
Let but their hidden sympathies be sought
Through the high medium of awakened thought;—
To England's Women! Ye, whose virtuous lives
Attest your worth as mothers and as wives,
Whose wise and calm sobriety commands
The praise and reverence of surrounding lands;
To you I plead! I urge you to redress
The wrongs, the pain, the thraldom, the distress,

Caused by your passive agency. Protect
The timid handmaids of your pomp; reflect
On their unceasing toils; and when you gaze
On the gay robe, intent on future praise,
Oh! do not proudly from your mind exclude
The thought of that pale, patient sisterhood,
Who, in the favoured kingdom of the free,
Droop in the chains of civic slavery!
You may not actively inflict the stroke,
But yet you give a sanction to the yoke
By silence. I require you not to slight
Their aid. I speak not as an anchorite,
Wishing the young and lovely to resign
The charm of bright attire. Still smile and shine
In graceful garb; but let your influence stay
The might of all, who with despotic sway,
Withhold from those who toil your taste to please,
Befitting seasons of repose and ease.
A cry appeals to every feeling breast:
Oh! hear it! 'tis the cry of the oppressed!
Arouse ye! strive a moral to extract
From verse that is the vehicle of fact!
So may ye bring a blessing on the page
Of one, who grieving for a thoughtless age,
Mingles with words of warning and advice
This record of the Pageant and its Price!

(1846)

84 THE EMBROIDERY FRAME

> The mind will easily straggle from the fingers, nor can its sorrows receive solace from silken flowers. [*Rasselas*]

In a lofty room a lady fair
   Sits plying the silken thread,
She doth not the bitter bondage share
   Of the tribe who toil for bread;
On the rich graceful folds of her rich attire
   The glittering sunbeam falls;
Not such are the sad ones who work for hire
   In the hovel's whitened walls:
The wreaths, that beneath her fingers bloom,
   Seem fresh from their native bowers,—
Why doth she wear such a glance of gloom
   As she bends o'er her silken flowers?

Around her are splendid works of taste,
   Yet to view them she never deigns,—

MARIA ABDY

By her side a golden harp is placed,
    But she doth not wake its strains:
She will not cast on the poet's lays,
    Or the scholar's page, a look,
Though wont from the dawn of her childish days
    To grasp, and to prize a book.
Strange that she thus should the pastimes slight
    So meet for her leisure hours!
Strange that she sadly from morn till night
    Sits weaving her silken flowers!

Oh! languor hath crept o'er that lady fair,
    Since she felt Affliction's sting,
And she may not walk in the free fresh air,
    And she may nor read or sing;
Indolence woos her with stealing spell,
    But the spell she would fain withstand,
So she strives her doleful thoughts to quell
    By the work of her active hand;
At her will, the rich red roses blow,
    And the stately lily towers,
But she cannot still the sense of woe
    By the charm of her silken flowers.

She thinks on the parents who once caressed
    The child of their hope and pride,—
She thinks on the time, more dear, more blessed,
    When she smiled as a joyous bride:
They are gone—the husband of her love,
    And her parents good and kind;
She knows that they live in bliss above,
    But she weeps to be left behind:
And the orphaned daughter and widowed wife
    Sighs over past happy hours,
As she wakes the fresh green leaves to life
    That circle her silken flowers.

She thinks on those who the needle ply
    In hunger, in want, and cold,
She gives them her gentle sympathy,
    And she gives them her ready gold;
Lavishly oft to the weary poor
    Is her kindly bounty shown,
But she feels that the sorrows that gold can cure
    Must be lighter than her own:
The gorgeous time-piece she sadly eyes
    That tells forth the lagging hours,
As she weaves bright threads of rainbow dyes
    In her vivid silken flowers.

MARIA ABDY

The woes of the poor have been sung full well,
  Who wearily sew and stitch,
But I wish that our minstrels would sometimes tell
  Of the sufferings of the rich!
I wish they would sing of the grief and gloom
  That may fill the heart and head,
When fragrance breathes through the gilded room,
  And the banquet is duly spread:
Labour might strengthen the sinking health,
  And might brace the mental powers,
Unnerved by the downy couch of wealth,
  And the frame of silken flowers.

And I fain would lead some bard of fame
  To the room where that lady fair
Daily is sitting alone at her frame,
  With a brow and a mind of care,—
Trembling to lift up her dark, soft eyes,
  From the work by her fingers wrought,
And nursing the bitter memories
  Of enduring, changeless thought,—
Pausing awhile in a bud or leaf,
  While her tears descend in showers,
And feeling that never can deep, true grief,
  Find a solace in silken flowers!

(1847)

CAROLINE NORTON (née SHERIDAN, later STIRLING-MAXWELL) (1808–1877)

She was born in London on 22 March 1808, the second of three daughters of Thomas Sheridan and Caroline (née Callander). All three sisters were famed for their beauty, and the eldest, Helen, also became famous as a poet. In 1817 her father died in public service at the Cape of Good Hope and the family experienced financial difficulty, which was partly relieved by a Crown apartment at Hampton Court. The family later moved to George Street, Westminster. She married George Chapple Norton on 30 June 1827 despite his lack of income and poor prospects. She experienced early success with *The sorrows of Rosalie*, 1829, *The undying one and other poems*, London 1830, *Poems*, Boston 1833, and edited two important Annuals, *Keepsake* and *Fisher's Drawing-room Scrapbook*. At one stage she claimed that she made £1400 a year from her contributions and editorial work and it appears that her writing soon became the main source of income for her family. Despite using her influence with Lord Melbourne to obtain a post for her husband, George Norton later accused her of adultery with Melbourne and a criminal conversation trial took place on 23 June 1836. The action was widely thought to be politically inspired and she and Melbourne were acquitted. She subsequently attempted a reconciliation but was rejected and the relationship degenerated into a custody battle over the three sons and financial settlements, resulting in further court action in 1853. As a result of these experiences, she produced a number of historically important works on divorce and child custody: *Separation of mother and child by the law of custody of infants considered*, London 1837, *A plain letter to the Lord Chancellor on the Infant Custody Bill*, London 1839, *English laws for women in the nineteenth century*, London 1854, and *A letter to the Queen on Lord Chancellor Cranworth's Marriage and Divorce Bill*, 1855. She also published three novels: *Stuart of Dunleath*, 3v. London 1851, *Lost and saved*, 3v. London 1863, and *Old Sir Douglas*, 3v. 1867, and two prose tales, *The wife, and woman's reward*, 3v. London 1835, which contain thinly disguised autobiographical elements.

Possibly as a result of her close connections with Melbourne and the reform-orientated nature of his administration, she developed a keen interest in factory reform and the question of child labour, followed the parliamentary proceedings closely, and published the long poem *A voice from the factories*, London 1836. In her later collections of poems, *The dream, and other poems*, London 1840, and *The child of the islands*, London 1845, she continued to raise the issue of the poor and the oppressed, but with the onset of Chartism, she became, like many Whigs, an advocate for parliamentary-led reform from above to mitigate the evils of industrial capitalism, but a firm opponent of extra-parliamentary agitation and democracy. By the time she published her *Letters to the mob*, London 1848, in which she attacked the 'dream of equality' and Chartist ideals, the liberal intellectual climate, while it still supported state action in areas of reform, was also looking to state action to stem agitation. Nevertheless, her contribution to central areas of reform—child labour, divorce, child custody and married women's property—remains significant and somewhat neglected.

George Norton died on 24 February 1875 and she soon married an old friend, Sir William Stirling-Maxwell, on 1 March 1877. At the time of the marriage she was already ill and she died on 15 June 1877 from a combination of catarrh, jaundice and local peritonitis, at 10 Upper Grosvenor Street, with a George Crowson present at her death.

85 THE CAPTIVE HEART

As the freed bird from its prison springs,
    With eager heart and glancing eye,
And, spreading out its quivering wings,
    Flies upward to the happy sky,
So my poor heart, so long thine own,
    At length from love's enchantment free,
Goes forth into the world alone,
    Exulting in its liberty.

But as that bird, a prisoner long,
    With weary wing, unused to soar,
Forgets to trill his joyous song,
    And feebly sinks to earth once more,
So from its bonds released in vain,

CAROLINE NORTON

My heart its fainting strength essays,
Then feels the recollected chain,
  And sinks—as in my prisoned days!

Alas! too like that wild bird's flight
  The heart which love at length sets free;
He seeks the greenwood's known delight,
  And I my youth's lost liberty;
Shunned by his mates, he flies alone,
  I, welcomed back by friends of yore,
Find each vain pleasure tedious grown—
  My heart hath lost the power to *soar*!

(1835)

86 SONNET

In the cold change which Time hath wrought on Love
  (The snowy winter of his summer prime),
Should a chance sigh, or sudden tear-drop, move
  Thy heart to memory of the olden time;
Turn not to gaze on me with pitying eyes,
  Nor mock me with a withered hope renewed;
But from the bower we both have loved, arise,
  And leave me to my barren solitude!
What boots it that a momentary flame
  Shoots from the ashes of a dying fire?
We gaze upon the hearth from whence it came,
  And know the exhausted embers *must* expire:
Therefore no pity, or my heart will break;
Be cold, be careless—for thy past love's sake!

(1836)

87 A VOICE FROM THE FACTORIES

  As sickly plants betray a niggard earth,
  Whose barren bosom starves her generous birth,
  Nor genial warmth, nor genial juice retains,
  Their roots to feed, and fill their verdant veins,
  And as in climes where winter holds his reign,
  The soil, though fertile, will not teem in vain,
  Forbids her gems to swell, her shades to rise,
  Nor trusts her blossoms to the churlish skies,—
  So draw Mankind in vain the vital airs,
  Unformed, unfriended by those kindly cares
  That health and vigour to the soul impart,
  Spread the young thought, and warm the opening heart.
    [Gray's 'Alliance of Education and Government']

CAROLINE NORTON

> The abuses even of such a business must be cautiously dealt with; lest in eradicating them, we shake or disorder the whole fabric. We admit, however, that the case of Children employed in the Cotton Factories is one of those which call fairly for legislative regulation. [McCulloch]

I

When fallen man from Paradise was driven
Forth to a world of labour, death, and care,
Still of his native Eden, bounteous Heaven
Resolved one brief memorial to spare,
And gave his offspring an imperfect share
Of that lost happiness, amid decay;
Making their first *approach* to life seem fair,
And giving, for the Eden past away,
Childhood, the weary life's long happy holiday.

II

Sacred to heavenly peace those years remain;
And when with clouds their dawn is overcast,
Unnatural seem the sorrow and the pain
(Which rosy joy flies forth to banish fast,
Because that season's sadness may not last).
Light is their grief! a word of fondness cheers
The unhaunted heart; the shadow glideth past;
Unknown to them the weight of boding fears,
And soft as dew on flowers their bright, ungrieving tears.

III

See the stage-wonder (taught to earn its bread
By the exertion of an infant skill)
Forsake the wholesome slumbers of its bed,
And mime, obedient to the public will.
Where is the heart so cold that does not thrill
With a vexatious sympathy, to see
That child prepare to play its part, and still
With simulated airs of gaiety
Rise to the dangerous rope, and bend the supple knee?

IV

Painted and spangled, trembling there it stands,
Glances below for friend or father's face,
Then lifts its small round arms and feeble hands
With the taught movements of an artist's grace;
Leaves its uncertain gilded resting-place—
Springs lightly as the elastic cord gives way—
And runs along with scarce perceptible pace—
Like a bright bird upon a waving spray,
Fluttering and sinking still, whene'er the branches play.

V

Now watch! a joyless and distorted smile
Its innocent lips assume (the dancer's leer!),
Conquering its terror for a little while;
Then lets the Truth of Infancy appear,
And with a stare of numbed and childish fear
Looks sadly towards the audience come to gaze
On the unwonted skill which costs so dear.
While still the applauding crowd, with pleased amaze,
Ring through its dizzy ears unwelcome shouts of praise.

VI

What is it makes us feel relieved to see
That hapless little dancer reach the ground;
With its whole spirit's elasticity
Thrown into one glad, safe, triumphant bound?
Why are we so sad, when, as it gazes round
At that wide sea of paint, and gauze, and plumes,
(Once more awake to sense, and sight, and sound,)
The nature of its age it re-assumes,
And one spontaneous smile at length its face illumes?

VII

Because we feel, for childhood's years and strength,
Unnatural and hard the task hath been;—
Because our sickened souls revolt at length,
And ask what infant innocence may mean
Thus toiling through the artificial scene;—
Because at that word, Childhood, start to birth
All dreams of hope and happiness serene—
All thoughts of innocent joy that visit earth—
Prayer—slumber—fondness—smiles—and hours of rosy mirth.

VIII

And therefore, when we hear the shrill faint cries
Which mark the wanderings of the little sweep;
Or when, with glittering teeth and sunny eyes,
The boy-Italian's voice, so soft and deep,
Asks alms for his poor marmoset asleep;
They fill our hearts with pitying regret,
Those little vagrants doomed so soon to weep,—
As though a term of joy for all was set,
And that *their* share of Life's long suffering was not yet.

IX

Ever a toiling *child* doth make us sad:
'Tis an unnatural and mournful sight,
Because we feel their smiles should be so glad,
Because we know their eyes should be so bright.

CAROLINE NORTON

What is it, then, when, tasked beyond their might,
They labour all day long for others' gain,—
Nay, trespass on the still and pleasant night,
While uncompleted hours of toil remain?
Poor little Factory Slaves—for You these lines complain!

X

Beyond all sorrow which the wanderer knows
Is that these little pent-up wretches feel;
Where the air thick and close and stagnant grows,
And the low whirring of the incessant wheel
Dizzies the head and makes the senses reel:
There, shut for ever from the gladdening sky,
Vice premature and Care's corroding seal
Stamp on each sallow cheek their hateful die,
Line the smooth open brow, and sink the saddened eye.

XI

For them the fervid summer only brings
A double curst of stifling withering heat;
For them no flowers spring up, no wild bird sings,
No moss-grown walks refresh their weary feet;—
No river's murmuring sound;—no wood-walk, sweet
With many a flower the Learned slight and pass;—
Nor meadow, with pale cowslips thickly set
Amid the soft leaves of its tufted grass,—
Lure *them* a childish stock of treasures to amass.

XII

Have we forgotten our own infancy,
That joys so simple are to them denied?—
Our boyhood's hopes—our wanderings far and free,
Where yellow gorse-bush left the common wide
And open to the breeze?—The active pride
Which made each obstacle a pleasure seem;
When, rashly glad, all danger we defied,
Dashed through the brook by twilight's fading gleam,
Or scorned the tottering plank, and leapt the narrow stream.

XIII

In lieu of this,—from short and bitter night,
Sullen and sad the infant labourer creeps
He joys not in the glow of morning's light,
But with an idle yearning stands and weeps,
Envying the babe that in its cradle sleeps
And ever, as he slowly journeys on,
His listless tongue unbidden silence keeps
His fellow-labourers (*playmates* hath he none)
Walk by, as sad as he, nor hail the morning sun.

XIV

Mark the result. Unnaturally debarred
All Nature's fresh and innocent delights,
While yet each germing energy strives hard,
And pristine good with pristine evil fights;
When every passing dream the heart excites,
And makes even *guarded* virtue insecure;
Untaught, unchecked, they yield as vice invites:
With all around them cramped, confined, impure,
Fast spreads the moral plague which nothing new shall cure.

XV

Yes, this reproach is added; (infamous
In realms which own a Christian monarch's sway!)
Not suffering *only* is their portion, thus
Compelled to toil their youthful lives away:
Excessive labour works the Soul's decay—
Quenches the intellectual light within—
Crushes with iron weight the mind's free play—
Steals from us Leisure purer thoughts to win—
And leaves us sunk and lost in dull and native sin.

XVI

Yet in the British senate men rise up,
(The freeborn and the fathers of our land!)
And, while these drink the dregs of Sorrow's cup,
Deny the sufferings of the pining band.
With nice-drawn calculations at command
They prove—rebut—explain—and reason long;
Proud of each shallow argument they stand,
And prostitute their utmost powers of tongue
Feebly to justify this great and glaring wrong.

XVII

So rose, with such a plausible defence
Of the unalienable Right of Gain,
Those who against Truth's brightest eloquence
Upheld the cause of torture and of pain:
And fear of property's decrease made vain,
For years, the hope of Christian charity
To lift the curse from Slavery's dark domain,
And send across the wide Atlantic sea
The watchword of brave men—the thrilling shout 'Be Free!'

XVIII

Oh! shall it then be said that Tyrant acts
Are those which cause our country's looms to thrive?
That Merchant England's prosperous trade exacts
This bitter sacrifice, e'er she derive

That profit due for which the feeble strive?
Is her commercial avarice so keen,
That in her busy multitudinous hive
Hundreds must die like insects, scarcely seen,
While the thick-thronged survivors work where they have been?

XIX

Forbid it, Spirit of the glorious Past
Which gained our Isle the surname of 'The Free,'
And made our shores a refuge at the last
To all who would not bend the servile knee,
The vainly-vanquished sons of Liberty!
Here ever came the injured, the oppressed,
Compelled from the Oppressor's face to flee—
And found a home of shelter and of rest
In the warm generous heart that beat in England's breast.

XX

Here came the Slave, who straightway burst his chain,
And knew that none could ever bind him more;
Here came the melancholy sons of Spain;
And here, more buoyant Gaul's illustrious poor
Waited the same bright day that shone before.
Here rests the Enthusiast Pole! and views afar
With dreaming hope, from this protecting shore,
The trembling rays of Liberty's pale star
Shine forth in vain to light the too-unequal war.

XXI

And shall Reproach cling darkly to the name
Which every memory so much endears?
Shall *we*, too, tyrannise,—and tardy Fame
Revoke the glory of our former years,
And stain Britannia's flag with children's tears?
So shall the mercy of the English throne
Become a by-word in the Nations' ears,
As one who pitying heard the stranger's groan,
But to these nearer woes was cold and deaf as stone.

XXII

Are there not changes made which grind the Poor?
Are there not losses every day sustained,—
Deep grievances, which make the spirit sore?
And what the answer, when *these* have complained?
'For crying evils there hath been ordained
The Remedy of Change; to obey its call
Some individual loss must be disdained,
And pass as unavoidable and small,
Weighed with the broad result of general good to all.'

XXIII

Oh! such an evil *now* doth cry aloud!
And Change should be by generous hearts begun,
Though slower gain attend the prosperous crowd,
Lessening the fortunes for their children won.
Why should it grieve a father, that his son
Plain competence must moderately bless?
That he must trade, even as his sire has done,
Not born to independent idleness,
Though honestly above all probable distress?

XXIV

Rejoice! Thou hast not left enough of gold
From the lined heavy ledger, to entice
His drunken hand, irresolutely bold,
To squander it in haggard haunts of vice:—
The hollow rattling of the uncertain dice
Eats not the portion which thy love bestowed;—
Unable to afford that Pleasure's price,
Far off he slumbers in his calm abode,
And leaves the Idle Rich to follow Ruin's road.

XXV

Happy his lot! For him there shall not be
The cold temptation given by vacant time;
Leaving his young and uncurbed spirit free
To wander through the feverish paths of crime!
For *him* the Sabbath bell's returning chime
Not vainly ushers in God's day of rest;
No night of riot clouds the morning's prime:
Alert and glad, not languid and oppressed,
He wakes, and with calm soul is the Creator blessed.

XXVI

Ye save for children! Fathers, is there not
A plaintive magic in the name of child,
Which makes you feel compassion for *their* lot
On whom Prosperity hath never smiled?
When with your Own an hour hath been beguiled
(For whom you hoard the still increasing store),
Surely, against the face of Pity mild,
Heart-hardening Custom vainly bars the door,
For that less favoured race—The Children of the Poor.

XXVII

'The happy homes of England!'—they have been
A source of triumph, and a theme for song;
And surely, if there be a hope serene
And beautiful, which may to Earth belong,

CAROLINE NORTON

'Tis when (shut out the world's associate throng,
And closed the busy day's fatiguing hum),
Still waited for with expectation strong,
Welcomed with joy, and overjoyed to come,
The good man goes to seek the twilight rest of home.

XXVIII

There sits his gentle Wife, who with him knelt
Long years ago at God's pure altar-place;
Still beautiful,—though all that she hath felt
Hath calmed the glory of her radiant face,
And given her brow a holier, softer grace.
Mother of Souls Immortal, she doth feel
A glow from Heaven her earthly love replace;
Prayer to her lip more often now doth steal,
And meditative hope her serious eyes reveal.

XXIX

Fondly familiar is the look she gives
As he returns, who forth so lately went,—
For they *together* pass their happy lives;
And many a tranquil evening have they spent
Since, blushing, ignorantly innocent,
She vowed, with downcast eyes and changeful hue,
To love him only. Love fulfilled hath lent
Its deep repose; and, when he meets her view
Her soft look only says,—'I trust—and I am true.'

XXX

Scattered like flowers, the rosy children play—
Or round her chair a busy crowd they press;
But, at the Father's coming, start away,
With playful struggle for his loved caress,
And jealous of the one he first may bless.
To each, a welcoming word is fondly said;
He bends and kisses some; lifts up the less;
Admires the little cheek, so round and red,
Or smooths with tender hand the curled and shining head.

XXXI

Oh! let us pause, and gaze upon them now.
Is there not one—beloved and lovely boy!
With Mirth's bright seal upon his open brow,
And sweet fond eyes, brimful of love and joy?
He, whom no measure of delight can cloy,
The daring and the darling of the set;
He who, though pleased with every passing toy,
Thoughtless and buoyant to excess, could yet
Never a gentle word or kindly deed forget?

XXXII

And one, more fragile than the rest, for whom—
As for the weak bird in a crowded nest—
Are needed all the fostering care of home
And the soft comfort of the brooding breast:
One, who hath oft the couch of sickness pressed!
On whom the Mother looks, as it goes by,
With tenderness intense, and fear suppressed,
While the soft patience of her anxious eye
Blends with 'God's will be done,'—'God grant thou may'st not die!'

XXXIII

And is there not the elder of the band?
She with the gentle smile and smooth bright hair,
Waiting, some paces back,—content to stand
Till these of Love's caresses have their share;
Knowing how soon his fond paternal care
Shall seek his violet in her shady nook,—
Patient she stands—demure, and brightly fair—
Copying the meekness of her Mother's look.
And clasping in her hand the favourite story-book.

XXXIV

Wake, dreamer!—Choose;—to labour Life away,
Which of these little precious ones shall go
(Debarred of summer-light and cheerful play)
To that receptacle for dreary woe,
The Factory Mill?—Shall He, in whom the glow
Of Life shines bright, whose free limbs' vigorous tread
Warns us how much of beauty that we know
Would fade, when *he* became dispirited,
And pined with sickened heart, and bowed his fainting head?

XXXV

Or shall the little quiet one, whose voice
So rarely mingles in their sounds of glee,
Whose life can bid no living thing rejoice,
But rather is a long anxiety;—
Shall he go forth to toil? and keep the free
Frank boy, whose merry shouts and restless grace
Would leave all eyes that used his face to see
Wistfully gazing towards that vacant space
Which makes their fireside seem a lone and dreary place?

XXXVI

Or, sparing these, send Her whose simplest words
Have power to charm,—whose warbled, childish song,
Fluent and clear and bird-like, strikes the chords
Of sympathy among the listening throng,—

Whose spirits light, and steps that dance along,
Instinctive modesty and grace restrain:
The fair young innocent who knows no wrong,—
Whose slender wrists scarce hold the silken skein
Which the glad Mother winds;—shall *She* endure this pain?

XXXVII

Away! The thought—the *thought* alone brings tears!
They labour—*they*, the darlings of our lives!
The flowers and sunbeams of our fleeting years;
From whom alone our happiness derives
A lasting strength, which every shock survives;
The green young trees beneath whose arching boughs
(When failing Energy no longer strives)
Our wearied age shall find a cool repose;—
They toil in torture!—No—the painful picture close.

XXXVIII

Ye shudder,—nor behold the vision more!
Oh, Fathers! is there then one law for these,
And one for the pale children of the Poor,—
That to their agony your hearts can freeze;
Deny their pain, their toil, their slow disease;
And deem with false complaining they encroach
Upon your time and thought? Is yours the Ease
Which misery vainly struggles to approach,
Whirling unthinking by, in Luxury's gilded coach?

XXXIX

Examine and decide. Watch through his day
One of these little ones. The sun hath shone
An hour, and by the ruddy morning's ray,
The last and least, he saunters on alone.
See where, still pausing on the threshold stone,
He stands, as loth to lose the bracing wind;
With wistful wandering glances backward thrown
On all the light and glory left behind,
And sighs to think that He must darkly be confined!

XL

Enter with him. The stranger who surveys
The little natives of that dreary place
(Where squalid suffering meets his shrinking gaze),
Used to the glory of a young child's face,
Its changeful light, its coloured sparkling grace,
(Gleams of Heaven's sunshine on our shadowed earth!)
Starts at each visage wan, and bold, and base,
Whose smiles have neither innocence nor mirth,—
And comprehends the Sin original from birth.

XLI

There the pale Orphan, whose unequal strength
Loathes the incessant toil it *must* pursue,
Pines for the cool sweet evening's twilight length,
The sunny play-hour, and the morning's dew:
Worn with its cheerless life's monotonous hue,
Bowed down, and faint, and stupefied it stands;
Each half-seen object reeling in its view—
While its hot, trembling, languid little hands
Mechanically heed the Task-master's commands.

XLII

There, sounds of wailing grief and painful blows
Offend the ear, and startle it from rest;
(While the lungs gasp, what air the place bestows;)
Or misery's joyless vice, the ribald jest.
Breaks the sick silence: staring at the guest
Who comes to view their labour, they beguile
The unwatched moment; whispers half suppressed
And mutterings low, their faded lips defile,—
While gleams from face to face a strange and sullen smile.

XLIII

These then are his Companions: he, too young
To share their base and saddening merriment,
Sits by: his little head in silence hung;
His limbs cramped up; his body weakly bent;
Toiling obedient, till long hours so spent
Produce Exhaustion's slumber, dull and deep.
The Watcher's stroke,—bold—sudden—violent,—
Urges him from that lethargy of sleep,
And bids him wake to Life,—to labour and to weep!

XLIV

But the day hath its End. Forth then he hies
With jaded, faltering step, and brow of pain;
Creeps to that shed,—his Home,—where happy lies
The sleeping babe that cannot toil for Gain;
Where his remorseful Mother tempts in vain
With the best portion of their frugal fare:
Too sick to eat—too weary to complain—
He turns him idly from the untasted share,
Slumbering sinks down unfed, and mocks her useless care.

XLV

Weeping she lifts, and lays his heavy head
(With all a woman's grieving tenderness)
On the hard surface of his narrow bed;
Bends down to give a sad unfelt caress,

And turns away;—willing her God to bless,
That, weary as he is, he need not fight
Against that long-enduring bitterness,
The Voluntary Labour of the Night,
But sweetly slumber on till day's returning light.

XLVI

Vain hope! Alas! unable to forget
The anxious task's long, heavy agonies,
In broken sleep the victim labours yet!
Waiting the boding stroke that bids him rise,
He marks in restless fear each hour that flies—
Anticipates the unwelcome morning prime—
And murmuring feebly, with unwakened eyes,
    'Mother! Oh Mother! is it yet The Time?'
Starts at the moon's pale ray—or clock's far distant chime.

XLVII

Such is *his* day and night! Now then return
Where your Own slumber in protected ease;
They whom no blast may pierce, no sun may burn;
The lovely, on whose cheeks the wandering breeze
Hath left the rose's hue. Ah! not like these
Does the pale infant-labourer ask to be:
He craves no tempting food—no toys to please—
    Not Idleness,—but less of agony;
Not Wealth,—but comfort, rest, Contented Poverty.

XLVIII

There is, among all men, in every clime,
A difference instinctive and unschooled:
God made the Mind unequal. From all time
By fierceness conquered, or by cunning fooled,
The World hath had its Rulers and its Ruled:—
Yea—uncompelled—men abdicate free choice,
Fear their own rashness, and, by thinking cooled,
    Follow the counsel of some trusted voice;—
A self-elected sway, wherein their souls rejoice.

XLIX

Thus, for the most part, willing to obey,
Men rarely set Authority at naught:
Albeit a weaker or a worse than they
May hold the rule with such importance fraught:
And thus the peasant, from his cradle taught
That some must *own*, while some must *till* the land,
Rebels not—murmurs not—even in his thought.
    Born to his lot, he bows to high command,
And guides the furrowing plough with a contented hand.

L

But, if the weight which habit renders light
Is made to gall the Serf who bends below—
The dog that watched and fawned, prepares to bite!
Too rashly strained, the cord snaps from the bow—
Too tightly curbed, the steeds their riders throw—
And so, (at first contented his fair state
Of customary servitude to know,)
Too harshly ruled, the poor man learns to hate
And curse the oppressive law that bids him serve the Great.

LI

Then first he asks his gloomy soul the Cause
Of his discomfort; suddenly compares—
Reflects—and with an angry Spirit draws
The envious line between his lot and theirs,
Questioning the Justice of the unequal shares;
And from the gathering of this discontent,
Where there is strength, Revolt his standard rears;
Where there is weakness, evermore finds vent
The sharp annoying cry of sorrowful complaint.

LII

Therefore should Mercy, gentle and serene,
Sit by the Ruler's side, and share his Throne:—
Watch with unerring eye the passing scene,
And bend her ear to mark the feeblest groan;
Lest due Authority be overthrown,
And they that ruled perceive (too late confessed!)
Permitted Power might still have been their own,
Had they but watched that none should be oppressed—
No just complaint despised—no Wrong left unredressed.

LIII

Nor should we, Christians in a Christian land,
Forget who smiled on helpless infancy,
And blessed them with divinely gentle hand.—
'Suffer that little children come to me':
Such were His words to whom we bow the knee!
These to our care the Saviour did commend;
And shall we His bequest treat carelessly,
Who yet our full protection would extend
To the lone Orphan child left by an Earthly Friend?

LIV

No! rather what the Inspired Law imparts
To guide our ways, and make our path more sure;
Blending with Pity (native to our hearts),
Let us to these, who patiently endure

CAROLINE NORTON

Neglect, and penury, and toil, secure
    The innocent hopes that to their age belong:
So, honouring Him, the Merciful and Pure,
    Who watches when the Oppressor's arm grows strong,—
And helpeth them to right—the Weak—who suffer wrong!

(1836)

88 SONNET

Like an enfranchised bird, who wildly springs,
    With a keen sparkle in his glancing eye
And a strong effort in his quivering wings,
    Up to the blue vault of the happy sky,—
So my enamoured heart, so long thine own,
    At length from Love's imprisonment set free,
Goes forth into the open world alone,
    Glad and exulting in its liberty:
But like that helpless bird, (confined so long,
    His weary wings have lost all power to soar,)
Who soon forgets to trill his joyous song,
    And, feebly fluttering, sinks to earth once more,—
So, from its former bonds released in vain,
My heart still feels the weight of that remembered chain.

(1841)

89 SONNET: THE DISDAINED LOVER

I stand beside the waves,—the mournful waves,—
    Where thou didst stand in silence and in fear,
For thou wert trained by custom's haughty slaves,
    And love, from such as I, disdained to hear;
Yet, with the murmur of the echoing sea,
    And the monotonous billows, rolling on,
Were mingled sounds of weeping,—for in thee
    All nature was not hardened into stone:
And from the shore there came a distant chime
    From the old village-clock;—ah! since that day,
Like a dull passing-bell each stroke of time
    Falls on my heart; and in the ocean spray
A voice of lamentation seems to dwell,
As in that bitter hour of agonised farewell!

(1841)

THE POET'S CHOICE

I
'Twas in youth, that hour of dreaming;
Round me, visions fair were beaming,
Golden fancies, brightly gleaming,
        Such as start to birth
When the wandering restless mind,
Drunk with beauty, thinks to find
Creatures of a fairy kind
        Realised on Earth!

II
Then, for me, in every dell
Hamadryads seemed to dwell
(They who die, as Poets tell,
        Each with her own tree);
And sweet mermaids, low reclining,
Dim light through their grottoes shining,
Green weeds round their soft limbs twining,
        Peopled the deep Sea.

III
Then, when moon and stars were fair,
Nymph-like visions filled the air,
With blue wings and golden hair
        Bending from the skies;
And each cave by echo haunted
In its depth of shadow granted,
Brightly, the Egeria wanted,
        To my eager eyes.

IV
But those glories passed away;
Earth seemed left to dull decay,
And my heart in sadness lay,
        Desolate, uncheered;
Like one wrapped in painful sleeping,
Pining, thirsting, waking, weeping,
Watch through Life's dark midnight keeping,
        Till Thy form appeared!

V
Then my soul, whose erring measure
Knew not where to find true pleasure,
Woke and seized the golden treasure
        Of thy human love;

CAROLINE
NORTON

And, looking on thy radiant brow,
My lips in gladness breathed the vow
Which angels, not more fair than thou,
    Have registered above.

VI
And now I take my quiet rest,
With my head upon thy breast,
I will make no further quest
    In Fancy's realms of light;
Fay, nor nymph, nor wingèd spirit,
Shall my store of love inherit;
More thy mortal charm doth merit
    Than dream, however bright:

VII
And my soul,—like some sweet bird
Whose song at summer eve is heard,
When the breeze, so lightly stirred,
    Leaves the branch unbent,—
Sits and all-triumphant sings,
Folding up her brooding wings,
And gazing out on earthly things
    With a calm content.

(1841)

CAROLINE CLIVE (née MEYSEY-WIGLEY) (1801–1873)

She was born on 24 June 1801 in London, the second daughter of Edmund Meysey-Wigley and Anna Maria Meysey. She was brought up in Shaken-hurst, Worcestershire, where her father had land and property and was MP for Worcester until 1802. She contracted polio when only three years old which left her permanently disabled. From 1829 to 1833 she managed the household of her brother Edmund, who had inherited Malvern Hall, Solihull. On inheriting property of her own, she moved to Olton Hall. In 1838 she toured France, visiting the poet and dramatist, Catherine Gore (1799–1861), for whom she felt 'nearly the strongest of all my passions'. She married the Revd Archer Clive, Rector of Solihull, in 1840. He later became Chancellor of Hereford Cathedral and died in 1878. They had two children, Charles Meysey (b. 1842) and Alice (b. 1843). Shortly after her marriage she published *IX poems. By V.*, London 1840, which was much admired by Hartley Nelson Coleridge in his review of modern British poetesses. She added nine other poems in a second edition, published the following year, and went on to produce longer poems in later years: *I watched the heavens*, London 1842, *The Queen's ball*, London 1847, *The valley of the Rea*, London 1851, and *The Morlas*,

CAROLINE CLIVE

London 1853. Further poems were added in editions of *IX poems* in 1856 and 1872 but these also omitted poems. In 1847 she moved to Whitfield, Herefordshire, after her husband inherited an estate. (They also owned other estates in Old Stratford and Hampton Lucy.) From 1848 until her death she kept an extensive diary (together with her husband), extracts of which were edited by Mary Clive in 1949. The original is in Solihull Central Library. She was best known for one of the first Victorian 'sensation' novels, *Paul Ferroll*, London 1855, in which a man murders his wife and escapes punishment by emigrating. Several critics found the moral injustice too hard to take and this may have led her to assuage criticism in a further novel, *Why Paul Ferroll killed his wife*, London 1860. She died on 14 July 1873 at Treville, Hereford in a domestic accident when her dress accidentally caught fire.

91 THE GRAVE

I stood within the grave's o'ershadowing vault;
    Gloomy and damp it stretched its vast domain;
Shades were its boundary; for my strained eye sought
    For other limit to its width in vain.

Faint from the entrance came a daylight ray,
    And distant sound of living men and things;
This, in the encountering darkness passed away,
    That, took the tone in which a mourner sings.

I lit a torch at a sepulchral lamp,
    Which shot a thread of light amid the gloom;
And feebly burning against the rolling damp,
    I bore it through the regions of the tomb.

Around me stretched the slumbers of the dead,
    Whereof the silence ached upon mine ear;
More and more noiseless did I make my tread,
    And yet its echoes chilled my heart with fear.

The former men of every age and place,
    From all their wanderings gathered, round me lay;
The dust of withered Empires did I trace,
    And stood 'mid Generations passed away.

I saw whole cities, that in flood or fire,
    Or famine or the plague, gave up their breath;
Whole armies whom a day beheld expire,
    Swept by ten thousands to the arms of Death.

CAROLINE CLIVE

I saw the old world's white and wave-swept bones,
  A giant heap of creatures that had been;
Far and confused the broken skeletons
  Lay strewn beyond mine eye's remotest ken.

Death's various shrines—the Urn, the Stone, the Lamp—
  Were scattered round, confused, amid the dead;
Symbols and Types were mouldering in the damp,
  Their shapes were waning and their meaning fled.

Unspoken tongues, perchance in praise or woe,
  Were charactered on tablets Time had swept;
And deep were half their letters hid below
  The thick small dust of those they once had wept.

No hand was here to wipe the dust away;
  No reader of the writing traced beneath;
No spirit sitting by its form of clay;
  No sigh nor sound from all the heaps of Death.

One place alone had ceased to hold its prey;
  A form had pressed it and was there no more;
The garments of the Grave beside it lay,
  Where once they wrapped him on the rocky floor.

He only with returning footsteps broke
  The eternal calm wherewith the Tomb was bound;
Among the sleeping Dead alone He woke,
  And blessed with outstretched hands the host around.

Well is it that such blessing hovers here,
  To soothe each sad survivor of the throng,
Who haunt the portals of the solemn sphere,
  And pour their woe the loaded air along.

They to the verge have followed what they love,
  And on the insuperable threshold stand;
With cherished names its speechless calm reprove,
  And stretch in the abyss their ungrasped hand.

But vainly there they seek their soul's relief,
  And of the obdurate Grave its prey implore,
Till Death himself shall medicine their grief,
  Closing their eyes by those they wept before.

All that have died, the Earth's whole race, repose,
   Where Death collects his Treasures, heap on heap;
O'er each one's busy day, the nightshades close;
   Its Actors, Sufferers, Schools, Kings, Armies—sleep.

CAROLINE
CLIVE

(1840)

9   WRITTEN IN ILLNESS

My bark floats on the sea of death,
   Of deepening waves the sport;
And dull disease, with heavy breath,
   Impels me from the port.

Wide and unknown, the ocean surge
   Outstretches to my ken;
Oh! when I reach yon cloudy verge,
   What sights will meet me then?

Thee, native world, full well I know;
   And as thy shores recede,
Mine eyes desert the onward prow,
   Thy well-known forms to read.

There shines the light that first I knew,
   The scenes that light displayed;
From which my soul the feelings drew,
   Whereof itself was made.

There lie the shapes of joys and ills,
   Which moved erewhile my mind;
Like storms and suns upon the hills
   The traveller leaves behind.

But still receding, wafted on,
   All indistinct they grow;
The busy crowd that moves thereon
   To me is silent now.

Its glittering ray mine eye escapes,
   The mists are round me furled;
Farewell, farewell, ye human shapes!
   Farewell, my native world!

(Wr. 1829, pub. 1840)

93 FORMER HOME

In scenes untrod for many a year,
    I stand again, the long estranged;
And gazing round me, ponder here
    On all that has, and has not changed.

The casual visitor would see
    Nought altered in the aspects round;
But long familiar shapes to me
    Are missing, which I fain had found.

Still stands the rock, still runs the flood,
    Which not an eye could pass unmoved;
The airy copse, the fringing wood,
    Which even the passer marked and loved.

But when mine eyes' delighted pride,
    Had dwelt the rock's high front upon;
I sought upon its warmer side,
    A vine we trained—and that was gone.

And though awhile content I gazed
    Upon the river quick and fair;
I sought ere long, a seat we raised
    In childhood—but it was not there.

Stones lay around, I know not whether
    Its relics, or the winter's snow—
And sitting where we sat together,
    Again I watched the torrent flow.

So whirled the waves that formed it then,
    In foam around yon jutting stone;
So arrowy shot they down the glen,
    When here was passed the hours long flown.

There in the waters dipped the tree
    From which, the day I parted hence,
I took a few green leaves, to be
    My solace still through time and chance.

Full many a spring the tree has shone
    In sunlight, air, and beauty here;
While I in cities gazed upon
    The withered leaves of that one year.

That year was fraught with heavy things,
    With deaths and partings, loss and pain;
And every object round me rings
    Its mournful epitaph again.

CAROLINE CLIVE

But most, those small familiar traits,
   Which only we have loved or known;
They flourished with our happier days—
   They withered because we were gone.

Their absence seems to speak of those
   Who're scattered far upon the earth;
At whose young hands they once arose,
   Whose eyes gazed gleeful on their birth.

Those hands since then have grasped the brand,
   Those eyes in grief grown dim and hot;
And wandering through a stranger's land,
   Oft yearned to this remembered spot.

How changed are they!—how changed am I!—
   I was a boy then—and 'tis gone;
Gone is each boyish vanity,
   But what in manhood have I won?

I know not—but while standing now,
   Where opened first the heart of youth,
I recollect how high would glow
   Its thoughts of Glory, Faith, and Truth—

How full it was of good and great,
   How true to heaven, how warm to men;
Alas! I scarce forbear to hate
   The colder breast I bring again.

Hopes disappointed, sin and time
   Have moulded me, since here I stood;
Ah! paint old feelings, rock sublime,
   Speak life's fresh accents, mountain flood!

(1840)

EMILY BRONTË (1818–1848)

She was born at Thornton, near Bradford on 30 July 1818, the fifth of six children of Patrick Brontë and Maria (née Branwell). In 1820 the family, which now consisted of Maria (b. 1814), Elizabeth (b. 1815), Charlotte (b. 1816), Patrick Branwell (b. 1817), Emily (b. 1818) and Anne (b. 1820), moved to Haworth, where Patrick Brontë had been appointed curate. The following year, Maria Brontë (the mother) died and her sister Elizabeth Branwell moved in and took over management of the household. In 1824 the two eldest daughters, Maria and Elizabeth, attended Cowan Bridge school, and were soon followed by Charlotte and Emily. However, the following year, both Maria and Elizabeth left the school in ill-health and died shortly afterwards.

EMILY
BRONTË

Returning from a clerical conference in Leeds in June 1826, Patrick Brontë brought gifts for the remaining children—a set of ninepins for Charlotte, a box of toy soldiers for Patrick Branwell, a toy village for Emily and a dancing doll for Anne. A new world of imagination seems to have opened up for the children, and over the next few years they began writing stories. These would eventually develop into the complex fictional worlds of Gondal in the South Pacific (Emily and Anne) and Angria in Africa (Charlotte and Patrick Branwell).

In 1835 Emily went briefly to Roe Head school but returned to Haworth because of ill-health. In 1838 she took up a position as teacher at Law Hill school, near Halifax, but lasted less than six months. In the summer of 1841 Charlotte and Emily and possibly Anne considered the possibility of setting up a school themselves. With a view to this, Charlotte and Emily spent nine months the following year at a private school in Brussels learning French. The idea of the school was eventually abandoned. In 1845 Charlotte discovered what is probably Emily's Gondal poems notebook (now in the British Library) and Charlotte, Emily and Anne published *Poems by Currer, Ellis and Acton Bell*, London 1846, but it passed largely unnoticed. The following year, Emily published *Wuthering Heights*, 2v. London 1847, still using the pseudonym 'Ellis Bell'. After attending her brother's funeral in September, she fell ill, never recovered, and died on 19 December 1848, the cause of death given as consumption from which she had been suffering for nine months, with John B. Woodhouse of Haworth present at her death.

94 'I'M HAPPIEST WHEN MOST AWAY'

I'm happiest when most away
I can bear my soul from its home of clay
On a windy night when the moon is bright
And the eye can wander through worlds of light—

When I am not and none beside—
Nor earth nor sea nor cloudless sky—
But only spirit wandering wide
Through infinite immensity.

(Wr. 1838)

95 'IT'S OVER NOW; I'VE KNOWN IT ALL'

It's over now; I've known it all;
I'll hide it in my heart no more,
But back again that night recall,
And think the fearful vision o'er.

The evening sun, in cloudless shine,
Had passed from summer's heaven divine;
And dark the shades of twilight grew,
And stars were in the depth of blue;

And in the heath on mountains far
From human eye and human care,
With thoughtful heart and tearful eye
I sadly watched that solemn sky.

EMILY
BRONTË

(Wr. 1838)

96 'HARP OF WILD AND DREAM-LIKE STRAIN'

Harp of wild and dream-like strain,
When I touch thy strings,
Why dost thou repeat again
Long-forgotten things?

Harp, in other, earlier days,
I could sing to thee;
And not one of all my lays
Vexed my memory.

But now, if I awake a note
That gave me joy before,
Sounds of sorrow from thee float,
Changing evermore.

Yet, still steeped in memory's dyes,
They come sailing on,
Darkening all my summer skies,
Shutting out my sun.

(Wr. 1838)

97 'I AM THE ONLY BEING WHOSE DOOM'

I am the only being whose doom
No tongue would ask, no eye would mourn;
I never caused a thought of gloom,
A smile of joy, since I was born.

In secret pleasure, secret tears,
This changeful life has slipped away,
As friendless after eighteen years,
As lone as on my natal day.

There have been times I cannot hide,
There have been times when this was drear,
When my sad soul forgot its pride
And longed for one to love me here.

EMILY
BRONTË

But those were in the early glow
Of feelings since subdued by care;
And they have died so long ago,
I hardly now believe they were.

First melted all the hope of youth,
Then fancy's rainbow fast withdrew;
And then experience told me truth
In mortal bosoms never grew.

'Twas grief enough to think mankind
All hollow, servile, insincere;
But worse to trust to my own mind
And find the same corruption there.

(Wr. 1839)

98 'IT IS NOT PRIDE, IT IS NOT SHAME'

It is not pride, it is not shame,
That makes her leave the gorgeous hall;
And though neglect her heart might tame
She mourns not for her sudden fall.

'Tis true she stands among the crowd
An unmarked and an unloved child,
While each young comrade, blithe and proud,
Glides through the maze of pleasure wild.

And all do homage to their will,
And all seem glad their voice to hear;
She heeds not that, but hardly still
Her eye can hold the quivering tear.

What made her weep, what made her glide
Out to the park this dreary day,
And cast her jewelled chains aside,
And seek a rough and lonely way,

And down beneath a cedar's shade
On the wet grass regardless lie,
With nothing but its gloomy head
Between her and the showery sky?

I saw her standing in the gallery long,
Watching the little children there,
As they were playing the pillars among
And bounding down the marble stair.

(Wr. 1839)

99 'THE WIND, I HEAR IT SIGHING'   EMILY BRONTË

The wind, I hear it sighing
With Autumn's saddest sound;
Withered leaves as thick are lying
As spring-flowers on the ground.

This dark night has won me
To wander far away;
Old feelings gather fast upon me
Like vultures round their prey.

Kind were they once, and cherished,
But cold and cheerless now;
I would their lingering shades had perished
When their light left my brow.

'Tis like old age pretending
The softness of a child,
My altered, hardened spirit bending
To meet their fancies wild.

Yet could I with past pleasures
Past woe's oblivion buy,
That by the death of my dearest treasures
My deadliest pains might die,

O then another daybreak
Might haply dawn above,
Another summer gild my cheek,
My soul, another love.

(Wr. 1839)

100 THE NIGHT-WIND

In summer's mellow midnight,
A cloudless moon shone through
Our open parlour window
And rosetrees wet with dew.

I sat in silent musing,
The soft wind waved my hair:
It tole me Heaven was glorious,
And sleeping Earth was fair.

I needed not its breathing
To bring such thoughts to me,
But still it whispered lowly,
'How dark the woods will be!

EMILY
BRONTË

'The thick leaves in my murmur
Are rustling like a dream,
And all their myriad voices
Instinct with spirit seem.'

I said, 'Go, gentle singer,
Thy wooing voice is kind,
But do not think its music
Has power to reach my mind.

'Play with the scented flower,
The young tree's supple bough,
And leave my human feelings
In their own course to flow.'

The wanderer would not leave me;
Its kiss grew warmer still—
'O come,' it sighed so sweetly,
'I'll win thee 'gainst thy will.

'Have we not been from childhood friends?
Have I not loved thee long?
As long as thou hast loved the night
Whose silence wakes my song.

'And when thy heart is laid at rest
Beneath the church-yard stone
I shall have time enough to mourn
And thou to be alone.'

(Wr. 1840)

101 'AND LIKE MYSELF LONE, WHOLLY LONE'

And like myself lone, wholly lone,
It sees the day's long sunshine glow;
And like myself it makes its moan
In unexhausted woe.

Give we the hills our equal prayer:
Earth's breezy hills and heaven's blue sea;
We ask for nothing further here
But our own hearts and liberty.

Ah! could my hands unlock its chain,
How gladly would I watch it soar,
And ne'er regret and ne'er complain
To see its shining eyes no more.

But let me think that if to-day
It pines in cold captivity,
To-morrow both shall soar away,
Eternally, entirely Free.

EMILY
BRONTË

(Wr. 1841)

102 'SHALL EARTH NO MORE INSPIRE THEE'

Shall Earth no more inspire thee,
Thou lonely dreamer now?
Since passion may not fire thee
Shall Nature cease to bow?

Thy mind is ever moving
In regions dark to thee;
Recall its useless roving—
Come back and dwell with me.

I know my mountain breezes
Enchant and soothe thee still—
I know my sunshine pleases
Despite thy wayward will.

When day with evening blending
Sinks from the summer sky,
I've seen thy spirit bending
In fond idolatry.

I've watched thee every hour;
I know thy mighty sway,
I know my magic power
To drive thy griefs away.

Few hearts to mortals given
On earth so wildly pine;
Yet none would ask a Heaven
More like this Earth than thine.

Then let my winds caress thee;
Thy comrade let me be—
Since nought beside can bless thee,
Return and dwell with me.

(Wr. 1841)

EMILY BRONTË

103 TO IMAGINATION

When weary with the long day's care,
    And earthly change from pain to pain,
And lost and ready to despair,
    Thy kind voice calls me back again:
Oh, my true friend! I am not lone,
While thou canst speak with such a tone!

So hopeless is the world without;
    The world within I doubly prize;
Thy world, where guile, and hate, and doubt,
    And cold suspicion never rise;
Where thou, and I, and Liberty,
Have undisputed sovereignty.

What matters it, that, all around,
    Danger, and guilt, and darkness lie,
If but within our bosom's bound
    We hold a bright, untroubled sky,
Warm with ten thousand mingled rays
Of suns that know no winter days?

Reason, indeed, may oft complain
    For Nature's sad reality,
And tell the suffering heart, how vain
    Its cherished dreams must always be;
And Truth may rudely trample down
The flowers of Fancy, newly-blown:

But, thou art ever there, to bring
    The hovering vision back, and breathe
New glories o'er the blighted spring,
    And call a lovelier Life from Death,
And whisper, with a voice divine,
Of real worlds, as bright as thine.

I trust not to thy phantom bliss,
    Yet, still, in evening's quiet hour,
With never-failing thankfulness,
    I welcome thee, Benignant Power;
Sure solacer of human cares,
And sweeter hope, when hope despairs!

(Wr. 1844, pub. 1846)

104 REMEMBRANCE

EMILY BRONTË

Cold in the earth—and the deep snow piled above thee,
Far, far, removed, cold in the dreary grave!
Have I forgot, my only Love, to love thee,
Severed at last by Time's all-severing wave?

Now, when alone, do my thoughts no longer hover
Over the mountains, on that northern shore,
Resting their wings where heath and fern-leaves cover
Thy noble heart for ever, ever more?

Cold in the earth—and fifteen wild Decembers,
From those brown hills, have melted into spring:
Faithful, indeed, is the spirit that remembers
After such years of change and suffering!

Sweet Love of youth, forgive, if I forget thee,
While the world's tide is bearing me along;
Other desires and other hopes beset me,
Hopes which obscure, but cannot do thee wrong!

No later light has lightened up my heaven,
No second morn has ever shone for me;
All my life's bliss from thy dear life was given,
All my life's bliss is in the grave with thee.

But, when the days of golden dreams had perished,
And even Despair was powerless to destroy;
Then did I learn how existence could be cherished,
Strengthened, and fed without the aid of joy.

Then did I check the tears of useless passion—
Weaned my young soul from yearning after thine;
Sternly denied its burning wish to hasten
Down to that tomb already more than mine.

And, even yet, I dare not let it languish,
Dare not indulge in memory's rapturous pain;
Once drinking deep of that divinest anguish,
How could I seek the empty world again?

(Wr. 1845, pub. 1846)

EMILY BRONTË

105 THE PRISONER. A FRAGMENT

In the dungeon-crypts, idly did I stray,
Reckless of the lives wasting there away;
'Draw the ponderous bars! open, Warder stern!'
He dared not say me nay—the hinges harshly turn.

'Our guests are darkly lodged,' I whispered, gazing through
The vault, whose grated eye showed heaven more grey than blue;
(This was when glad spring laughted in awaking pride;)
'Aye, darkly lodged enough!' returned my sullen guide.

Then, God forgive my youth; forgive my careless tongue;
I scoffed, as the chill chains on the damp flag-stones rung:
'Confined in triple walls, art thou so much to fear,
That we must bind thee down and clench thy fetters here?'

The captive raised her face, it was as soft and mild
As sculptured marble saint, or slumbering unweaned child;
It was so soft and mild, it was so sweet and fair,
Pain could not trace a line, nor grief a shadow there!

The captive raised her hand and pressed it to her brow;
'I have been struck,' she said, 'and I am suffering now;
Yet these are little worth, your bolts and irons strong,
And, were they forged in steel, they could not hold me long.'

Hoarse laughed the jailor grim: 'Shall I be won to hear;
Dost think, fond, dreaming wretch, that *I* shall grant thy prayer?
Or, better still, wilt melt my master's heart with groans?
Ah! sooner might the sun thaw down these granite stones.

'My master's voice is low, his aspect bland and kind,
But hard as hardest flint, the soul that lurks behind;
And I am rough and rude, yet not more rough to see
Than is the hidden ghost that has its home in me.'

About her lips there played a smile of almost scorn,
'My friend,' she gently said, 'you have not heard me mourn;
When you my kindred's lives, *my* lost life, can restore,
Then may I weep and sue,—but never, friend, before!

Still, let my tyrants know, I am not doomed to wear
Year after year in gloom, and desolate despair;
A messenger of Hope, comes every night to me,
And offers for short life, eternal liberty.

He comes with western winds, with evening's wandering airs,
With that clear dusk of heaven that brings the thickest stars.
Winds take a pensive tone, and stars a tender fire,
And visions rise, and change, that kill me with desire.

Desire for nothing known in my maturer years,   EMILY
When Joy grew mad with awe, at counting future tears.   BRONTË
When, if my spirit's sky was full of flashes warm,
I knew not whence they came, from sun, or thunder storm.

But, first, a hush of peace—a soundless calm descends;
The struggle of distress, and fierce impatience ends.
Mute music soothes my breast, unuttered harmony,
That I could never dream, till Earth was lost to me.

Then dawns the Invisible; the Unseen its truth reveals;
My outward sense is gone, my inward essence feels:
Its wings are almost free—its home, its harbour found,
Measuring the gulf, it stoops, and dares the final bound.

Oh, dreadful is the check—intense the agony—
When the ear begins to hear, and the eye begins to see;
When the pulse begins to throb, the brain to think again,
The soul to feel the flesh, and the flesh to feel the chain.

Yet I would lose no sting, would wish no torture less,
The more that anguish racks, the earlier it will bless;
And robed in fires of hell, or bright with heavenly shine,
If it but herald death, the vision is divine!'

She ceased to speak, and we, unanswering, turned to go—
We had no further power to work the captive woe:
Her cheek, her gleaming eye, declared that man had given
A sentence, unapproved, and overruled by Heaven.

                                      (Wr. 1845, pub. 1846)

106 'NO COWARD SOUL IS MINE'

No coward soul is mine
No trembler in the world's storm-troubled sphere
I see Heaven's glories shine
And Faith shines equal arming me from Fear

O God within my breast
Almighty ever-present Deity
Life, that in me hast rest
As I Undying Life, have power in Thee

Vain are the thousand creeds
That move men's hearts, unutterably vain,
Worthless as withered weeds
Or idlest froth amid the boundless main

EMILY BRONTË

To waken doubt in one
Holding so fast by thy infinity
So surely anchored on
The steadfast rock of Immortality

With wide-embracing love
Thy spirit animates eternal years
Pervades and broods above,
Changes, sustains, dissolves, creates and rears

Though Earth and moon were gone
And suns and universes ceased to be
And thou wert left alone
Every Existence would exist in thee

There is not room for Death
Nor atom that his might could render void
Since thou art Being and Breath
And what thou art may never be destroyed.

(Wr. 1846)

107 'OFTEN REBUKED, YET ALWAYS BACK RETURNING'

Often rebuked, yet always back returning
    To those first feelings that were born with me,
And leaving busy chase of wealth and learning
    For idle dreams of things which cannot be:

To-day, I will seek not the shadowy region;
    Its unsustaining vastness waxes drear;
And visions rising, legion after legion,
    Bring the unreal world too strangely near.

I'll walk, but not in old heroic traces,
    And not in paths of high morality,
And not among the half-distinguished faces,
    The clouded forms of long-past history.

I'll walk where my own nature would be leading:
    It vexes me to choose another guide:
Where the grey flocks in ferny glens are feeding;
    Where the wild wind blows on the mountain side.

What have those lonely mountains worth revealing?
    More glory and more grief than I can tell:
The earth that wakes *one* human heart to feeling
    Can centre both the worlds of Heaven and Hell.

(date unknown)

ANNE BRONTË (1820–1849)

She was born on 17 January 1820 at Thornton, near Bradford, the youngest child of six to Patrick Brontë and Maria (née Branwell). Three months after she was born the family moved to Haworth where Patrick Brontë had been appointed perpetual curate. Her mother died in 1821 and she was brought up by her mother's sister, Elizabeth Branwell, as were the other children, although they were often left to their own devices. After the deaths of her sisters Maria and Elizabeth in 1825, and Charlotte and Emily's withdrawal from Cowan Bridge school in the same year, she was educated almost entirely at home, except for a brief spell at Roe Head school (1835–1837). She briefly became governess to the Ingham family at Blake Hall near Roe Head (April–December 1839) but was unfairly dismissed and returned to Haworth where she fell in love with her father's new curate Willie Weightman. However, he died two years later. She took up a new post as governess to the Robinson family at Thorp Green, near York, in March 1840, and worked there until 1845. As 'Acton Bell' she contributed to the volume *Poems by Currer, Ellis and Acton Bell*, London 1846. Her two novels, *Agnes Grey*, London 1847, and *The tenant of Wildfell Hall*, 2v. London 1848, have been overshadowed by her sisters' novels and have attracted less attention, although *The tenant of Wildfell Hall* is an important treatment of miserable marriage, domestic violence and female independence.

She died on a visit to Scarborough on 28 May 1849 at 2 St Nicholas Cliff, Scarborough, the cause of death consumption, from which she had been suffering for six months, with Ellen Nussey present at her death.

108 THE NORTH WIND

That wind is from the North, I know it well;
No other breeze could have so wild a swell.
Now deep and loud it thunders round my cell,
    Then faintly dies,
    And softly sighs,
And moans and murmurs mournfully.
I know its language; thus it speaks to me—

'I have passed over thy own mountains dear,
Thy northern mountains—and they still are free,
Still lonely, wild, majestic, bleak and drear,
And stern and lovely, as they used to be

When thou, a young enthusiast,
As wild and free as they,
O'er rocks and glens and snowy heights
Didst often love to stray.

I've blown the wild untrodden snows
In whirling eddies from their brows,
And I have howled in caverns wild
Where thou, a joyous mountain child,
Didst dearly love to be.
The sweet world is not changed, but thou

ANNE
BRONTË

Art pining in a dungeon now,
Where thou must ever be;
No voice but mine can reach thine ear,
And Heaven has kindly sent me here,
To mourn and sigh with thee,
And tell thee of the cherished land
Of thy nativity.'

Blow on, wild wind, thy solemn voice,
However sad and drear,
Is nothing to the gloomy silence
I have had to bear.

Hot tears are streaming from my eyes,
But these are better far
Than that dull gnawing tearless [time]
The stupor of despair.

Confined and hopeless as I am,
O speak of liberty,
O tell me of my mountain home,
And I will welcome thee.

(Wr. 1838)

109 TO COWPER

Sweet are thy strains, celestial Bard;
   And oft, in childhood's years,
I've read them o'er and o'er again,
   With floods of silent tears.

The language of my inmost heart,
   I traced in every line;
My sins, *my* sorrows, hopes, and fears,
   Were there—and only mine.

All for myself the sigh would swell,
   The tear of anguish start;
I little knew what wilder woe
   Had filled the Poet's heart.

I did not know the nights of gloom,
   The days of misery;
The long, long years of dark despair,
   That crushed and tortured thee.

But, they are gone; from earth at length
   Thy gentle soul is passed,
And in the bosom of its God
   Has found its home at last.

ANNE BRONTË

It must be so, if God is love,
    And answers fervent prayer;
Then surely thou shalt dwell on high,
    And I may meet thee there.

Is he the source of every good,
    The spring of purity?
Then in thine hours of deepest woe,
    Thy God was still with thee.

How else, when every hope was fled,
    Couldst thou so fondly cling
To holy things and holy men?
    And how so sweetly sing,

Of things that God alone could teach?
    And whence that purity,
That hatred of all sinful ways—
    That gentle charity?

Are *these* the symptoms of a heart
    Of heavenly grace bereft:
For ever banished from its God,
    To Satan's fury left?

Yet, should thy darkest fears be true,
    If Heaven be so severe,
That such a soul as thine is lost,—
    Oh! how shall *I* appear?

(Wr. 1842, pub. 1846)

110 **LINES COMPOSED IN A WOOD ON A WINDY DAY**

My soul is awakened, my spirit is soaring
And carried aloft on the wings of the breeze;
For above and around me the wild wind is roaring,
Arousing to rapture the earth and the seas.

The long withered grass in the sunshine is glancing,
The bare trees are tossing their branches on high;
The dead leaves, beneath them, are merrily dancing,
The white clouds are scudding across the blue sky.

I wish I could see how the ocean is lashing
The foam of its billows to whirlwinds of spray;
I wish I could see how its proud waves are dashing,
And hear the wild roar of their thunder to-day!

(Wr. 1842, pub. 1846)

ANNE BRONTË

111 THE CAPTIVE DOVE

Poor restless dove, I pity thee;
And when I hear thy plaintive moan,
I mourn for thy captivity,
And in thy woes forget mine own.

To see thee stand prepared to fly,
And flap those useless wings of thine,
And gaze into the distant sky,
Would melt a harder heart than mine.

In vain—in vain! Thou canst not rise:
Thy prison roof confines thee there;
Its slender wires delude thine eyes,
And quench thy longings with despair.

Oh, thou were made to wander free
In sunny mead and shady grove,
And, far beyond the rolling sea,
In distant climes, at will to rove!

Yet, had thou but one gentle mate
Thy little drooping heart to cheer,
And share with thee thy captive state,
Thou couldst be happy even there.

Yet, even there, if, listening by,
One faithful dear companion stood,
While gazing on her full bright eyem
Thou might forget thy native wood.

But thou, poor solitary dove,
Must make, unheard, thy joyless moan;
The heart, that Nature formed to love,
Must pine, neglected, and alone.

(Wr. 1842–1843, pub. 1846)

112 IF THIS BE ALL

O God! if this indeed be all
    That Life can show to me;
If on my aching brow may fall
    No freshening dew from Thee,—

If with no brighter light than this
    The lamp of hope may glow,
And I may only *dream* of bliss,
    And wake to weary woe;

ANNE BRONTË

If friendship's solace must decay,
   When other joys are gone,
And love must keep so far away,
   While I go wandering on,—

Wandering and toiling without gain,
   The slave of others' will,
With constant care, and frequent pain,
   Despite, forgotten still;

Grieving to look on vice and sin,
   Yet powerless to quell
The silent current from within,
   The outward torrent's swell:

While all the good I would impart,
   The feelings I would share,
Are driven backward to my heart,
   And turned to wormwood, there;

If clouds must *ever* keep from sight
   The glories of the Sun,
And I must suffer Winter's blight,
   Ere Summer is begun;

If Life must be so full of care,
   Then call me soon to Thee;
Or give me strength enough to bear
   My load of misery.

(Wr. 1845, pub. 1846)

113 DREAMS

While on my lonely couch I lie
I seldom feel myself alone,
For fancy fills my dreaming eye
With scenes and pleasures of its own.

Then I may cherish at my breast
An infant's form beloved and fair,
May smile, and soothe it into rest
With all a mother's fondest care.

How sweet to feel its helpless form
Depending thus on me alone;
And while I hold it safe and warm,
What bliss to think it is my own!

ANNE BRONTË

And glances then may meet my eyes
That daylight never showed to me,
What raptures in my bosom rise
Those earnest looks of love to see!

To feel my hand so kindly pressed,
To know myself beloved at last,
To think my heart has found a rest,
My life of solitude is past.

But then to wake and find it flown,
The dream of happiness destroyed,
To find myself unloved, alone,
What tongue can speak the dreary void?

A heart whence warm affections flow,
Creator, thou hast given to me,
And am I only thus to know
How sweet the joys of love would be?

(Wr. 1845)

CHARLOTTE BRONTË (later NICHOLLS) (1816–1855)

She was born on 21 April 1816 at Thornton, near Bradford, the third of six children of Patrick Brontë and Maria (née Branwell). In August 1824 she entered Cowan Bridge school, following her sisters Maria and Elizabeth who had begun the month before. Emily joined them in November and for a short time the four sisters were at school together. Ill-health forced first Maria and then Elizabeth to leave the school in 1825. When Maria died in May 1825 Charlotte and Emily were removed and educated at home. Elizabeth died a month after their return. In 1831 Charlotte attended Roe Head school for just over a year where she began a lifelong friendship with Ellen Nussey. She returned there in 1835 as a teacher, with Emily also attending as a pupil, although she soon returned to Haworth. In 1839 she was briefly governess to the Sidgwick family at Stonegappe, near Skipton, and in 1840 governess to the White family at Upperwood House, Rawdon. In 1842 she and Emily went to a private school in Belgium to learn French in preparation for setting up a school at Haworth. Returning to England in 1844 the project failed to arouse much interest and was dropped. In the autumn of 1845 she discovered a manuscript notebook containing Emily's poems, and the three sisters, Charlotte, Emily and Anne, published at their own expense *Poems by Currer, Ellis and Acton Bell*, London 1846. The following year she published *Jane Eyre: an autobiography*, 3v. London 1847, which proved an immediate success. Further novels followed which were well received but not so popular: *Shirley*, 3v. London 1849, and *Villette*, 3v. 1853. *The Professor*, 2v. London 1857, which had been rejected in 1847, was posthumously published with a foreword by her husband. By 1849 all her sisters and her brother had died and she was subject to increasing depression. After initial opposition from her father, she married the Revd Arthur Bell Nicholls, who had been her father's curate at Haworth, on 19 June 1854. She died at Haworth on 31 March 1855, the cause of death phthisis from which she had been suffering for three months, with Amos Ingham of Haworth present at her death.

CHARLOTTE BRONTË

114 ON THE DEATH OF EMILY JANE BRONTË

My darling, thou wilt never know
The grinding agony of woe
   That we have borne for thee.
Thus may we consolation tear
Even from the depth of our despair
   And wasting misery.

The nightly anguish thou art spared
When all the crushing truth is bared
   To the awakening mind,
When the galled heart is pierced with grief,
Till wildly it implores relief,
   But small relief can find.

Not know'st thou what it is to lie
Looking forth with streaming eye
   On life's lone wilderness.
'Weary, weary, dark and drear,
How shall I the journey bear,
   The burden and distress?'

Then since thou art spared such pain
We will not wish thee here again;
   He that lives must mourn.
God help us through our misery
And give us rest and joy with thee
   When we reach our bourne!

(Wr. 1848)

115 ON THE DEATH OF ANNE BRONTË

There's little joy in life for me,
   And little terror in the grave;
I've lived the parting hour to see
   Of one I would have died to save.

Calmly to watch the failing breath,
   Wishing each sigh might be the last;
Longing to see the shade of death
   O'er those belovèd features cast.

CHARLOTTE
BRONTË

The cloud, the stillness that must part
The darling of my life from me;
And then to thank God from my heart,
To thank Him well and fervently;

Although I knew that we had lost
The hope and glory of our life;
And now, benighted, tempest-tossed,
Must bear alone the weary strife.

(Wr. 1849)

ELIZABETH BARRETT BROWNING (née BARRETT) (1806–1861)
She was born on 6 March 1806 at Coxhoe Hall, Kelloe, Durham, the eldest of eleven children of Edward Barrett Moulton-Barrett and Mary (née Graham-Clarke). Her father had extensive plantation interests in Jamaica although his wealth later declined steadily owing to legal complications and the abolition of slavery. In 1809 the family moved to a large estate at Hope End, Ledbury, Hertfordshire, where Elizabeth Barrett was educated at home with her brother and soon became proficient in Latin and Greek (to which she later added Hebrew). A riding accident resulted in a spinal injury (the exact nature of which is not known) and for many years she was a semi-invalid. In 1832 her father's financial difficulties forced the sale of Hope End and she stayed for three years at Sidmouth. In 1835 the family moved to Wimpole Street, London, where she was to remain until her marriage and elopement with the poet Robert Browning in 1846. In 1840 she was recuperating from illness in Torquay and insisted her brother stay with her. They argued one day and he went sailing and was drowned. The exact psychological effect on her is difficult to establish but there is evidence in her poems and letters of a tremendous sense of guilt which recurred throughout her life. After the publication of *Poems*, 2v. London 1844, she met Robert Browning and married him secretly at Marylebone Church in 1846 against her father's wishes, eloping with him first to Paris but finally settling in Italy. They lived for a short time in Pisa, then in Florence, at Casa Guidi, in the Via Maggio, from May 1847 until her death in 1861. In Florence they had a wide circle of friends and received many visitors from Hans Christian Andersen to Nathaniel Hawthorne.

Her early poems display her formidable knowledge of Ancient Greek and contemporary concerns over Greek independence and Byron's intervention. Her first work, *The battle of Marathon. A poem*, London 1820, was privately printed and was followed by *An essay on mind*, London 1826, and *Prometheus bound. Translated from the Greek of Aeschylus. And miscellaneous poems*, London 1833. Her first periodical contributions, 'Stanzas, excited by some reflection on the present state of Greece', and 'Thoughts awakened by contemplating a piece of the palm which grows on the summit of the Acropolis at Athens', appeared in the *New Monthly Magazine*, 1 (1821), 523, and 2 (1821), 59. She also contributed two poems in 1825–1826 to the *Literary Gazette* where Letitia Landon was a major contributor. Thereafter, she published several of her more important poems in the *New Monthly Magazine* ('Stanzas addressed to Miss Landon', 45 (1835), 82; 'The romaunt of Margret', 47 (1836), 316–20; 'The poet's vow', 48 (1836), 209–18; 'The island', 49 (1837), 22–5). She also contributed a number of poems to the *Athenaeum*. Her first major collection, *The seraphim, and other poems*, London 1838, reprinted many of these contributions and aroused some interest but it was not until *Poems*, 2v. London 1844, appeared that her reputation was established. However, she was by no means unknown before then, having contributed two important poems to the Annual edited by her friend, Mary Russell Mitford, *Finden's Tableaux* ('A romance of the Ganges' (1838), 29–31, and 'The romaunt of the page' (1839), 1–5) and had begun to publish in America in *Graham's Magazine*. She had also contributed a widely admired poem, 'The cry of the children', to *Blackwood's* (54 (1843), 260–2). She continued to publish many of her poems after 1844 in *Blackwood's* and *Graham's* but placed two of her fiercest anti-slavery poems in the Boston-based abolitionist magazine, *The Liberty Bell* ('The runaway slave at Pilgrim's Point' (1848), 29–44, and 'A curse for the nation' (1856), 1–9). Her 'Sonnets from the Portuguese', first published in *Poems*, London 1850, exhibit a baroque wit—she was also widely read in seventeenth-century English poetry—and quickly became popular. These long overshadowed her radicalism and feminism and it has been only in the last twenty years that her narrative of a nineteenth-century woman poet, *Aurora Leigh*, London 1856, has attracted critical attention. (On its appearance, *Aurora Leigh* evoked sharply different reactions—Coventry Patmore and William Roscoe objected to its forthright presentation of an independent woman—but it was also greatly admired by Leigh Hunt, George Eliot and Elizabeth Gaskell.) Similarly, her engagement with Italian independence in *Casa Guidi Windows*, London 1851, and, more intensely, in *Poems before Congress*, London 1860, has rarely been studied or linked to her earlier metaphysical and social concerns. Despite a number of editions of her work, no critical edition exists. *The complete works*, ed. Charlotte Porter and Helen A. Clarke, 6v. New York 1900, gives useful annotations but contains no textual work. She died in Florence on 30 June 1861.

116 STANZAS ADDRESSED TO MISS LANDON, AND SUGGESTED BY HER 'STANZAS ON THE DEATH OF MRS HEMANS'

Thou bay-crowned living one—who o'er
    The bay-crowned dead art bowing,
And o'er the shadeless, moveless brow
    Thy human shadow throwing;
And o'er the sighless, songless lips
    The wail and music wedding—
Dropping o'er the tranquil eyes
    Tears not of *their* shedding!

Go! take thy music from the dead,
    Whose silentness is sweeter;
Reserve thy tears for living brows,
    For whom such tears are meeter;

ELIZABETH BARRETT BROWNING

And leave the violets in the grass,
    To brighten where thou treadest,
No flowers for *her!* Oh! bring no flowers—
    Albeit 'Bring flowers,' thou saidest.

But bring not near her solemn corse
    A type of human seeming;
Lay only dust's stern verity
    Upon her dust undreaming.
And while the calm perpetual stars
    Shall look upon it solely;
Her spherèd soul shall look on *them*,
    With eyes more bright and holy.

Nor mourn, oh living one, because
    Her part in life was mourning:
Would she have lost the poet's flame,
    For anguish of the burning?
The minstrel harp, for the strained string?
    The tripod, for the afflated
Woe? or the vision, for those tears
    Through which it shone dilated?

Perhaps she shuddered while the world's
    Cold hand her brow was wreathing:
But wronged she ne'er that mystic breath
    Which breathed in all her breathing,—
Which drew from rocky earth and man
    Abstractions high and moving,—
Beauty, if not the beautiful,—
    And love, if not the loving.

Such visionings have paled in sight
    The *Saviour* she descrieth,
And little reeks who wreathed the brow
    That on His bosom lieth.
The whiteness of His innocence
    O'er all her garments flowing,
There learneth she that sweet 'new song'
    She will not mourn in knowing.

Be blessed, crowned and living one:
    And when thy dust decayeth,
May thine own England say for thee
    What now for her it sayeth,—
'Albeit softly in our ears
    Her silver song was ringing,
The footsteps of her parting soul
    Were softer than her singing.'

(1835)

117 THE SOUL'S TRAVELLING
Ἤδη νοερούς
πετάσαι ταρσούς [Synesius]

ELIZABETH BARRETT BROWNING

I

I dwell amid the city ever,
The great humanity which beats
Its life along the stony streets,
Like a strong and unsunned river
In a self-made course,
I sit and hearken while it rolls.
   Very sad and very hoarse
   Certes is the flow of souls:
Infinitest tendencies,
By the finite, pressed and pent,—
In the infinite, turbulent.
And how we tremble in surprise,
When sometimes, with an awful sound,
God's great plummet strikes the ground!

II

The champ of the steeds on the silver bit,
As they whirl the rich man's chariot by;
The beggar's whine as he looks at it,—
But it goes too fast for charity.
The trail, on the street, of the poor man's broom,
That the lady, who walks to her palace-home,
On her silken skirt, may catch no dust:
The tread of the business-men who must
Count their per cents by the paces they take:
The cry of the babe, unheard of its mother
Though it lie on her breast, while she thinks of the other
Laid yesterday where it will not wake.
The flower-girl's prayer to buy roses and pinks,
Held out in the smoke, like stars by day;
The gin-door's oath, that hollowly chinks
Guilt upon grief, and wrong upon hate:
The cabman's cry to get out of the way;
The dustman's call down the area-grate:
The young maid's jest, and the old wife's scold,
The haggling talk of the boys at a stall;
The fight in the street, which is backed for gold,—
The plea of the lawyers in Westminster Hall;
The drop on the stones, of the blind man's staff,
As he trades in his own grief's sacredness;
The brothel's shriek, and the Newgate laugh,
The hum upon 'Change, and the organ's grinding,
The grinder's face being nevertheless
Dry and vacant of even woe,

ELIZABETH BARRETT BROWNING

While the children's hearts are leaping so
At the merry music's winding!
The black-plumed funeral's creeping train,
Long and slow (and yet they will go
As fast as Life, though it hurry and strain!)
Creeping the populous houses through,
And nodding their plumes at either side,—
At many a house where an infant, new
To the sunshiny world, has just struggled and cried:
At many a house, where sitteth a bride
Trying the morrow's coronals,
With a scarlet blush, to-day.—
   Slowly creep the funerals,
As none should hear the noise and say,
The living, the living, must go away
      To multiply the dead!
   Hark! an upward shout is sent!
In grave strong joy from tower to steeple
      The bells ring out—
The trumpets sound, the people shout,
The young Queen goes to her parliament.
She turneth round her large blue eyes,
More bright with childish memories
Than royal hopes, upon the people:
On either side she bows her head
   Lowly, with a Queenly grace,
And smile most trusting-innocent,
As if she smiled upon her mother!
The thousands press before each other
      To bless her to her face:
And booms the deep majestic voice
Through trump and drum,—'May the Queen rejoice
   In the people's liberties!'—

        III
   I dwell amid the city,
   And hear the flow of souls in act and speech,
For pomp or trade, for merrymake or folly:
I hear the confluence and sum of each,
   And that is melancholy!—
Thy voice is a complaint, O crownèd city,
The blue sky covering thee, like God's great pity.

        IV
   O blue sky! it mindeth me
   Of places where I used to see
   Its vast unbroken circle thrown
   From the far pale-peakèd hill

Out to the last verge of ocean—
As by God's arm it were done
Then for the first time, with the emotion
Of that first impulse on it still.
Oh, we spirits fly at will,
Faster than the winged steed
Whereof in old book we read,
With the sunlight foaming back
From him, to a misty wrack,
And his nostril reddening proud
As he breatheth the steep thundercloud!
Smoother than Sabrina's chair
Gliding up from wave to air,
While she smileth debonair
Yet holy, coldly and yet brightly,
Like her own mooned waters nightly,
   Through her dripping hair.

V

Very fast and smooth we fly,
Spirits, though the flesh be by.
All looks feed not from the eye,
Nor all hearings from the ear;
We can hearken and espy
Without either; we can journey,
Bold and gay, as knight to tourney;
And though we wear no visor down
To dark our countenance, the foe
Shall never chafe us as we go.

VI

I am gone from peopled town!
It passeth its street-thunder round
My body, which yet hears no sound;
For now another sound, another
Vision, my soul's senses have.
O'er a hundred valleys deep,
Where the hills' green shadows sleep,
Scarce known, because the valley trees
Cross those upland images—
O'er a hundred hills, each other
Watching, to the western wave—
I have travelled,—I have found
The silent, lone, remembered ground.

VII

I have found a grassy niche,
Hollowed in a seaside hill,
As if the ocean-grandeur, which

Is aspectable from the place,
Had struck the hill as with a mace
Sudden and cleaving. You might fill
That little nook with the little cloud
Which sometimes lieth by the moon
To beautify a night of June;
A cavelike nook, which, opening all
To the wide sea, is disallowed
From its own earth's sweet pastoral;
Cavelike, but roofless overhead,
And made of verdant banks instead
Of any rocks, with flowerets spread,
Instead of spar and stalactite . . .
Cowslips and daisies, gold and white, . . .
Such pretty flowers on such green sward,
You think, the sea, they look toward,
Doth serve them for another sky,
As warm and blue as that on high.

VIII

And in this hollow is a seat,
And when you shall have crept to it,
Slipping down the banks too steep
To be o'erbrowsèd by the sheep,—
Do not think—though at your feet
The cliff's disrupt—you shall behold
The line where earth and ocean meet:
You sit too much above to view
The solemn confluence of the two:
You can hear them as they greet;
You can hear that evermore
Distance-softened noise, more old
Than Nereid's singing,—the tide spent
Joining soft issues with the shore
In harmony of discontent,—
And when you hearken to the grave
Lamenting of the underwave,
You must believe in their communion,
Albeit you witness not the union.

IX

Except that sound, the place is full
Of silences, which when you cull
By any word, it thrills you so
That presently you let them grow
To meditation's fullest length,
Across your soul with a soul's strength:
And as they touch your soul, they borrow
As of its grandeur, so its sorrow,—

That deathly odour which the clay
Leaves on its deathlessness alway.

ELIZABETH
BARRETT
BROWNING

X

Alway! alway! must this be?
Rapid Soul from city gone,
Dost thou carry inwardly
What doth make the ciry's moan?
Must this deep sigh of thine own
Haunt thee with humanity?
Green-visioned banks, that are too steep
To be o'erbrowsèd by the sheep,
May all sad thoughts adown you creep
Without a shepherd?—Mighty sea,
Can we dwarf thy magnitude,
And fit it to our straitest mood?—
O fair, fair Nature! are we thus
Impotent and querulous
Among thy workings glorious,
Wealth and sanctities,—that still
Leave us vacant and defiled,
And wailing like a kissed child,
Kissed soft against his will?

XI

God, God!—
With a child's voice I cry,
Weak, sad, confidingly—
God, God!
Thou knowest eyelids raised not always up
Unto Thy love, (as none of ours are) droop,
As ours, o'er many a tear!
Thou knowest, though thy universe is broad,
Two little tears suffice to cover all.
Thou knowest,—Thou, who are so prodigal
Of beauty,—we are oft but stricken deer,
Expiring in the woods—that care for none
Of those delightsome flowers they die upon.

XII

O blissful Mouth, which breathed the mournful breath
We name our souls,—self spoilt!—by that strong passion
Which paled thee once with sighs,—by that strong death
Which made thee once unbreathing—from the wrack,
Themselves have called around them, call them back
Back to thee in continuous aspiration!
For here, O Lord,
For here they travel vainly,—vainly pass
From city pavement to untrodden sward,

ELIZABETH
BARRETT
BROWNING

Where the lark finds her deep nest in the grass
Cold with the earth's last dew. Yea, very vain
The greatest speed of all these souls of men,
Unless they travel upward to Thy Throne!
There, sittest Thou, the satisfying One,
With help for sins, and holy perfectings
For all requirements—while the archangel, raising
Unto Thy face, his full ecstatic gazing,
Forgets the rush and rapture of his wings!

(1838, rev. & repr. 1850)

118 COWPER'S GRAVE

> I will invite thee, from thy envious hearse
> To rise, and 'bout the world thy beams to spread,
> That we may see there's brightness in the dead.   [Habington]

It is a place where poets crowned
   May feel the heart's decaying—
It is a place where happy saints
   May weep amid their praying—
Yet let the grief and humbleness,
   As low as silence, languish;
Earth surely now may give her calm
   To whom she gave her anguish.

O poets! from a maniac's tongue
   Was poured the deathless singing!
O Christians! at your cross of hope
   A hopeless hand was clinging!
O men! this man, in brotherhood,
   Your weary paths beguiling,
Groaned inly while he taught you peace,
   And died while ye were smiling!

And now, what time ye all may read
   Through dimming tears his story—
How discord on the music fell,
   And darkness on the glory—
And how, when one by one, sweet sounds
   And wandering lights departed,
He wore no less a loving face,
   Because so broken-hearted—

He shall be strong to sanctify
   The poet's high vocation,
And bow the meekest Christian down
   In meeker adoration:

ELIZABETH
BARRETT
BROWNING

Nor ever shall he be in praise,
  By wise or good forsaken;
Named softly, as the household name
  Of one whom God hath taken!

With sadness that is calm, not gloom,
  I learn to think upon him;
With meekness that is gratefulness,
  On God whose heaven hath won him—
Who suffered once the madness-cloud,
  Toward His love to blind him;
But gently led the blind along
  Where breath and bird could find him;

And wrought within his shattered brain,
  Such quick poetic senses,
As hills have language for, and stars,
  Harmonious influences!
The pulse of dew upon the grass,
  His own did calmly number;
And silent shadow from the trees
  Fell o'er him like a slumber.

The very world, by God's constraint,
  From falsehood's chill removing,
Its women and its men became
  Beside him, true and loving!—
And timid hares were drawn from woods
  To share his home-caresses,
Uplooking to his human eyes
  With sylvan tendernesses.

But while, in blindness he remained
  Unconscious of the guiding,
And things provided came without
  The sweet sense of providing,
He testified this solemn truth,
  Through frenzy desolated—
Nor man, nor nature satisfy,
  When only God created!

Like a sick child that knoweth not
  His mother while she blesses,
And droppeth on his burning brow
  The coolness of her kisses;
That turns his fevered eyes around—
  'My mother! where's my mother?'—
As if such tender words and looks
  Could come from any other!

ELIZABETH BARRETT BROWNING

The fever gone, with leaps of heart
    He sees her bending o'er him;
Her face all pale from watchful love,
    The unweary love she bore him!
Thus, woke the poet from the dream
    His life's long fever gave him,
Beneath these deep pathetic eyes
    Which closed in death, to save him!

Thus! oh, not *thus*! no type of earth
    Could image that awaking,
Wherein he scarcely heard the chant
    Of seraphs, round him breaking—
Or felt the new immortal throb
    Of soul from body parted;
But felt *those eyes alone*, and knew
    '*My* Saviour! *not* deserted!'

Deserted! who hath dreamt that when
    The cross in darkness rested,
Upon the Victim's hidden face
    No love was manifested?
What frantic hands outstretched have e'er
    The atoning drops averted—
What tears have washed them from the soul—
    That *one* should be deserted?

Deserted! God could separate
    From His own essence rather:
And Adam's sins *have* swept between
    The righteous Son and Father—
Yea! once, Immanuel's orphaned cry,
    His universe hath shaken—
It went up single, echoless,
    'My God, I am forsaken!'

It went up from the Holy's lips
    Amid his lost creation,
That of the lost, no son should use
    Those words of desolation;
That earth's worst frenzies, marring hope,
    Should mar not hope's fruition;
And I, on Cowper's grave, should see
    His rapture, in a vision!

(1838)

119 THE CRY OF THE HUMAN

ELIZABETH BARRETT BROWNING

'There is no God,' the foolish saith,—
　But none, 'There is no sorrow;'
And nature oft, the cry of faith,
　In bitter need will borrow:
Eyes, which the preacher could not school,
　By wayside graves are raised;
And lips say, 'God be pitiful,'
　Who ne'er said, 'God be praised.'
　　　　　　　Be pitiful, O God!

The tempest stretches from the steep
　The shadow of its coming—
The beasts grow tame, and near us creep,
　As help were in the human—
Yet, while the cloud-wheels roll and grind,
　We spirits tremble under!—
The hills have echoes; but we find
　No answer for the thunder.
　　　　　　　Be pitiful, O God!

The battle hurtles on the plains—
　Earth feels new scythes upon her:
We reap our brothers for the wains,
　And call the harvest ... honour,—
Draw face to face, front line to line,
　One image all inherit,—
Then kill, curse on, by that same sign,
　Clay, clay,—and spirit, spirit.
　　　　　　　Be pitiful, O God!

The plague runs festering through the town,—
　And never a bell is tolling;
And corpses, jostled 'neath the moon,
　Nod to the dead-cart's rolling!
The young child calleth for the cup—
　The strong man brings it weeping;
The mother from her babe looks up,
　And shrieks away its sleeping.
　　　　　　　Be pitiful, O God!

The plague of gold strikes far and near,—
　And deep and strong it enters:
This purple chimar which we wear,
　Makes madder than the centaur's
Our thoughts grow blank, our words grow strange;
　We cheer the pale gold-diggers—
Each soul is worth so much on 'Change,

245

And marked, like sheep, with figures.
      Be pitiful, O God!

The curse of gold upon the land,
 The lack of bread enforces—
The rail-cars snort from strand to strand,
 Like more of Death's White horses!
The rich preach 'rights' and future days,
 And hear no angel scoffing:
The poor die mute—with starving gaze
 On corn-ships in the offing.
      Be pitiful, O God!

We meet together at the feast—
 To private mirth betake us—
We stare down in the winecup, lest
 Some vacant chair should shake us!
We name delight, and pledge it round—
 'It shall be ours to-morrow!'
God's seraphs! do your voices sound
 As sad in naming sorrow?
      Be pitiful, O God!

We sit together, with the skies,
 The steadfast skies, above us:
We look into each other's eyes,—
 'And how long will you love us?'—
The eyes grow dim with prophecy,
 The voices, low and breathless—
'Till death us part!'—O words, to be
 Our *best* for love the deathless!
      Be pitiful, O God!

We tremble by the harmless bed
 Of one loved and departed—
Our tears drop on the lips that said
 Last night, 'Be stronger-hearted!'
O God,—to clasp those fingers close,
 And yet to feel so lonely!—
To see a light on dearest brows,
 Which is the daylight only!
      Be pitiful, O God!

The happy children come to us,
 And look up in our faces:
They ask us—Was it thus, and thus,
 When we were in their places?—
We cannot speak:—we see anew
 The hills we used to live in;

And feel our mother's smile press through
   The kisses she is giving.
               Be pitiful, O God!

We pray together at the kirk,
   For mercy, mercy, solely—
Hands weary with the evil work,
   We lift them to the Holy!
The corpse is calm below our knee—
   Its spirit, bright before Thee—
Between them, worse than either, we—
   Without the rest or glory!
               Be pitiful, O God!

We leave the communing of men,
   The murmur of the passions;
And live alone, to live again
   With endless generations.
Are we so brave?—The sea and sky
   In silence lift their mirrors;
And, glassed therein, our spirits high
   Recoil from their own terrors.
               Be pitiful, O God!

We sit on hills our childhood wist,
   Woods, hamlets, streams, beholding!
The sun strikes, through the farthest mist,
   The city's spire to golden.
The city's golden spire it was,
   When hope and health were strongest,
But now it is the churchyard grass,
   We look upon the longest.
               Be pitiful, O God!

And soon all vision waxeth dull—
   Men whisper, 'He is dying:'
We cry no more, 'Be pitiful!'—
   We have no strength for crying!—
No strength, no need! Then, Soul of mine,
   Look up and triumph rather—
Lo! in the depth of God's Divine,
   The Son adjures the Father—
               Be pitiful, O God!

ELIZABETH BARRETT BROWNING

(1842, rev. & repr. 1844)

ELIZABETH BARRETT BROWNING

120 THE CRY OF THE CHILDREN

Do ye hear the children weeping, O my brothers!
    Ere the sorrow comes with years?
They are leaning their young heads against their mothers,
    And *that* cannot stop their tears.
The young lambs are bleating in the meadows,
The young birds are chirping in the nest,
The young fawns are playing with the shadows,
The young flowers are blowing from the west;
But the young young children, O my brothers!
    They are weeping bitterly!
They are weeping in the playtime of the others—
    In the country of the free.

Do you question the young children in the sorrow,
    Why their tears are falling so?
The old man may weep for his to-morrow
    Which is lost in long ago.
The old tree is leafless in the forest—
The old year is ending in the frost;
The old wound, if stricken, is the sorest—
The old hope is hardest to be lost!
But the young young children, O my brothers!
    Do ye ask them why they stand
Weeping sore before the bosoms of their mothers,
    In our happy fatherland?

They look up with their pale and sunken faces,
    And their looks are sad to see;
For the man's grief untimely draws and presses
    Down the cheeks of infancy.
'Your old earth,' they say, 'is very dreary—
Our young feet,' they say, 'are very weak!
Few paces have we taken, yet are weary—
Our grave-rest is very far to seek!
Ask the old why they weep, and not the children;
    For the outside earth is cold—
And we young ones stand without, in our bewildering,
    And the graves are for the old.

'True,' say the young children, 'it may happen
    That we die before our time!
Little Alice died last year—the grave is shapen
    Like a snowball, in the rime.
We looked into the pit prepared to take her—
Was no room for any work in the close clay!
From the sleep wherein she lieth none will wake her,
    Crying—"Get up, little Alice, it is day!"

ELIZABETH BARRETT BROWNING

If you listen by that grave in sun and shower,
With your ear down, little Alice never cries;
Could we see her face, be sure we should not know her,
For the new smile which has grown within her eyes.
For merry go her moments, lulled and stilled in
    The shroud, by the kirk-chime!
It is good when it happens,' say the children,
    'That we die before our time!'

Alas, the young children! they are seeking
    Death in life, as best to have!
They are binding up their hearts away from breaking,
    With a cerement from the grave.
Go out, children, from the mine and from the city—
Sing out, children, as the little thrushes do!
Pluck your handfuls of the meadow cowslips pretty—
Laugh aloud to feel your fingers let them through!
But the children say—'Are cowslips of the meadows
    Like the weeds anear the mine?
Leave us quiet in the dark of our coal-shadows,
    From your pleasures fair and fine.

'For oh!' say the children, 'we are weary—
    And we cannot run or leap;
If we cared for any meadows, it were merely
    To drop down in them and sleep.
Our knees tremble sorely in the stooping—
We fall upon our face, trying to go;
And underneath our heavy eyelids drooping,
The reddest flower would look as pale as snow.
For, all day, we drag our burden tiring,
    Through the coal-dark underground—
Or, all day, we drive the wheels of iron
    In the factories, round and round.

'All day long, the wheels are droning, turning—
    Their wind comes in our faces!
Till our hearts turn, and our heads with pulses burning,
    And the walls turn in their places!
Turns the sky in the high window blank and reeling—
Turns the long light that droppeth down the wall—
Turn the black flies that crawl along the ceiling—
All are turning all the day, and we with all!
All day long, the iron wheels are droning—
    And sometimes we could pray—
"O ye wheels" (breaking off in a mad moaning)
    "Stop! be silent for to-day!"'

ELIZABETH BARRETT BROWNING

Ay! be silent! let them hear each other breathing,
    For a moment, mouth to mouth;
Let them touch each other's hands, in a fresh wreathing
    Of their tender human youth;
Let them feel that this cold metallic motion
Is not all the life God giveth them to use;
Let them prove their inward souls against the notion
That they live in you, or under you, O wheels!
Still, all day, the iron wheels go onward,
    As if Fate in each were stark!
And the children's souls, which God is calling sunward,
    Spin on blindly in the dark.

Now, tell the weary children, O my brothers!
    They they look to Him, and pray
For the blessed One, who blesseth all the others,
    To bless *them* another day.
They answer, 'Who is God that he should hear us,
While this rushing of the iron wheels is stirred?
When we sob aloud, the human creatures near us
Pass unhearing—at least, answer not a word;
And *we* hear not (for the wheels in their resounding)
    Strangers speaking at the door.
Is it likely God, with angels singing round him,
    Hears our weeping any more?

'Two words, indeed, of praying we remember;
    And, at midnight's hour of harm,
Our Father, looking upward in the chamber,
    We say softly for a charm.
We say no other words except *Our Father!*
And we think that, in some pause of angels' song,
He may pluck them with the silence sweet to gather,
And hold both within his right hand, which is strong.
Our Father! If he heard us, he would surely
    (For they call him good and mild)
Answer—smiling down the steep world very purely—
    "Come and rest with me, my child."

'But no,' say the children, weeping faster;
    'He is silent as a stone,
And they tell us, of his image is the master
    Who commands us to work on.
Go to!' say the children; 'up in heaven,
Dark, wheel-like, turning clouds are all we find!
We look up for Him—but tears have made us blind.'
Do ye hear the children weeping and disproving,
    O my brothers, what ye teach?
For God's possible is taught by his world's loving—
    And the children doubt of each!

ELIZABETH BARRETT BROWNING

And well may the children weep before ye—
    They are weary ere they run!
They have never seen the sunshine, nor the glory
    Which is brighter than the sun!
They know the grief of men, but not the wisdom—
They sink in the despair, with hope at calm—
Are slaves, without the liberty in christdom—
Are martyrs by the pang without the palm!
Are worn as if with age; yet unretrievingly
    No joy of memory keep—
Are orphans of the earthly love and heavenly—
    Let them weep—let them weep!

They look up with their pale and sunken faces,
    And their look is dread to see;
For you think you see their angels in their places,
    With eyes meant for Deity.
'How long,' they say, 'how long, O cruel nation!
Will you stand, to move the world, on a child's heart,
Trample down with a mailed heel its palpitation,
And tread onward to your throne amid the mart?
Our blood splashes upward, O our tyrants!
    And your purple shows your path—
But the child's sob curseth deeper in the silence,
    Than the strong man in his wrath!'

(1843)

121 SONNET: THE SOUL'S EXPRESSION

With stammering lips and insufficient sound,
I strive and struggle to deliver right
That music of my nature, day and night
With dream and thought and feeling interwound;
And inly answering all the senses round
With octaves of a mystic depth and height,
Which step out grandly to the infinite
From the dark edges of the sensual ground.
This song of soul I struggle to outbear
Through portals of the sense, sublime and whole,
And utter all myself into the air:
But if I did it,—as the thunder roll
Breaks its own cloud,—my flesh would perish there,
Before that dread apocalypse of soul.

(1843, repr. 1844)

ELIZABETH BARRETT BROWNING

122 SONNET: THE SERAPH AND POET

The seraph sings before the manifest
God-one, and in the burning of the Seven,
And with the full life of consummate Heaven
Heaving beneath him like a mother's breast
Warm with her first-born's slumber in that nest!
The poet sings upon the earth grave-riven;
Before the naughty world soon self-forgiven
For wronging him; and in the darkness pressed
From his own soul by worldly weights. Even so,
Sing, seraph with the glory! Heaven is high—
Sing, poet with the sorrow! Earth is low!
The universe's inward voices cry
'Amen' to either song of joy and woe—
Sing seraph,—poet,—sing on equally.

(1843, repr. 1844)

123 THE RUNAWAY SLAVE AT PILGRIM'S POINT

I

I stand on the mark, beside the shore,
   Of the first white pilgrim's bended knee;
Where exile changed to ancestor,
   And God was thanked for liberty.
I have run through the night—my skin is as dark—
I bend my knee down on this mark—
   I look on the sky and the sea.

II

O, pilgrim-souls, I speak to you:
   I see you come out proud and slow
From the land of the spirits, pale as dew,
   And round me and round me ye go.
O, pilgrims, I have gasped and run
All night long from the whips of one
   Who, in your names, works sin and woe!

III

And thus I thought that I would come
   And kneel here where ye knelt before,
And feel your souls around me hum
   In undertone to the ocean's roar;
And lift my black face, my black hand,
Here in your names, to curse this land
   Ye blessed in Freedom's, heretofore.

ELIZABETH
BARRETT
BROWNING

IV

I am black, I am black,
    And yet God made me, they say:
But if He did so—smiling, back
    He must have cast his work away
Under the feet of His white creatures,
With a look of scorn, that the dusky features
    Might be trodden again to clay.

V

And yet He has made dark things
    To be glad and merry as light;
There's a little dark bird sits and sings,
    There's a dark stream ripples out of sight;
And the dark frogs chant in the safe morass,
And the sweetest stars are made to pass
    O'er the face of the darkest night.

VI

But we who are dark, we are dark!
    O God, we have no stars!
About our souls, in care and cark,
    Our blackness shuts like prison-bars!
And crouch our souls so far behind,
That never a comfort can they find,
    By reaching through their prison-bars.

VII

Howbeit God's sunshine and His frost
    They make us hot, they make us cold,
As if we were not black and lost;
    And the beasts and birds in wood and wold,
Do fear us and take us for very men;—
Could the whippoorwill or the cat of the glen
    Look into my eyes and be bold?

VIII

I am black, I am black,
    And once I laughed in girlish glee;
For one of my colour stood in the track
    Where the drivers' drove, and looked at me
And tender and full was the look he gave!
A Slave looked so at another Slave,—
    I look at the sky and the sea.

IX

And from that hour our spirits grew
    As free as if unsold, unbought;
We were strong enough, since we were two,

ELIZABETH BARRETT BROWNING

    To conquer the world, we thought.
The drivers drove us day by day:
We did not mind; we went one way,
    And no better a liberty sought.

X

In the open ground between the canes,
    He said 'I love you,' as he passed:
When the shingle-roof rang sharp with the rains,
    I heard how he vowed it fast.
While others trembled, he sat in the hut
And carved me a bowl of the coconut,
    Through the roar of the hurricanes.

XI

I sang his name instead of a song;
    Over and over I sang his name:
Backward and forward I sang it along,
    With my sweetest notes, it was still the same!
But I sang it low, that the slave-girls near
Might never guess, from what they could hear,
    That all the song was a name.

XII

I look on the sky and the sea!
    We were two to love, and two to pray,—
Yes, two, O God, who cried on Thee,
    Though nothing didst thou say.
Coldly thou sat behind the sun,
And now I cry, who am but one,—
    Thou will not speak to-day!

XIII

We were black, we were black,
    We had no claim to love and bliss—
What marvel, ours was cast to wrack?
    They wrung my cold hands out of his—
They dragged him—why, I crawled to touch
His blood's-mark in the dust—not much,
    Ye pilgrim-souls,—though plain as This!

XIV

Wrong, followed by a greater wrong!
    Grief seemed too good for such as I;
So the white men brought the shame ere long
    To stifle the sob in my throat thereby.
They would not leave me for my dull
Wet eyes!—it was too merciful
    To let me weep pure tears, and die.

ELIZABETH BARRETT BROWNING

XV

I am black, I am black!
   I wore a child upon my breast,—
An amulet that hung too slack,
   And, in my unrest, could not rest!
Thus we went moaning, child and mother,
One to another, one to another,
   Until all ended for the best.

XVI

For hark! I will tell you low—low—,
   I am black, you see;
And the babe, that lay on my bosom so,
   Was far too white—too white for me.
As white as the ladies who scorned to pray
Beside me at church but yesterday,
   Though my tears had washed a place for my knee.

XVII

And my own child—I could not bear
   To look in his face, it was so white:
So I covered him up with a kerchief rare,
   I covered his face in, close and tight!
And he moaned and struggled as well as might be,
For the white child wanted his liberty,—
   Ha, ha! he wanted his master's right.

XVIII

He moaned and beat with his head and feet—
   His little feet that never grew!
He struck them out as it was meet
   Against my heart to break it through.
I might have sung like a mother mild,
But I dared not sing to the white-faced child
   The only song I knew.

XIX

And yet I pulled the kerchief close:
   He could not see the sun, I swear,
More then, alive, than now he does
   From between the roots of the mangles—where?
I know where!—close!—a child and mother
Do wrong to look at one another,
   When one is black and one is fair.

XX

Even in that single glance I had
   Of my child's face,—I tell you all,—
I saw a look that made me mad,—

ELIZABETH BARRETT BROWNING

The master's look, that used to fall
On my soul like his lash,—or worse,—
Therefore, to save it from my curse,
    I twisted it round in my shawl.

XXI

And he moaned and trembled from foot to head,—
    He shivered from head to foot,—
Till, after a time, he lay, instead,
    Too suddenly still and mute;
And I felt, beside, a creeping cold,—
I dared to lift up just a fold,
    As in lifting a leaf of the mango fruit.

XXII

But My fruit! ha, ha!—there had been
    (I laugh to think on it at this hour!)
Your fine white angels,—who have seen
    God's secret nearest to His power,—
And gathered my fruit to make them wine,
And sucked the soul of that child of mine,
    As the humming-bird sucks the soul of the flower.

XXIII

Ha, ha! for the trick of the angels white!
    They freed the white child's spirit so;
I said not a word, but day and night
    I carried the body to and fro;
And it lay on my heart like a stone—as chill;
The sun may shine out as much as he will,—
    I am cold, though it happened a month ago.

XXIV

From the white man's house and the black man's hut
    I carried the little body on;
The forest's arms did around us shut,
    And silence through the trees did run!
They asked no questions as I went,—
They stood too high in astonishment,—
    They could see God rise on his throne.

XXV

My little body, kerchiefed fast,
    I bore it on through the forest—on—
And when I felt it was tired at last,
    I scooped a hole beneath the moon.
Through the forest-tops the angels far,
With a white fine finger in every star
    Did point and mock at what was done.

XXVI

Yet when it all was done aright,
    Earth twixt me and my baby strewed,—
All changed to black earth,—nothing white,—
    A dark child in the dark,—ensued
Some comfort, and my heart grew young;
I sat down smiling there, and sung
    The song I told you of, for good.

XXVII

And thus we two were reconciled,
    The white child and black mother, thus:
For, as I sang it,—soft and wild,
    The same song, more melodious,
Rose from the grave whereon I sat!
It was the dead child singing that,
    To join the souls of both of us.

XXVIII

I look on the sea and the sky!
    Where the Pilgrims' ship first anchored lay,
The great sun rideth gloriously!
    But the Pilgrims' ghosts have slid away
Through the first faint streaks of the morn!
My face is black, but it glares with a scorn
    Which they dare not meet by day.

XXIX

Ah, in their stead their hunter-sons!
    Ah, ah! they are on me! they form in a ring!
Keep off,—I brave you all at once,—
    I throw off your eyes like a noisome thing!
You have killed the black eagle at nest, I think;
Did you never stand still in your triumph, and shrink
    From the stroke of her wounded wing?

XXX

(Man, drop that stone you dared to lift!—)
    I wish you, who stand there, seven abreast,
Each for his own wife's grace and gift,
    A little corpse as safely at rest,
Hid in the mangles! yes, but *she*
May keep live babies on her knee,
    And sing the song she liketh best.

XXXI

I am not mad,—I am black!
    I see you staring in my face,—
I know you staring, shrinking back,—

Ye are born of the Washington race!
And this land is the Free America,—
And this mark on my wrist,—(I prove what I say)
    Ropes tied me up here to the flogging-place.

XXXII

You think I shrieked there? not a sound!
    I hung as a gourd hangs in the sun;
I only cursed them all around
    As softly as I might have done
My own child after. From these sands
Up to the mountains, lift your hands
    O Slaves, and end what I begun.

XXXIII

Whips, curses! these must answer those!
    For in this Union, ye have set
Two kinds of men in adverse rows,
    Each loathing each! and all forget
The seven wounds in Christ's body fair;
While He sees gaping everywhere
    Our countless wounds that pay no debt.

XXXIV

Our wounds are different—your white men
    Are, after all, not gods indeed,
Nor able to make Christs again
    Do good with bleeding. We who bleed,—
(Stand off!)—we help not in our loss,—
We are too heavy for our cross,
    And fall and crush you and your seed.

XXXV

I fall,—I swoon,—I look at the sky!
    The clouds are breaking on my brain:
I am floated along, as if I should die
    Of Liberty's exquisite pain!
In the name of the white child waiting for me
In the deep black death where our kisses agree,—
White men, I leave you all curse-free,
    In my broken heart's disdain!

(Wr. 1846, pub. 1848)

124 MAUDE'S SPINNING

ELIZABETH BARRETT BROWNING

I

He listened at the porch that day
  To hear the wheel go on, and on,
And then it stopped—ran back away—
  While through the door he brought the sun.
  But now my spinning is all done.

II

He sat beside me, with an oath
  That love ne'er ended, once begun;
I smiled—believing for us both,
  What was the truth for only one.
  And now my spinning is all done.

III

My mother cursed me that I heard
  A young man's wooing as I spun.
Thanks, cruel mother, for that word,
  For I have, since, a harder known!
  And now my spinning is all done.

IV

I thought—O God!—my first-born's cry
  Both voices to my ear would drown!
I listened in mine agony—
  It was the *silence* made me groan!
  And now my spinning is all done.

V

Bury me 'twixt my mother's grave,
  Who cursed me on her death-bed lone,
And my dead baby's—(God it save!)
  Who, not to bless me, would not moan.
  And now my spinning is all done.

VI

A stone upon my heart and head,
  But no name written on the stone!
Sweet neighbours! whisper low instead,
  'This sinner was a loving one—
  And now her spinning is all done.'

VII

And let the door ajar remain,
  In case that he should pass anon;
And leave the wheel out very plain,
  That He, when passing in the sun,
  May *see* the spinning is all done.

(1846)

ELIZABETH BARRETT BROWNING

125 THE POET

The poet hath the child's sight in his breast,
And sees all *new*. What oftenest he has viewed,
He views with the first glory. Fair and good
Pall never on him, at the fairest, best,
But stand before him, holy, and undressed
In week-day false conventions; such as would
Drag other men down from the altitude
Of primal types, too early dispossessed.
Why, God would tire of all his heavens as soon
As thou, O childlike, godlike poet! did'st
Of daily and nightly sights of sun and moon!
And therefore hath He set thee in the midst
Where men may hear thy wonder's ceaseless tune,
And praise His world for ever as thou bidst.

(1847)

126 HIRAM POWERS'S GREEK SLAVE

They say Ideal Beauty cannot enter
The house of anguish. On the threshold stands
An alien Image with the shackled hands,
Called the Greek Slave: as if the artist meant her,
(That passionless perfection which he lent her,
Shadowed, not darkened, where the sill expands)
To, so, confront man's crimes in different lands,
With man's ideal sense. Pierce to the centre,
Art's fiery finger!—and break up ere long
The serfdom of this world! Appeal, fair stone,
From God's pure heights of beauty, against man's wrong!
Catch up in thy divine face, not alone
East griefs but west,—and strike and shame the strong,
By thunders of white silence, overthrown.

(Wr. *c.*1847, pub. 1850)

Notes

ABBREVIATIONS

BD   A biographical dictionary of the living authors of Great Britain and Ireland, . . . [ed. John Watkins and Frederic Shoberl], London 1816.

Boyle   Andrew Boyle, An index to the annuals (1820-1850), Worcester: Andrew Boyle 1967.

Davis & Joyce   Gwen Davis and Beverley A. Joyce (eds), Poetry by women to 1900: a bibliography of American and British writers, London: Mansell 1991.

DNB   The dictionary of national biography, ed. Leslie Stephen and Sidney Lee, 63v. London 1885-1900.

FC   The feminist companion to English literature, ed. Virginia Blain, Patricia Clements and Isobel Grundy, London: Batsford 1990.

GM   The Gentleman's Magazine, 1731–.

GRO   General Register Office, St Catherine's House, London (births, deaths, and marriages, after 1837).

HCR   Edith J. Morley (ed.), Henry Crabb Robinson on books and their writers, 3v. London 1938.

Helsinger, Sheets & Veeder   Elizabeth K. Helsinger, Robin Lauterbach Sheets and William Veeder, The woman question: Society and literature in Britain and America, 1837–1883, 3v. Manchester 1983, ii.109–64.

HNC   Hartley Nelson Coleridge, 'Modern English poetesses', Quarterly Review, 66 (1840), 374–418.

IGI   International Genealogical Index, Genealogical Society of Utah, Salt Lake City. Version 3.05, 1994.

Jackson   J. R. de J. Jackson, Romantic poetry by women: a bibliography, 1770–1835, Oxford: Clarendon Press 1993.

LLC   The library of literary criticism, ed. C. W. Moulton, 8v. New York: Moulton 1901–1905.

LR   Location register of English literary manuscripts and letters, ed. David C. Sutton, 2v. London: The British Library 1995.

Michell   Nicolas Michell, Living poets and poetesses: a biographical and critical poem. Second edition, London 1832.

MM   Monthly Magazine, and British Register, 1796–

NCBEL   New Cambridge bibliography of English literature, vols II–III, ed. George Watson, Cambridge: Cambridge University Press 1969–1971.

NOTES   Nichols, *Anecdotes*   John Nichols, *Literary anecdotes of the eighteenth century*, 9v. London 1812–1815.

Nichols, *Illustrations*   John Nichols, *Illustrations of the literary history of the eighteenth century*, 8v. London 1817–1858.

NMM   *New Monthly Magazine*, new series, 1821–.

WW CL   *The letters of William and Dorothy Wordsworth* [1787–1853], ed. E. de Selincourt, second edition, rev. C. L. Shaver, Mary Moorman and A. G. Hill, 7v. Oxford: Clarendon Press 1967–1988.

HELEN MARIA WILLIAMS (later STONE?) (1761–1827)
DNB; *FC*; *NCBEL*, ii.693–4; Jackson, 374–5; Davis & Joyce, 302; *LR*, ii.1000–1; *LLC*, v.74–5; *HCR*, 147–8; *GM* 98.i (1828), 373; *Monthly Repository*, N.S. II (1828), 136–7; *Thraliana: the diary of Mrs Hester Lynch Piozzi, 1776–1809*, ed. K. C. Balderston, 2v. Oxford 1951, ii.730, 791, 849, 894n, 922; *WW CL*, i.68–9; L. D. Woodward, *Une adhérente anglaise de la révolution française: Hélène-Maria Williams et ses amis*, Paris 1930; M. Ray Adams, 'Helen Maria Williams and the French Revolution', in E. L. Griggs (ed.), *Wordsworth and Coleridge: studies in honor of G. M. Harper*, Princeton 1939, pp.87–117; Julie Ellison, 'Redoubled feeling: politics, sentiment and the sublime in Williams and Wollstonecraft', in L. E. Brown and P. Craddock (eds) *Studies in Eighteenth-century Culture*, 20 (1990), 197–215; Matthew Bray, 'Helen Maria Williams and Edmund Burke: radical critique and complicity', *Eighteenth-century Life*, 16 (1992), 1–24.

1. Text: *A poem on the bill lately passed for regulating the slave trade*, London 1788.

The quality of mercy is not strained]   Shakespeare, *The merchant of Venice*, Act IV, Scene i, line 180.

O, Pitt,]   William Pitt (1759–1806), British politician and friend of William Wilberforce. On 9 May 1788, owing to Wilberforce's illness he brought forward the resolution for the regulation of the slave-trade. He continued to support the cause and on 2 April 1792, despite strong opposition within his own party, he made a widely admired speech in favour of immediate abolition.

And Richmond, he!]   Charles Lennox, Third Duke of Richmond and Lennox (1759–1806), British politician and advocate of parliamentary reform, who supported Wilberforce in the House of Lords.

Britain's Senate]   'I trust an English House of Commons will never persist in thinking, that what is morally wrong, can ever be politically right; that the virtue and the prosperity of a people are things at variance with each other; and that a country which abounds with so many sources of wealth, cannot afford to close one polluted channel, which is stained with the blood of our fellow creatures. . . . The Africans have not long to suffer, nor their oppressors to triumph. Europe seems hastening towards a period too enlightened for the perpetuation of such monstrous abuses. The mists of ignorance and error are falling away, and the benign beams of philosophy are spreading their lustre over the nations.' *Letters written in France, in the summer 1790 . . .* , London 1790, pp.48–9.

'There is not one argument, one invective, levelled by you at the confiscators of the church revenue, which could not, with the strictest propriety, be applied by the planters and negro-drivers to our Parliament, if it gloriously dared to shew the world that British senators were men: if natural feelings of humanity silenced the old cautions of timidity, till this stigma on our nature was wiped off, and all men were allowed to enjoy their birth-right—liberty, till by their crimes they had authorized society to deprive them of the blessing they had abused.' Mary Wollstonecraft, *A vindication of the rights of men, in a letter to the right honourable Edmund Burke* (1790), in *The works of Mary Wollstonecraft*, ed. Janet Todd and Marilyn Butler, 7v. London 1989, v.51.

On slavery in the period, see Thomas Clarkson, *The history of the rise, progress, and accomplishment of the African slave-trade by the British parliament*, 2v. London 1808; F. J. Klingberg, *The anti-slavery movement in England: a study in English humanitarianism*, New Haven 1926; David Brion Davis, *The problem of slavery in the age of revolution, 1770–1823*, Ithaca, New York 1975; A. J. Barker, *The African link: British attitudes to the negro in the era of the Atlantic slave trade, 1150–1807*, London 1978; Robin Blackburn, *The overthrow of colonial slavery, 1776–1848*, London 1988. On women's involvement specifically, see Moira Ferguson, *Subject to others: British women writers and colonial slavery, 1670–1834*, London 1992; Clare Midgley, *Women against slavery: the British campaigns, 1780–1870*, London 1992; J. R. Oldfield, *Popular politics and British anti-slavery*, Manchester 1995.

For literary works relating to slavery and the slave-trade in the period, see Peter C. Hogg, *The African slave trade and its suppression: a classified and annotated bibliography of books, pamphlets and periodical articles*, London, Frank Cass 1973, pp.324–38. For an overview of the subject, see Wylie Sypher, *Guinea's captive kings: British anti-slavery literature of the XVIIIth century*, Chapel Hill 1942, especially Part II, Chapter 4, 'Anti-slavery verse', pp.156–230, and on women specifically see Ferguson and Midgley cited above.

For other poems, see William Roscoe, *The wrongs of Africa*, 2 parts, London 1787–1788; Edward Rushton, *West-Indian eclogues*, London 1787; Eliza Knipe, 'Atombola and Omoza; an African story', in *Six narrative poems*, London 1787, pp.51–60; William Cowper, 'The morning dream' (1788), 'Pity for the poor African' (1788), 'The negro's complaint' (1789), 'Sonnet to William Wilberforce' (1792), in *The poetical works*, ed. H. S. Milford, London 1967, pp.373–4, 375–6, 371–2, 415–16; Hugh Mulligan, *Poems chiefly on slavery and oppression*, London 1788; J. N. Puddicombe, *Poem . . . for the suppression of the slave trade*, London 1788, Maria and Harriet Falconar, *Poems on slavery*, London 1788; John Jamieson, *The sorrows of slavery, a poem*, London 1789; Thomas Wilkinson, *An appeal to England, on behalf of the abused Africans*, London 1789; Mary Leadbeater, 'The negro' (1789), in *Poems*, Dublin 1808, pp.87–93; M. Birkett, *A poem on the African slave trade. Addressed to her own sex*, 2 parts, Dublin 1792; Charles Lloyd, 'The Slave—an Ode', in *Poems on various subjects*, Carlisle 1795, pp.62–4; Robert Southey, 'Poems on the slave trade', in *Poems*, Bristol 1797, pp.29–43; Mary Robinson, 'The negro girl', in *Lyrical tales*, London 1800, pp.107–14; Amelia Opie, 'The negro boy's tale', in *Poems*, London 1802, pp.61–79; Elizabeth Benger, 'A poem, occasioned by the abolition of the slave trade, in 1806,' in *Poems on the abolition of the slave trade, by James Montgomery, James Grahame and Elizabeth Benger*, London 1809, pp.101–41; Charlotte Richardson, 'The negro', 'Ode on the abolition of the slave trade', 'After reading Clarkson on the abolition of the slave trade', in *Poems, chiefly composed during the pressure of severe illness. Vol.II*, York 1809, pp.38–40, 66–9, 103–4.

HANNAH MORE (1745–1833)
DNB; *FC*; *NCBEL*, 2. 1598–1600; Jackson, 225–39; Davis & Joyce, 200; Boyle, 204; *LR*, ii.666–9; *LLC*, v.190–6; *Thraliana: the diary of Mrs Hester Lynch Piozzi, 1776–1809*, ed. K. C. Balderston, 2v. Oxford 1951, ii.1000, n.3; W. Roberts, *Memoirs of . . . Hannah More*, 4v. London 1834; H. Thompson, *Life of Hannah More* . . . , London 1838; Joseph Cottle, *Reminiscences of Coleridge and Southey*, London 1847, pp.52–4; Thomas De Quincey, 'Recollections of Hannah More', *Collected writings*, ed. David Mason, 14v. Edinburgh 1889–1890, xiv.94–131; M. A. Hopkins, *Hannah More and her circle*, New York 1947; M. G. Jones, *Hannah More*, Cambridge 1952; Elizabeth Kowaleski-Wallace, *Their fathers' daughters: Hannah More, Maria Edgeworth, and patriarchal complicity*, Oxford 1991.

2. Text: *Slavery, a poem*, London 1788.
—O great design!] The epigraph is not from Thomson's *Liberty* but from *Winter* (1730), lines 376–81 with omissions and misquotation. For More's other poems on the slave trade, see **3** and 'The petition of a negro boy', *Amulet* (1828), 169–70.

For the significance of Bristol as a slave-trade centre in the eighteenth century, see Roger Anstey, *The Atlantic slave trade and Bristol abolition*, London 1975; C. M. MacInnes, *Bristol and the slave trade*, Bristol 1963; W. E. Minchinton, 'The slave trade of Bristol with the mainland colonies in North America, 1699–1770', in Roger Anstey and P. E. H. Hair (eds), *Liverpool, the African slave trade and abolition*, Historical Society of Lancashire and Cheshire, Occasional Series, vol.2, 1976, pp.38–59; David Richardson (ed.), *Bristol and the eighteenth-century African slave-trade, vol. 1, the years of expansion, 1698–1729*, Bristol 1986, *vol.2, the years of ascendancy, 1730–1745*, Bristol 1987, *vol.3, the years of decline, 1746–1769*, Bristol 1991.

O, plaintive Southerne!] Thomas Southerne (1660–1746), dramatist, whose 1696 dramatisation of Aphra Behn's *Oronooko; or, the Royal Slave* (1688), was popular throughout the eighteenth century.

No Muse, O Qua-shi] 'It is a point of honour among negroes of a high spirit to die rather than to suffer their glossy skin to bear the mark of the whip. Qua-shi had somehow offended his master, a young planter with whom he had been bred up in the endearing intimacy of a play-fellow. His services had been faithful; his attachment affectionate. The master resolved to punish him, and pursued him for that purpose. In trying to escape Qua-shi stumbled and fell; the master fell upon him; they wrestled long with doubtful victory; at length Qua-shi got uppermost, and, being firmly seated on his master's breast, he secured his legs with one hand, and with the other drew a sharp knife, then said, "Master, I have been bred up with you from a child; I have loved you as myself; in return you have condemned me to a punishment of which I must ever have borne the marks: thus only I can avoid them;" so saying, he drew the knife with all his strength across his own throat, and fell down dead, without a groan, on his master's body.' Ramsay's *Essay on the treatment of African slaves* (HM).

Tempe] The beautiful valley in Thessaly (north-east Greece).

Their fertile fields, their arts] 'Besides many valuable productions of the soil, clothes and carpets of exquisite manufacture are brought from the coast of Guinea' (HM).

Their sense of feeling] 'Nothing is more frequent than this cruel and stupid argument, that they do not *feel* the miseries inflicted on them as Europeans would do' (HM).

Zeno] Zeno of Elea, ancient Greek philosopher (fl. *c*.470 BC). A disciple of Parmenides, admired by Plato and Aristotle, he was tortured by the tyrant Nearchus and responded by biting his tongue off and spitting it in Nearchus' face.

When the sharp iron] 'This is not said figuratively. The writer of these lines has seen a complete set of chains, fitted to every separate limb of these unhappy, innocent men; together with instruments for wrenching open the jaws, contrived with such ingenious cruelty as would shock the humanity of an inquisitor' (HM).

Cortez] Hernando Cortez (1485–1547), conqueror of Mexico.

Cook] James Cook (1728–1779), circumnavigator, explorer of the Pacific, who was killed by native Hawaiians at Karakakowa Bay.

Penn] William Penn (1644–1718), English Quaker, founder of Pennsylvania. Although a slave-holder, he introduced measures to extend criminal justice to slaves and for the protection of· the native Indian population. Quaker opposition to slavery in America and elsewhere grew steadily throughout the eighteenth century. See J. W. Frost (ed.), *The Quaker origins of antislavery*, Norwood, Pennsylvania 1980, and 'The origins of the Quaker crusade against slavery: a review of recent literature', *Quaker History*, 67 (1978), 42–58. For two Quaker women's contributions to abolition, see *Memoir of the life of Catherine Phillips*, London 1797, and *Some account of the life and religious exercises of Mary Neale*, Dublin 1797.

Still thy meek spirit in thy flock survives] 'The Quakers have emancipated all their slaves throughout America' (HM).

3. Text: *The sorrows of Yamba, or, the negro woman's lamentation*, Bath 1795 (complete). The first edition adds 'To the tune of Hosier's Ghost' to the text title, but this was dropped in later reprintings. The first edition was illustrated.

British Tar] British sailor (abbreviation from *tarpaulin*).

Smack the Cat about the Deck] Cat o' nine tails, a rope whip with nine knotted lashes used for flogging. The flogging of female slaves became a public issue after Wilberforce's speech had drawn attention to the case of Captain Kimber who had flogged a female slave to death for refusing to dance naked.

'the weary are at rest'] Job 3.17.

ANN YEARSLEY (née CROMARTIE) (1752–1806)
DNB; *FC*; *NCBEL*, ii.698; Jackson, 383–5; Davis & Joyce, 310; *LR*, ii. 1031; *GM*, 1784, ii.897, 1785, i.304, 1806, i.485; William Roberts, *Memoirs of Hannah More*, 4v. London 1834, i.361–75, 383–91; Robert

NOTES Southey, *The lives and works of the uneducated poets*, ed. J. S. Childers, Oxford 1925; Joseph Cottle, *Reminiscences of Coleridge and Southey*, London 1847, pp.47–51; J. M. S. Tomkins, 'The Bristol milkwoman', in her *The polite marriage*, Cambridge 1938, pp.58–102; Donna Landry, *The muses of resistance: laboring-class women's poetry in Britain, 1739–1796*, Cambridge 1990, pp.120–85; Mary Waldron, '"By no means milk and water matters": the contribution to English poetry of Ann Yearsley', *Studies in Voltaire and the Eighteenth-Century*, 304 (1992), 801–4, and 'Ann Yearsley and the Clifton records', *The Age of Johnson*, 3 (1990), 301–29; Moira Ferguson, 'Resistance and power in the life and writings of Ann Yearsley', *The Nineteenth-Century: Theory and Interpretation*, 27 (1986), 247–68, and 'The unpublished poems of Ann Yearsley', *Tulsa Studies in Women's Literature*, 12 (1993), 13–46; Patricia Demers, '"For mine's a stubborn and savage will": "Lactilla" (Ann Yearsley) and "Stella" (Hannah More) reconsidered', *Huntington Library Quarterly*, 56 (1993), 135–50.

Ann Yearsley's birth date was first established by J. M. S. Tompkins (1938, p.60), where it is given as 15 July 1752, correcting the *DNB* error of 1756. Mary Waldron (1990, p.301), however, states '[Tompkins] pursues her subject to Clifton where she was born in 1753'. At first glance this looks like a misreading of Tompkins. However, there is evidence that 1753 is correct. The Parish Register Transcript (PR) under Baptisms for 1753, reads, 'Ann daug. of Jn. & Ann Cromarty [possibly Cremarty] July 15.' The PR clearly states the date; the surname is less clear. This conflicts with Tompkins reading of 1752 and Cromartie, indicating that perhaps she did not use the PR but the Bishop's Transcript (BT). Most of the PRs and BTs were badly burnt in the 1940 bombing and subsequent transcriptions of both have proved difficult. Tompkins certainly saw the documentation before the bombing. It seems therefore to be 'insolent pedantry', in Gibbon's fine phrase, to correct Tompkins, despite some evidence to the contrary, and I have therefore followed her in giving 1752 and Cromartie.

4. Text: *A poem on the inhumanity of the slave-trade...*, London 1788.
Bristol]   See above note to 2.
Lactilla]   A milkmaid, hence Yearsley herself.
Philomel]   A nightingale.
Sol]   The sun.
Their erring minds]   'Indians have often been heard to say, in their complaining moments, "God Almighty no love us well; he be good to buckers; he bid buckers burn us; he no burn buckers."' (AY).
buckers]   White man (AY).
Gorgon]   In classical mythology, there were three gorgons, Medusa, Stheno and Euryale. Their gaze turned victims to stone and they had serpents for hair.
The name of Mussulman]   'The Turk gives freedom to his slave on condition that he embraces Mahometism' (AY).
The Spaniard]   'The Spaniard, immediately on purchasing an Indian, gives him baptism' (AY).
Another gasps]   'A Coromantin slave in Jamaica (who had frequently escaped to the mountains), was, a few years since, doomed to have his leg cut off. A young practitioner from England (after the surgeon of the

estate had refused to be an executioner) undertook the operation, but after the removal of the limb, on the slave's exclaiming, "You buckers! God Almighty made dat leg; you cut it off! You put it on again?" was so shocked, that the other surgeon was obliged to take up the vessels, apply the dressings, &c. The Negro suffered without a groan, called for his pipe, and calmly smoked, till the absence of his attendant gave him an opportunity of tearing off his bandages, when he bled to death in an instant. Many will call this act of the Negro's stubbornness; under *such* circumstances, I dare give it a more *glorious* epithet, and that is *fortitude*' (AY). Compare Adam Smith's famous description of American Indians' 'fortitude' which ends with an attack on slavery: 'The same contempt of death and torture prevails among all other savage nations. There is not a negro from the coast of Africa who does not, in this respect, possess a degree of magnanimity which the soul of his sordid master is too often scarce capable of conceiving. Fortune never exerted more cruelly her empire over mankind, than when she subject those nations of heroes to the refuse of the jails of Europe, to wretches who possess the virtues neither of the countries which they came from, nor those which they go to, and whose levity, brutality and baseness, so justly expose them to the contempt of mankind.' *The theory of moral sentiments*, ed. D. D. Raphael and A. L. Macfie, Oxford 1976, pp.206–7.

ANNA LAETITIA BARBAULD (née AIKIN) (1743–1825)
DNB; *FC*; *NCBEL*, ii.639–40; Jackson, 17–19; Davis & Joyce, 14–15; Boyle 17; *LR*, i.38; *LLC*, v.22–6; *HCR*, *Monthly Repository*, XX (1825), 185–6; Lucy Aikin, 'Memoir', in *The works of Anna Laetitia Barbauld*, 2v. London 1825, i.[v]–lxxii; [William Turner], 'Mrs Barbauld', *Newcastle Magazine*, N.S. IV. (1825), 182–6, 229–32; Anna Letitia LeBreton, *Memoir of Mrs Barbauld*, London 1874; Betsy Rodgers, *Georgian chronicle: Mrs Barbauld and her family*, London 1958; Catherine A. Moore, *The literary career of Anna Laetitia Barbauld*, Ph.D. Unpublished Dissertation, University of North Carolina 1969; William McCarthy and Elizabeth Kraft, *The poems of Anna Laetitia Barbauld*, Athens, Georgia 1994.

5. Text: *Epistle to William Wilberforce, Esq. on the rejection of the bill for abolishing the slave trade*, London 1791 (complete). For details of the debate see *The debate on a motion for the abolition of the slave-trade, in the House of Commons, on . . . April 18 and 19, 1791*, London 1791. For Barbauld, as for Helen Maria Williams, Mary Wollstonecraft and, later, Elizabeth Barrett Browning, the question of slavery was firmly enmeshed in other questions concerning the nature of moral virtue, particularly civic and political virtue, religious toleration, the spirit of inquiry and the significance of the French Revolution. 'We appeal to the certain, sure operation of increasing light and knowledge, which it is no more in your power to stop, than to repel the tide with your naked hand, or to wither with your breath, the genial influence of vegetation. The spread of that light is in general gradual and imperceptible; but there are periods when its progress is accelerated, when it seems with a sudden flash to open the firmament, and pour in day at one. Can ye not discern the signs of the times? The minds of men are in movement from the Borysthenes to the Atlantic. Agitated with new and strong emotions, they swell and heave

beneath oppression, as the sea within the polar circle, when, at the approach of spring, they grow impatient to burst their icy chains; when what, but an instant before, seemed so firm,—spread for many a dreary league like a floor of solid marble,—at once with a tremendous noise gives way, long fissures spread in every direction, and the air resounds with the clash of floating fragments, which every hour are broken from the mass. The genius of Philosophy is walking abroad, and with the touch of Ithuriel's spear is trying the establishments of the earth. The various forms of Prejudice, Superstition, and Servility start up in their true shapes, which had long imposed upon the world the revered semblances of Honour, Faith, and Loyalty. Whatever is loose must be shaken, whatever is corrupted must be lopt away; whatever is not built on the broad basis of public utility must be thrown to the ground. Obscure murmurs gather, and swell into a tempest; the spirit of inquiry, like a severe and searching wind, penetrates every part of the great body polititc; and whatever is unsound, whatever is infirm, shrinks at the visitation. Liberty, here with the lifted crosier in her hand, and the crucifix conspicuous on her breast; there, led by Philosophy, and crowned with the civic wreath, animates men to assert their long-forgotten rights. With a policy, far more liberal and comprehensive than the boasted establishments of Greece and Rome, she diffuses her blessings to every class of men; and even extends a smile of hope and promise to the poor African, the victim of hard, impenetrable avarice. Man, as man, becomes an object of respect . . . . May you [the French Revolution] never lose sight of the great principle you have held forth,—the natural equality of men. May you never forget that without public spirit there can be no liberty; that without virtue there may be a confederacy, but cannot be a community. May you, and may we, consigning to oblivion every less generous competition, only contest who shall set the brightest example to the nations; and may its healing influence be diffused, till the reign of Peace shall spread

. . . from shore to shore,
Till wars shall cease, and slavery be no more.'

[Alexander Pope, 'Windsor Forest' (1713), ll.407–8, *The poems of Alexander Pope*, ed. John Butt, London 1963, p.210.], *An address to the opposers of the repeal of the Corporation and Test Acts (1790). Works* (ed. Lucy Aikin), 2v. London 1825, ii.371–2, 376.

'London is extremely full now: the trial, the parliamentary business, and fetes and illuminations, and the Shakespeare Gallery, have all contributed to fill the great hive. But among these various objects, none is surely so interesting as the noble effort making for the abolition of the slave-trade. Nothing, I think, for centuries past, has done the nation so much honour; because it must have proceeded from the most liberal motives,—the purest love of humanity and justice. The voice of the Negroes could not have made itself heard but by the ear of pity; they might have been oppressed for ages more with impunity, if we had so pleased.' To Judith Beecroft (née Dixon), May 1789, *Works*, ii.81.

Wilberforce] William Wilberforce (1759–1833) took up the abolition of the slave-trade cause in Parliament. On 18 April 1791 a bill was defeated and again in 1799. It finally became law on 25 March 1807.

A new Astrean reign] In the Golden Age, Astrea, the goddess of justice and innocence, left the earth because of sin and corruption and was metamorphosed into the constellation Virgo.

the Scythian, the Sybarite] The Scythians were the ancient inhabitants of Eastern European and Asiatic Russia and were notorious for their savagery. The Sybarites, from Southern Italy, were notorious for their self-indulgence and luxury.

Augusta] London.

Fasti] chronological list of events.

Howard's honoured name] John Howard (1726–1790), prison reformer, whose *State of the prisons in England and Wales*, Warrington 1777, was widely admired. Barbauld's brother, John Aikin, was a close friend and assisted him in the publication of his works and, after his death, published *View of the character and public services of the late John Howard*, Warrington 1792. Barbauld later refers to him in *Eighteen hundred and eleven*, London 1812, 'Howard's sainted feet'.

MARY LEADBEATER (née SHACKLETON) (1758–1826)

DNB; *FC*; Jackson, 196; Davis & Joyce, 169; Boyle, 168; *LR*, ii.565–7; *Memoirs and letters of Richard and Elizabeth Shackleton, late of Ballitore, Ireland* . . . , London 1822, *The Leadbeater papers*, 2v. London 1862 (A memoir of Mary Leadbeater', i.1–12). IGI.

6–8 Texts: *Poems*, Dublin 1808, pp.259–63, 285–7, 309–11.

6–8. For a retrospective account of the Irish rebellion, see Thomas De Quincey, *The collected writings*, ed. David Mason, 14v. Edinburgh 1889–1890, i.227–66.

6. Zephyr] the west wind.

7. Bellona] the Roman goddess of war, and wife of Mars.

MARY ROBINSON (née DARBY) (1758–1800)

DNB; *FC*; *NCBEL*, ii.680–1; Jackson, 276–9; Davis & Joyce, 240–1; *LR*, ii.803; *LLC*, iv.411–12; P. H. Highfill, K. A. Burnim and E. A. Langhans (eds), *A biographical dictionary of actors, actresses, musicians, dancers, managers & other stage personnel in London 1660–1800*, vol.XIII, Carbondale 1991; M. Steen, *The lost one: a biography of Mary Robinson*, London 1937; M. Ray Adams, 'Mrs Mary Robinson: a study of her later career', in his *Studies in the literary backgrounds of English radicalism*, Philadelphia 1947, pp.104–29; L. W. Koengeter, *Mrs Mary Robinson: a biographical and critical appraisal*, Ph.D. Harvard University 1975; Stuart Curran, 'Mary Robinson's *Lyrical tales* in context', in Carol Shiner Wilson and Joel Haefner (eds), *Re-visioning romanticism: British women writers, 1776–1837*, Philadelphia 1994.

9. Text: *Poems*, vol.II, London 1793, pp.27–32. On the eighteenth-century background to madness, see Max Byrd, *Visits to Bedlam: madness and literature in the eighteenth-century*, Charleston 1974.

10–12. Texts: *Lyrical tales*, London 1800, pp.30–48, 139–48, 156–61.

10. Lascar] East Indian sailor, often press-ganged into service in the British Navy:

13. Text: *Memoirs of the late Mrs Robinson, written by herself. With some posthumous pieces*, [ed. Maria Elizabeth Robinson], 4v. London 1801, iii. 174–84. Maria Elizabeth Robinson prefixed the following note, iii. 173–4: 'The following Poem, which by the *date* the Reader will perceive to have been written a very short time previous to the dissolution of its excellent

Author, will require no apology for its insertion in this publication. The correctness of the metre, and the plaintive harmony which pervades every stanza, clearly evinces the mild philosophy with which a strong mind can smooth a journey to the grave. This LAST offspring of Mrs. ROBINSON'S Muse was produced at intervals of favourable symptoms of her fatal malady. The *subject was interesting to her heart.* She adopted it with all the enthusiasm of mournful ANTICIPATION. The story first suggested itself to her after perusing various accounts of a SAVAGE BOY, lately discovered in the *Forest of Averyon,* in the department of *Tarn,* and said to be then existing at *Paris.* Frequent instances of this kind have occurred in the history of Man, and conjecture has almost uniformly been bewildered respecting the origin of such fugitives. In countries where BANDITTI have been known to reside, imagination may be allowed the exercise of its powers; and Reason may ruminate on the possibility, as well as the probability, of such an interesting history as that of [The savage of Averyon].' For further details on the discovery of and reaction to the boy found living wild, see Harlan Lane, *The wild boy of Averyon,* Cambridge, Mass. 1976; Roger Shattuck, *The forbidden experiment: the story of the wild boy of Averyon,* New York 1980.

ANNE BANNERMAN (1765–1829)

DNB; FC; NCBEL; Jackson, 16–17; Davis & Joyce, 14; *LR,* i.37; *BD,* 13; IGI; Nichols, *Illustrations,* vii.97, 112, 123, 133, 135, 138, 164, 181–2. BL. MSS. Loan No. 96.

14–17. Texts: *Poems,* Edinburgh 1800, pp.25–34, 55–60, 61–5, 78.

14. naval victory]   Admiral Richard Howe (1726–1799), whose victory over the French, off the coast of Brest, on 1 June 1794, was followed by a royal visit to welcome him at Portsmouth on 20 June and subsequent celebrations. It is also possible that the naval victory referred to was Nelson's at the Nile on 1 August 1798, after which there were also celebrations but the early position of the text in the volume seems to favour Howe's victory.

Quels traits]   Jean-Baptiste Rousseau (1671–1741), 'Ode VI: A la fortune', *Oeuvres diverses,* Soleure 1712, p.80, with significant omissions. *Trans* 'In such scenes do your splendours appear, merciless conquerors? [Unbounded desires, vast schemes, Kings vanquished by Titans.] City walls ablaze, victors steeped in blood, a people put to the sword. [Mothers ashen and bloody, snatching their trembling daughters from the arms of a soldier.] Bewildered spectators that we are, we admire such exploits.'

He leaves]   'A single warrior, prompted by caprice or revenge, will take the field alone, and march several hundred miles to surprise and cut off a straggling enemy.' Robertson's *History of America,* vol. II (AB).

O! for a lodge]   'O! for a lodge in some vast wilderness, / Some boundless contiguity of shade.' Cowper's *Task* (AB).

15. Zembla's ice]   The Nova Zembla, a group of islands in the Arctic ocean, to the north of Archangel in Russia.

Zaara's burning sands]   The Sahara.

Cancer]   The sign of the zodiac which appears when the sun has reached its highest northern limit in mid-June.

Magellan]   Ferdinand Magellan (1480–1521), Portuguese navigator

who first attempted to circumnavigate the globe and discovered the Straits of Magellan in 1520. He was killed in the Philippines the following year.
16. When at last . . . the sea] Samuel Johnson, *The Rambler*, 187, 31 December 1751.

Alone, by night,] "'Tis thine to sing, how, framing hideous spells, / In Skye's lone isle the gifted wizard sits, / Waiting in wint'ry cave his wayward fits.' Collins' 'Ode on the superstitions of the Highlands' (AB).
18. Text: *Tales of superstition and chivalry*, London 1802, pp.1–16. Compare Coleridge's 'The ballad of the dark ladie' (1798) and 'Christabel' (1797–1801), in his *Poetical works*, ed. E. H. Coleridge, London 1967, pp.293–5, 550–7, 213–36.

FANNY HOLCROFT (1780–1844)
BD, 160; *GM*, N.S. 23.i (1845), 212; GRO; *HCR*, 11, 56, 68, 116–17; William Kegan Paul, *Godwin, his friends and contemporaries*, 2v. London 1876; Thomas Moore, *Memoirs, journal and correspondence*, ed. Lord John Russell, 8v. London 1853–1856; *The letters of Charles Lamb, to which are added those of his sister*, ed. E. V. Lucas, 3v. London 1935, ii. 358, iii.8; J. A. Froude, *Thomas Carlyle: a history of the first forty years of his life, 1795–1835*, 2v. London 1882, ii.168, 175; Edwin W. Marrs, *The letters of Charles and Mary Anne Lamb*, 3v. Ithaca 1975–1978, ii. 72n, 208, 209n, 221–2, iii.3, 37, 119, 166n, 207, 230; Peter Marshall, *William Godwin*, New Haven 1984, pp.206, 209, 234, 253; *DNB* (Thomas Holcroft); William Hazlitt, *Memoirs of the late Thomas Holcroft* (1816); *The complete works of William Hazlitt*, ed. P. P. Howe, 21v. London 1930–1934, iii.70, 106, 170, 174, 195, 198–9, 206–7, 218–21, 232, 236, 275–7. BL. MSS. Loan 96.

19. Text: *MM*, III, January 1797, p.54.
20. Text: *MM*, III, February 1797, p.142. 'The poem entitled "Annabella", in the last *Monthly Magazine*, and the present, are early efforts by Miss Holcroft. She was under seventeen when they were written' (*MM*).
21. Text: *MM*, III, April 1797, p.289.
22. Text: *MM*, IV, October 1797, p.286. 'The lines in italic excepted' (*MM*). These lines were possibly by her father, Thomas Holcroft, but it is pure speculation.
23. Text: *MM*, XII, November 1801, p.328.
24. Text: *MM*, XIV, December 1802, p.413.
25. Text: *MM*, XV, April 1803, p.243. Reprinted in [Elizabeth Scott, ed.], *Specimens of British poetry* . . . , Edinburgh 1823, pp.143–4.

JANE ELIZABETH ROSCOE (later HORNBLOWER) (1797–1853)
DNB (William Roscoe, Mary Anne Jevons); Jackson, 280; Davis & Joyce, 144; Boyle, 245–6; *GM*, N.S. 40.ii (1853), 326; George Chandler, *William Roscoe of Liverpool*, London 1953; F. W. Dunston, *Roscoeana*, [Liverpool] [1907]; GRO.

26–28. Texts: *Poems*, London 1820, p.15, pp.41–3, 64–6.
28. Llanberis Pass] A series of large steep crags, near the town of Llanberis in North Wales, now a major climbing area.

29–35. Texts: *Poems*, London 1843, pp.32, 63, 98–9, 106, 110–13, 126–8, 171–2.

29. Pent in the city's darksome walls] 'in populous city pent', Milton, *Paradise Lost*, ix.445, 'In the great city, pent 'mid cloisters dim', Coleridge, *Frost at Midnight*.

CAROLINE BOWLES (later SOUTHEY) (1786–1854)
DNB; *FC*; *NCBEL*, iii.268–9; Jackson, 37–8; Davis & Joyce, 264; Boyle, 33–5; *LR*, i.83–5; *HNC*, 402–4; Courtney, 33–43; Michell, 63–4; Edward Dowden (ed.), *The correspondence of Robert Southey with Caroline Bowles*, Dublin 1881; *Athenaeum*, 5 August 1854; GRO.

36. Text: *Blackwood's*, XIII (1823), p.275. Reprinted, *Solitary hours* . . . , Edinburgh and London 1826, pp.148–50.

37. Text: *Winter's Wreath* (1829), 240.

'Records of Woman'] Felicia Hemans, *Records of woman: with other poems*, London 1828. For other women's responses to Hemans, see the thematic index in this volume. On women's reading, see Sally Mitchell, *The fallen angel: chastity, class and women's reading, 1835–1880*, Bowling Green, Ohio 1981; and Kate Flint, *The woman reader, 1837–1914*, Oxford 1993.

Is it some twilight] See Hemans' 'The spirit's mysteries', in *Records of woman: with other poems*, London 1828, pp.264–6, and Landon's variation on the theme in 'A history of the lyre', in *The Venetian bracelet . . . and other poems*, London 1829, p.106, 'Methinks we must have known some former state . . .'.

38–39. Texts: *Tales of the factories:* . . . , London 1833, pp.5–15, 16–26.

38. Moloch] God of the Ammonites, to whom children were sacrificed, 2 Kings 23.10. 'First Moloch, horrid king besmeared with blood / Of human sacrifice and parents' tears.' Milton, *Paradise Lost*, i.392–3.

Jaggernaut] Hindu god, a cult title for Vishnu. On the last day of a festival worshippers were thought to throw themselves under the wheels of the procession car but the anecdotal evidence for this is doubtful.

Mammon] God of this world, hence riches. 'Ye cannot serve God and Mammon', Matthew, vi.24. Mammon 'admiring more / The riches of heaven's pavement, trodden gold, / Than aught divine or holy.' Milton, *Paradise Lost*, i.681–3. Robert Southey's fierce attack on the 'temples of Mammon' in *Sir Thomas More: or, colloquies on the progress and prospects of society*, 2v. London 1829, starkly contrasted agricultural and industrial life, the older agricultural colleges 'raised by the magic of some indigenous Amphion's music', the 'new cottages of the manufacturers . . . naked, and in a row . . . From the largest of Mammon's temples down to the poorest hovel in which his helotry are stalled, these edifices have all one character . . . always offensive to the eye as to the mind.' Caroline Bowles, deeply attached to Buckland Cottage, was probably sympathetic to Southey's attacks on Mammon and the contrast between country and city life. Others, such as Macaulay, in the *Edinburgh Review* (1830), responded with contempt, although Mammon was a constant theme throughout the period from Sterling's *The state of society in England* (1829) to Kingsley's famous sermon *God and Mammon* (1874).

on *this* side the salt waves / No lack of slavery, nor of *Infant Slaves*] Compare William Cowper, *The Task* (1785) Book II, lines 35–7, 'I had much rather be myself the slave, / And wear the bonds, than fasten them on him. / We have no slaves at home.—Then why abroad?'

guilty Tyre] The destruction of Tyre, punished for its ungodly prosperity and trading, is told in Isaiah 23. Bowles' apocalyptic vision shares certain similarities with Barbauld's in *Eighteen hundred and eleven*, London 1812.

For the background to factory reform and child labour, see John Fielden, *The curse of the factory system*, London [1836]; Samuel Kydd, *The history of the factory movement, from the year 1802 to the enactment of the ten hours' bill in 1847*, London 2v. 1857; Barbara Leigh Hutchins and Amy Harris, *A history of factory legislation*, London 1903; J. T. Ward, *The factory movement, 1830–1855*, London 1962. See also notes to **86** and **119**. Despite strong opposition, mainly on the economic grounds used to oppose the abolition of slavery, a parliamentary Select Committee was set up in 1832, followed by a Royal Commission in 1833, resulting in the Factory Act 1833, which limited to an eight-hour day the employment of nine- to twelve-year-olds.

FELICIA DOROTHEA HEMANS (née BROWNE) (1793–1835)
DNB; *FC*; *NCBEL*, iii.283–4; Jackson, 152-6; Davis & Joyce, 134–5; Boyle, 120–3; *LR*, i. 452–54; *LLC*, v.254–62; Michell, 90–1; IGI; [Maria Jane Jewsbury], 'Original papers. Literary sketches No. 1. Felicia Hemans', *Athenaeum*, 171 (5 February 1831), 104–5; Letitia Elizabeth Landon, 'On the character of Mrs. Hemans' writings', *NMM*, XLIV (1835), 425–33; H. F. Chorley, *Memorials of Mrs. Hemans*, 2v. London 1836; Harriet Hughes, *The poetical works of Mrs. Hemans, with a memoir of her life*, 7v. Edinburgh 1839; S. C. Hall, *Retrospect of a long life: from 1815 to 1883*, 2v. London 1883, ii. 56–72; *Poetical works*, Oxford 1914 (*PW*); For recent comment on Felicia Hemans see: Norma Clarke, *Ambitious heights: writing, friendship, love: the Jewsbury sisters, Felicia Hemans and Jane Carlyle*, London 1990; Glennis Stephenson, 'Poet construction: Mrs Hemans, L. E. L., and the image of the nineteenth-century woman', in Shirley Neuman and Glennis Stephenson (eds), *Reimagining women: representations of women in culture*, Toronto 1993, pp.61–73; Tricia Lootens, 'Hemans and the home: Victorianism, feminine "internal enemies", and the domestication of national identity', *PMLA*, 109 (1994), 238–53; Susan J. Wolfson, '"Domestic affections" and "the spear of Minerva": Felicia Hemans and the dilemma of gender', in Carol Shiner Wilson and Joel Haefner (eds) *Re-visioning romanticism: British women writers, 1776–1837*, Philadelphia, University of Pennsylvania Press 1994, pp.128–66; Nanora Sweet, 'History, imperialism, and the aesthetics of the beautiful: Hemans and the post-Napoleonic moment' in Mary A Favrer and Nicola J. Watson (eds), *At the limits of romanticism: essays in cultural and materialist criticism*, Bloomington, Indiana 1994, 170–84.

40. Text: *The forest sanctuary: and other poems*, London 1825, pp.189–90. For the significance of flowers and botany in the period, see Ann B. Shteir, 'Botany in the breakfast room: women and early nineteenth-century British plant study', in Pnina G. Abir-Am and Dorinda Outram (eds), *Uneasy careers and intimate lives: women in science, 1789–1979*, New Brunswick, NJ 1987, pp.31–43; Alan Bewell, '"Jacobin plants": botany as social theory in the 1790s', *Wordsworth Circle*, 20 (1989),

132–9, 'Keats' "Realm of Flora"',*Studies in Romanticism,* 31 (1992), 71–98; Judith Pascoe, 'Female botanists and the poetry of Charlotte Smith', in Carol Shiner Wilson and Joel Haefner (eds), *Re-visioning Romanticism: British women writers, 1776–1837,* Philadelphia 1994, pp.193–209. See also Hemans' 'Flowers and music in a room of sickness', *Blackwood's,* XXXIV (1833), 861–6 (*PW,* 569–73), a poem which moved Wordsworth whose sister, Dorothy, was ill at the time (Wordsworth to Felicia Hemans, 30 April 1834), 'The dying girl and flowers' (*PW,* 338–9), 'The flower of the desert' (*PW,* 556–7), 'The day of flowers' (*PW,* 605–9), 'Flowers' (*PW,* 649). See also Maria Jane Jewsbury, 'On receiving a bunch of flowers from the author of the "Excursion"', *Forget-Me-Not* (1830), 46–7.

41. Text: *NMM,* XVI (1826), 407–8. Reprinted, *Records of woman: with other poems,* Edinburgh and London 1828, pp.131–5, where an epigraph was added, 'A fearful gift upon thy heart is laid, / Woman!—a power to suffer and to love, / Therefore thou so canst pity.' Untraced. Compare Hemans' 'Indian woman's death-song' in the same collection, pp.103–8. American Indians had long featured in eighteenth-century thought. See B: Bissell, *The American Indian in English literature of the eighteenth century,* New Haven 1925; C. B. Tinker, *Nature's simple plan,* Princeton 1922; H. N. Fairchild, *The noble savage,* New York 1928; L. Whitney, *Primitivism and the idea of progress,* Baltimore 1934. One of the major philosophical defences of American Indian virtues, Adam Smith's *The theory of moral sentiments,* highlighted the links between them and classical virtues of self-command, magnanimity and contempt of death. Hemans imposes the theme of 'woman's love' on to these virtues. Smith, and other writers had remarked on the absence of love in this moral economy, 'The weakness of love, which is so much indulged in ages of humanity and politeness, is regarded among savages as the most unpardonable effeminacy', *The theory of moral sentiments,* ed. D. D. Raphael and A. L. Macfie, Oxford 1976, p.205.

42. Text: *Literary Souvenir* (1827), 189–91. Reprinted, *Songs of the affections, with other poems,* Edinburgh and London 1830, pp.156–9.

Corinne] The heroine of Madame de Stael's novel *Corinne ou l'Italie,* 2v. Paris 1807, a central figure for Hemans and Landon, raising important difficulties of the cost of fame, the value of improvisation, the fantasy of becoming a heroine, the freedom of the south, and a series of complex gender issues. The centrality of the myth (and its line of descent from Rousseau) was first demonstrated by Ellen Moers, *Literary women: the great writers,* New York 1963, and has been re-examined by Angela Leighton, *Victorian women poets: writing against the heart,* Brighton, 1992, pp.30–4, although the complex structural relationships between the reading of *Corinne* and the reading of Rousseau's *Nouvelle Heloise* by an earlier generation await fuller investigation. Compare Letitia Elizabeth Landon, 'Corinne at the Cape of Misena', *The Amulet* (1832), 251–5 and **64**.

Les femmes doivent] *Trans.* 'Women must think that there is very little in this career which could be considered as worthy as the most obscure life of a beloved woman and happy mother.'

O'er three hundred triumphs gone] 'The trebly hundred triumphs', Byron (FDH) ['Childe Harold's pilgrimage', Canto IV. St.82].

43. Text: *NMM,* XX (1827), pp.69–70. Reprinted, *Records of woman:*

with other poems, Edinburgh and London 1828, pp.160–3.

Ne me plaignez pas . . .] *Trans.* 'Do not pity me—if you knew how much pain this grave has spared me! Mary Tighe (1772–1810), author of *Psyche: or, the legend of love*, London 1805 (second edn, London 1811) whose work and early death affected a number of poets, notably Keats and Hemans.

'Extrinsic interest has lately attached to the fine scenery of Woodstock, near Kilkenny, on account of its having been the last residence of *Psyche*. Her grave is one of many in the churchyard of the village. The river runs smoothly by. The ruins of an ancient abbey, that have been partially converted into a church, reverently throw their mantle of tender shadow over it. Tales by the O'Hara Family' (FDH).

'I heard much of her unhappiness was caused by her own excessive love of admiration and desire to shine in society, which quite withdrew her from Hearth and Home and all their holy enjoyments, and that her mother, standing by her deathbed passionately exclaimed—"My Mary, my Mary, the pride of literature has destroyed you".' Letter to Robert Graves, 26 July 1831, in Norma Clarke, *Ambitious heights: writing, friendship, love: the Jewsbury sisters, Felicia Hemans, and Jane Welsh Carlyle*, London: 1990, pp.50–1.

Hemans admired Tighe's poetry at a deeply personal level and visited her tomb when in Ireland, 'her poetry has always touched me greatly from a similarity which I imagine I discover between her destiny and my own', Henry F. Chorley, *Memorials of Mrs Hemans* . . . , 2v. London 1836, ii.212. See Hemans' other responses to Tighe, 'Lines written for the album at Rosanna' (*PW*, 537) and 'On records of immature genius' (*PW*, 633).

44. Text: *Blackwood's*, XXII (1827), 585–6. Reprinted, *Songs of the affections, with other poems*, London and Edinburgh 1830, pp.123–6.

Where hath not woman stood] Untraced. Compare Tennyson, 'The princess' (1847), Part V, lines 437–41: 'Man for the field and woman for the hearth; / Man for the sword, and for the needle she; Man with the head, and woman with the heart; / Man to command, woman to obey; / All else confusion.'

45. Text: *The Amulet* (1829), 89–90.

Happy—happier far than thou] Hemans, 'Corinne at the Capitol'. As with many of the Annuals, though not all, *The Amulet* for 1829 was published in December 1828, so the correct date for this poem is 1828 and Hemans used the verse, 'Thou hast a charmed cup, O Fame!', as the epigraph to Joan of Arc in Rheims, *Records of woman: with other poems*, Edinburgh and London 1828, p.109. For reasons of simplicity and clarity, I have not altered the dates of poems published in Annuals to the previous year, although it is of more significance in this case.

Thou hast a charmed cup, O Fame!] See Landon, 'A history of the lyre', *The Venetian bracelet . . . and other poems*, London 1829, pp.87–115, and 'On the character of Mrs. Hemans' writings', *NMM*, XLIV (1835), 425–33, which also take up the issue of fame in a female context. See also Hemans' comments on Mary Tighe's fame, **43** note above. See also **78**.

46. Text: *Records of woman: with other poems*, Edinburgh and London 1828, pp.3–20.

And is not love in vain] Byron, *Prophecy of Dante*, Canto III, line 148.

NOTES

Fermossi al fin il cor che balzò tanto]   Trans. 'The heart which leapt so much, came to rest at last.' Quoted by Madame de Stael in 'Fragments des pensées de Corinne', *Corinne ou l'Italie* (1807), ed. Simone Balaye, Paris 1985, p.526.

47.   Text: *Records of woman: with other poems*, Edinburgh and London 1828, pp.286–8.

There blend the ties that strengthen]   Bernard Barton, 'Home', in *Poetic vigils*, London 1824, p.295.

48.   Text: *NMM*, XXII (1828), 555–6. Reprinted, *Songs of the affections, with other poems*, Edinburgh and London 1830, pp.212–16.

The Beings of the Mind are not of clay]   Byron, 'Childe Harold's Pilgrimage', Canto IV, St. 5. The epigraph later contracted to 'The Beings of the mind . . . mortal bondage'.

'a smiling with a sigh']   'Nobly he yokes / A smiling with a sigh', *Cymbeline*, Act IV (FDH).

Thou of the soft low voice]   'Her voice was ever soft, / Gentle and low', *King Lear*, Act V (FDH).

And pansies for sad thought]   'There is pansies, that's for thoughts', *Hamlet*, Act IV (FDH).

49.   Text: *Blackwood's*, XXIV (1828), 783–4. Reprinted, *Songs of the affections, with other poems*, Edinburgh and London 1830, pp.119–22.

And dreams, in their development, have breath]   Byron, 'The dream', St. 1 slightly misquoted.

50.   Text: *Literary Souvenir* (1828), 62–4. Reprinted, *The forest sanctuary: with other poems. The second edition, with additions*, Edinburgh and London 1829, pp.313–16.

Oh! that I had the wings of a dove,]   Psalms, 56, v. 6.

51.   Text: *Blackwood's*, XXV (1829), 500. Reprinted, *Songs of the affections, with other poems*, Edinburgh and London 1830, pp.109–11.

Oh! if the soul immortal be,]   Amelia Opie, 'Song'. 'Fond dream of love by love repaid', in *Poems*, London 1802, p.158. Compare Mary Ann Browne, 'The two homes', *Repentance: and other poems*, London 1829, pp.89–92. See also **47** and **51**.

52.   Text: *Blackwood's*, XXV (1829), 716. Reprinted, *Songs of the affections, with other poems*, Edinburgh and London 1830, pp.96–8.

Alas! what kind of grief should thy years know?]   Beaumont and Fletcher, *Philaster* (1620), Act II, Scene iii, line 39.

53.   Text: *The forest sanctuary: with other poems. The second edition, with additions*, Edinburgh and London 1829, pp.310–16.

There is no such thing as *forgetting*]   De Quincey, *Confessions of an English opium-eater, the collected writings*, ed. David Masson, 14v. Edinburgh 1889–1890, iii. 437.

Thou hast been called, O, Sleep, the friend of woe]   Southey, 'The curse of Kehama', XV. 'The city of Baly', St. 12.

54.   Text: *Blackwood's*, XXVIII (1830), 750. Reprinted, *Poetical remains of the late Mrs Hemans* [ed. David Moir], Edinburgh and London 1836, pp.83–5.

—How divine]   Wordsworth, *The Excursion*, Book IV, lines 513–21.

55.   Text: *Blackwood's*, XXVI (1834), 800. Reprinted, *Poetical remains of the late Mrs Hemans* [ed. David Moir], Edinburgh and London 1836, p.49.

56–57.   Texts: *NMM*, XLIII (1835), 328, 329. Reprinted, *The works of*

Mrs Hemans; with a memoir of her life, by her sister, 7v. Edinburgh and London 1839, vii.283, 285.

MARIANNE PROWSE (née JEFFERY) (1798–1850)
DNB (William Jeffery Prowse); IGI; GRO; Jackson, 263; Davis & Joyce, 231; Boyle, 150; Keats, Letters; GM, 1850, ii. 560; Transactions of the Devonshire Association (1918) 310; Maurice Buxton Forman, The letters of John Keats, fourth edition revised, London 1952, lvi–lviii; H. E. Rollins, The Letters of John Keats, 2v. Cambridge, Mass. 1958, i. 78–80; Robert Gittings (ed.) Letters of John Keats. A new selection, London 1975, p.402; Angus Graham Campbell, 'John Keats and Marian Jeffery', Keats Shelley Journal, 33 (1984), 40–50; Michell, 66.
58–63. Texts: Poems, London 1830, pp.43–4, 100, 101–2, 126–7, 151–3, 173–6.
61. * * * * *] Person unknown.
summer luxury] 'And scarce the luxury of summer fruits', Byron, The Corsair, Canto I.ii. 'In summer luxury', Keats, 'On the Grasshopper and Cricket'.
63. And scorn, and laughter] 'Where laughter is not mirth', [Goethe's] Lament of Tasso (MP).

LETITIA ELIZABETH LANDON (later MACLEAN) (1802–1838)
DNB; FC; NCBEL, iii.351–2; Jackson, 191–4; Davis & Joyce, 165–6; Boyle, 162–6; LR, ii.556–7; LLC, v.322–8; Michell, 32–5; W. B. Scott (ed.), Poetical works of Letitia Elizabeth Landon, London 1873 (repr. with an introduction by F. J. Sypher, New York 1990). Mrs Cornwall Baron-Wilson, 'Elegaic tribute to the memory of L. E. L.', in A volume of lyrics, London and Edinburgh 1840, pp.49–50; Alicia Jane Sparrow, 'Lines written on hearing of the death of L. E. L.', Friendship's Offering (1843), pp.105–6; Mary Ann Browne (later Gray), 'Stanzas suggested by the death of Mrs. McLean (L. E. L.)', in Sketches from the antique: and other poems, Dublin 1844, pp.148–51; Elizabeth Scaife, 'On the death of L. E. L.', in Poems on various subjects, Liverpool [1846], pp.180–2; Maria Abdy, 'The destiny of the gifted', in Keepsake (1841), pp.213–14; Emma Roberts, 'Memoir of L. E. L.', in The zenana and minor poems, London 1839, pp.5–33; H. F. Chorley, 'Mrs MacLean', in Athenaeum, 14, 5 January 1839; William Howitt, 'L. E. L.', Fisher's Drawing-Room Scrapbook (1840), pp.5–8; William Howitt, Homes and haunts of the most eminent British poets, 2v. London 1847; Laman Blanchard, Life and literary remains of L. E. L., 2v. London 1841; S. Sheppard, Characteristics of the genius and writings of L. E. L., London 1841; William Jerdan, The autobiography of William Jerdan, 4v. London 1852–1854, iii.169–206; Katherine Thomson, Recollections of literary characters and celebrated places, 2v. London 1854; [Katherine Thomson and A. Todd Thomson], Queens of society, London 1860; R. R. Madden, The literary life and correspondence of the Countess of Blessington, 3v. London 1855; S. C. Hall, Book of memories, London 1871; S. C. Hall, Retrospect of a long life: from 1815 to 1883, 2v. London 1883, ii.157–62; B. Cruikshank, Eighteen years on the Gold Coast of Africa, London 1873; A. A. Watts, Alaric Watts, a narrative of his life, 2v. London 1884; H. Ashton, Letty Landon, London 1951; G. E. Metcalfe, Maclean of the Gold Coast: the life and times of George Maclean, 1801–1847, London 1962. For recent comment on

Landon, see Glennis Stephenson, *Letitia Landon: the woman behind L. E. L.*, Manchester 1995.

64. Text: *The fate of Adelaide, a Swiss romantic tale; and other poems*, London 1821, pp.97–8.

Erato] The muse of erotic poetry, often represented with a lyre.

Psyche] Venus, jealous of Psyche's beauty, sent Cupid to make her fall in love with a monster but he himself fell in love with her and put her in a palace where he visited her at night, forbidding her to see him in the light. One night she looked at him with the aid of a lamp but some of the oil spilled and woke him. Abandoned and wandering the earth in search of him, Psyche was required to complete a series of superhuman tasks, all but the last of which she accomplished. Descending into Hades to bring back Persephone's casket of beauty, curiosity overcame her again and she opened it, immediately falling into a deep sleep. Cupid and Psyche were finally reunited and brought to heaven. The story, from Apuleus' *Golden Ass* (Books iv–vi) was often interpreted as an allegory of the soul's progress but after Mary Tighe's *Psyche; or, the legend of love*, London 1805 (usually read in one of the editions of 1811, containing additional poems), for Hemans and Landon it became something of an allegory of female destiny, mixed with the myth of Corinne and Mary Tighe's fate. There is a brief discussion of the significance of the fable for the romantics in Marilyn Butler, *Romantics, rebels, and reactionaries*, Oxford 1981, pp.132–7, and a full-length study of Keats' linguistic links to Mary Tighe's poem, in E. V. Weller, *Keats and Mary Tighe*, New York 1928. See also **43** note. Landon later contributed poems to Isabel Hill (trans.), *Corinne; or Italy, by Mme de Stael*, London 1833.

65. Text: *The troubadour: catalogue of pictures, and historical sketches*, London 1825, pp.280–3. One of a series of 'poetical pictures' Landon wrote in response to contemporary paintings. *The Enchanted Island* by Francis Danby (1793–1861) was exhibited in 1825.

Sultana] Most obviously, the sweet seedless raisin but also perhaps the daughter of a king.

Nautilus] Small mollusc, the female of which has a thin shell and webbed sail-like arms.

66. Text: *NMM*, XLIV (1835), 286–8. Reprinted, Laman Blanchard, *Life and literary remains of L. E. L.*, 2v. London 1841, ii.245–8.

The rose—the glorious rose is gone.] Hemans, 'The nightingale's death song'.

Bring flowers] See **40** above.

67–68. Texts: *Ethel Churchill: or, the two brides*, 3v. London 1837, ii. 117, ii.157. Reprinted, with supplied titles, Laman Blanchard, *Life and literary remains of L. E. L.*, 2v. London 1841, [77], ii. 277, [78], ii. 277.

69. Text: *NMM*, LV (1839), 28–9. Reprinted, Laman Blanchard, *Life and literary remains of L. E. L.*, 2v. London 1841, i.190–1. Compare Mary Ann Browne, 'To the polar star', in *Ignatia, and other poems*, London and Liverpool 1838, pp.110–12.

CATHERINE GRACE GODWIN (née GARNETT) (1798–1845)

DNB; *DNB* (Thomas Garnett); Jackson, 134; Davis & Joyce, 110; Boyle, 103–4; *LR*, i.404; IGI; GRO; WW *CL*, v.57–9; Michell, 92; A. Cleveland Wigan, 'Memoir of the author', *The poetical works . . .* , London 1854, i–viii.

70. Text: *Friendship's Offering* (1830), 284–7. Reprinted, *The poetical works . . .* , ed. A. Cleveland Wigan, London 1854, pp.438–40.
Bright names will hallow song] 'And bright names will hallow song', Byron, 'Childe Harold's pilgrimage', Canto III, St. 29.
71. Text: *The Literary Gazette*, 8 October 1836, pp.652–3. Reprinted, *The poetical works . . .* , ed. A. Cleveland Wigan, London 1854, pp.433–5. A manuscript at Northumberland Record Office (ZAN M12 Brook Autographs, v. 165A–B) is wrongly attributed to Mary Wollstonecraft. An epigraph, not present in either the manuscript or the *Literary Gazette* (1836) version, was added in *The poetical works . . .* ed. A. Cleveland Wigan, London 1854, pp.433–5, possibly by the editor:
  Who in her chamber sate,
Musing with Plato, though the horn was blown,
And every ear and every heart was won,
And all in green array were chasing down the sun. [Rogers]
Samuel Rogers, *Human life, a poem*, London 1819, p.24.

MARY ANN BROWNE (later GRAY) (1812–1845)
FC; Jackson, 42–3; Davis & Joyce, 115; Boyle, 40–1; *Dublin University Magazine*, XXV (1845), 327–31, XXIX (1847), 360–71; *The autobiography of William Jerdan*, 4v. London 1852, iii.169–206, iv.313–16; Mary Russell Mitford, *Recollections of a literary life; or, books, places, and people*, 3v. London 1852, ii. 32–40; Michell, 63; Letitia Elizabeth Landon, 'Stanzas to the author of "Mont Blanc", "Ada", &c.', in *The Venetian bracelet, the lost pleiad, a history of the lyre, and other poems*, London 1829, pp.287–94; Mrs Robert Wilson, 'To the memory of Mrs. James Gray', in *New Zealand and other poems*, London 1851, pp.77–80; Frances Browne, 'To the memory of Mrs James Gray', *Dublin University Magazine*, XXV (1845), 330–1.

72–74. Texts: *Winter's Wreath* (1832), 158–62, 211, 226–31.
72. Yesternight I prayed aloud] Coleridge, 'The pains of sleep'.
75. Text: *The birth-day gift*, London and Liverpool 1834, pp.162–72.
76. Text: *Ignatia, and other poems*, London 1838, pp.116–20.
A change came o'er the spirit of my dream.] Byron, 'The dream', first line of verses iii–viii.
77. Text: *Dublin University Magazine*, XXI (1843), 121–2. Reprinted, *Sketches from the antique: and other poems*, Dublin 1844, pp.140–2. This poem predates Thomas Hood's more famous poems, 'The song of the shirt' (1844) and 'The lady's dream' (1844). All these responses were probably due to the Report of the Commissioners on Child Employment 1843, which had drawn attention to the plight of seamstresses. Compare texts **84** and **124** below. See also, Charlotte Elizabeth Tonna, *The wrongs of women. In four parts. Part I. Milliners and dressmakers. Part II. The forsaken home. Part III. The little pin-headers. Part IV. The lace runners*, 4 parts, London 1843–1844. For a discussion of seamstresses in painting, see T. J. Edelstein, 'They sang "The Song of the Shirt": the visual iconography of the seamstress', *Victorian Studies*, 23 (1980), 183–210. For the significance of needlework, see Laurie Yager Lieb, '"The works of women are symbolical": needlework in the eighteenth-century', *Eighteenth-century Studies*, 10 (1986), 28–44; Cecilia Macheski, 'Penelope's daughters: images of needlework in eighteenth-century

literature', in Mary Anne Schofield and Cecilia Macheski (eds), *Fetter'd or free? British women novelists, 1670–1815*, Athens, Ohio 1986, pp.85–100; Carol Shiner Wilson, 'Lost needles, tangled threads: stitchery, domesticity, and the artistic enterprise in Barbauld, Edgeworth, Taylor, and Lamb', in Carol Shiner Wilson and Joel Haefner (eds), *Revisioning romanticism: British women writers, 1776–1837*, Philadelphia 1994, pp.167–90. For women workers in the period, see Ivy Pinchbeck, *Women workers and the industrial revolution, 1750–1850*, London 1930; Wanda Fraiken Neff, *Victorian working women: an historical and literary study of women in British industries and professions, 1832–1850*, New York 1929, esp. pp.115–50; Helsinger, Sheets & Veeder, ii.109–64; Kathleen Hickok, *Representations of women: nineteenth-century British women's poetry*, Westport, Conn. 1984, pp. 132–58.

MARIA ABDY (née SMITH) (*c.*1797–1867)
DNB; *FC*; Jackson, 3; Davis & Joyce, 3; Boyle, 3–6; *GM*, 1867, ii.399; IGI; GRO; Will at Somerset House. A. H. Bevan, *James and Horace Smith: a family narrative* . . . , London 1899.

78. Text: *Forget-Me-Not* (1833), pp.317–18.

Enchanted ground] A critical term in the eighteenth century, along with 'fairy land', used to describe the scene of reading where the reader was 'ravished' or 'transported' and entered into an imaginative world in a state of enchantment. The centrality of romance reading to this experience, particularly among eighteenth-century literary scholars and historians, has been documented in Arthur Johnston, *Enchanted ground: the study of medieval romance in the eighteenth century*, London 1964, although the link between enchantment and poetry is much older. See George R. Walsh, *The varieties of enchantment: early Greek views of the nature and function of poetry*, Chapel Hill 1984. As with so much in the eighteenth century, the imaginative landscape of the older romances became enmeshed in and reinforced by notions of 'the spirit of the place', novel reading, spectatorship, Newtonian 'new worlds', landscape gardening and much else. A further critical term, 'ideal presence', emerged in the 1760s out of moral sense theory to describe the dream-like reality of imaginative reading where the reader seemed to be entering a different world, and a complicated duality of living in the two worlds—one real, one imaginary but seemingly more real and vivid—develops. Abdy's poem recalls the romance origins of 'enchanted ground' but also has close links to the 'woman and fame' theme in Hemans and Landon.

79. Text: *Forget-Me-Not* (1834), 269–72.

Not idly did the Muses' choir] Franz Grillparzer, *Sappho* (1818), tr. J. Bramsen, London 1820.

80. Text: *Metropolitan*, XIII (1835), 257–8. Reprinted, *Poetry. Second series*, London 1838, pp.24–7.

81. Text: *Metropolitan*, XXVI (1839), 264–5. Reprinted, *Poetry. Third series*, London 1842, pp.99–102. On the theme of abandonment, see Lawrence Lipking, *Abandoned women and poetic tradition*, Chicago 1988. On the contrast between man's love and woman's love, ever present in Hemans and Landon, see also Caroline Bowles, 'Man's love', *Literary Souvenir* (1827), 250–1; Mary Ann Browne, 'Man's love' and 'Woman's love', in *The birthday gift*, London 1834, pp.93–4, 95–7; Fanny Kemble,

'Woman's love', in *Poems*, Philadelphia 1844, p.78; Caroline Lamb, 'Woman's love', *Keepsake* (1830), 316–17; Caroline Norton, 'Woman's love', Sarah Josepha Hale (ed.), *The ladies' wreath*, Boston 1837, p.147; Mary Cockle, 'Woman's love', *Forget-Me-Not* (1829); Maria Jane Jewsbury, 'Woman's love', in *Phantasmagoria* . . ., 2v., London 1825, i. 187–8; Elizabeth Barrett Browning, 'A woman's shortcomings' and 'A man's requirements', in *Poems. New edition*, 2v. London 1850, ii. 398–9, ii.400–2. On the subject of love generally, see Walter E. Houghton, *The Victorian frame of mind, 1830–1870*, New Haven 1957, pp.341–93; Kathleen Hickok, *Representations of women: nineteenth-century British women's poetry*, Westport, Conn. 1984; Kathleen Blake, *Love and the woman question in Victorian literature*, Hemel Hempstead 1983.

82.   Text: *Metropolitan*, XXXVI (1843), 269. Reprinted, *Poetry. Fourth series*, London 1846, pp.35–7.

Pluto . . . Proserpine]   Pluto, the Latin form of the Greek Hades, god of the Underworld; Proserpine, the Latin form of the Greek Persephone, snatched by Hades in the Greek myth while picking flowers and taken to the Underworld. In the second century BC there were Roman festivals of appeasement.

83.   Text: *Monthly Prize Essays* (1846), pp.319–23. Reprinted, *Poetry. Fifth series*, London 1850, pp.48–56.

'when unadorned, adorned the most']   James Thomson, *The seasons* (1744), 'Autumn', line 206.

84.   Text: *Keepsake* (1847), pp.103–5. Reprinted, *Poetry. Fifth series*, London 1850, pp.101–4.

CAROLINE NORTON (née SHERIDAN, later STIRLING-MAXWELL) (1808–1877)

DNB; *FC*; *NCBEL*, iii.544; Jackson, 243–4; Davis & Joyce, 208–9; Boyle, 211–12; *LR*, ii.708–11; *LLC*, vii.101–6; GRO. Michell, 16–19; R. H. Horne, 'Miss E. B. Barrett and Mrs Norton', in *A new spirit of the age*, 2v. London 1844, ii.129–40; J. G. Perkins, *The life of Mrs Norton*, London 1909; A. S. Acland, *Caroline Norton*, London 1948; Alan Chedzoy, *A scandalous woman: the story of Caroline Norton*, London 1992.

85.   Text: *New Monthly Magazine*, XLIII (1835), 230.
86.   Text: *Keepsake* (1836), 216.
87.   Text: *A voice from the factories. In serious verse. Dedicated to the right honourable Lord Ashley*, London 1836. The first epigraph was added when the poem was reprinted in *The dream, and other poems*, London 1840, pp.305–34.

In her dedication to Lord Ashley, Norton drew attention to the links between child labour, prison conditions and slavery:

For the *mode* in which I have done so, some apology is perhaps necessary, since the application of serious poetry to the passing events of the day has fallen into disuse, and is if not absolutely contemned, at least discouraged. Doubtless there are those to whose tastes and understandings, dry and forcible arguments are more welcome than reasonings dressed in the garb of poetry. Yet as poetry is the language of feeling, it should be the language of the multitude; since all men can feel, while comparatively few can reason acutely, and still fewer reduce their reasoning theories to practicable schemes of improvement. . . .

I will only add, that I have in *no* instance overcharged or exaggerated, by poetical fictions, the picture drawn by the Commissioners appointed to inquire into the subject. I have strictly adhered to the printed Reports; to that which I believe to be the melancholy truth; and that which I have, in some instances, myself had an opportunity of witnessing.

I earnestly hope I shall live to see this evil abolished. There will be delay—there will be opposition: such has ever been the case with all questions of conflicting interests, and more especially where the preponderating interest has been on the side of the existing abuse. Yet, as the noble-hearted and compassionate Howard became immortally connected with the removal of the abuses which for centuries disgraced our prison discipline; as the perserverance of Wilberforce created the dawn of the long-delayed emancipation of the negroes;—so, my Lord, I trust to see *your* name enrolled with the names of these great and good men, as the Liberator and Defender of those helpless beings, on whom are inflicted many of the evils both of slavery and imprisonment, without the odium of either.' *Dedication*, vi, viii–ix.

Norton was to continue her interest in the question of child labour (and also poor agricultural workers) in *The child of the islands*, London 1845, partly in response to the Shaftesbury Commission's 1842 report, to which 119 is also a response. In both poems, she responded not merely to the moral questions but to the physical texts of the Commissioners' Reports.

XXVII. 'The happy homes of England'] See Felicia Hemans, 'The homes of England', *Blackwood's*, XX (1827), 392. Reprinted with a different epigraph, *Records of woman: with other poems*, Edinburgh 1828, pp.169–71.

88–90. Texts: *The dream, and other poems*, London 1841, pp.289, 294, 153–6.

CAROLINE CLIVE (née WIGLEY) (1801–1873)
DNB; *FC*; *NCBEL*, iii.922–3; Davis & Joyce, 55; *LR*, i.208–9; HNC; Mary Clive (ed.), *From the diary and family papers of Mrs. Archer Clive*, London 1949.

91–93. Texts: *IX Poems by V.*, London 1840, pp.7–11, 18–19, 20–4.

92. For other women's poems on the theme of sickness, see especially the last eight sonnets by Felicia Hemans, 'Thoughts during sickness', originally published in the *New Monthly Magazine*, XLIII (1835), of which two examples are given above, **56–57**. See also Dorothy Wordsworth, 'Thoughts on my sick-bed' (wr. 1832), *Wordsworth Circle*, 9 (1978), 38–40.

EMILY BRONTË (1818–1848)
DNB; *FC*; *NCBEL*, iii.864–73; Davis & Joyce, 36; *LR*, i.91–2; *LLC*, v. 521–7; GRO. Winifred Gerin, *Emily Brontë: a biography*, Oxford 1971; Edward Chitham, *A Life of Emily Brontë*, Oxford 1987; Janet M. Barclay, *Emily Brontë criticism, 1900–1982: an annotated check list*, Westport, Conn., 1984; Helen Brown, 'The influence of Byron on Emily Brontë', *Modern Language Review*, 34 (1939), 374–81; Jacques Blondel, *Emily Brontë: expérience spirituelle et création poétique*, Paris 1956; C. Day Lewis, 'The poetry of Emily Brontë', *Brontë Society Transactions*, 13

(1965), 83–95; Anne Smith (ed.), *The Art of Emily Brontë*, London 1976; Margaret Homans, *Women writers and poetic identity: Dorothy Wordsworth, Emily Brontë, and Emily Dickinson*, Princeton, N.J. 1980; Lawrence Lipking *Abandoned women and poetic tradition*, Chicago 1988; Irene Taylor, *Holy ghosts: the male muses of Emily and Charlotte Brontë*, New York 1990.
Copy text: *The complete poems of Emily Jane Brontë*, ed. C. W. Hatfield, New York: Columbia University Press 1941. Texts have sometimes been amended to take into account the recent editorial work of *Emily Jane Brontë: the complete poems*, ed. Janet Gezari, Harmondsworth: Penguin Books 1992.

94. Text: Hatfield, pp.63–4, Gezari, pp.62–3. Probably written February 1838. First published, 1910.
95. Text: Hatfield, pp.66–7, Gezari, pp.64–5. Probably written March 1838. First published, 1902.
96. Text: Hatfield, p.69, Gezari, p.67. Probably written May 1838. First published, 1910.
97. Text: Hatfield, p.36, Gezari, pp.99–100. Dated 17 May 1839. First published, 1910.
98. Text: Hatfield, pp.124–5, Gezari, p.112. Dated 13 August 1839. First published, 1910/1923.
99. Text: Hatfield, pp.129–30, Gezari, p.117. Dated 29 October 1839. First published, 1902.
100. Text: Hatfield, pp.146–7, Gezari, pp.126–7. Dated 11 September 1840. First published, 1850.
101. Text: Hatfield, pp.161–2, Gezari, p.129. Dated 27 February 1841. First published, 1910.
102. Text: Hatfield, pp.163–4, Gezari, p.130. Dated 16 May 1841. First published, 1850.
103. Text: *Poems by Currer, Ellis, and Acton Bell*, London 1846, pp.96–7, Hatfield, pp.205–6, Gezari, pp.19–20. Dated 3 September 1844.
104. Text: *Poems by Currer, Ellis, and Acton Bell*, London 1846, pp.31–2, Hatfield, pp.222–3, Gezari, pp. 8–9. Dated 3 March 1845.
105. Text: *Poems by Currer, Ellis, and Acton Bell*, London 1846, pp.76–9, Gezari, pp.14–16. These lines were selected from a longer poem by Emily Brontë for the 1846 volume. For the complete text of the longer poem, see Hatfield, pp.236–41, 242, Gezari, pp.177–81. Dated 9 October 1845.
106. Text: Hatfield, pp.243–4, Gezari, p.182. Dated 2 January 1846. First published, 1850.
107. Text: Hatfield, pp.255–6, Gezari, p.198. First published, 1850. Possibly written 1846. Serious doubts about Emily's authorship have been raised and a strong case for Charlotte's authorship can be made. Anne has also been advanced as a candidate. For a succinct and judicious summary of the evidence, see Gezari, pp.284–5.

ANNE BRONTË (1820–1849)
DNB; *FC*; *NCBEL*, iii.864–73; Davis & Joyce, 36; *LR*, i.89; GRO. Winifred Gerin, *Anne Brontë*, London 1959; Elizabeth Langland, *Anne Brontë: the other one*, Basingstoke 1989; J. P. M. Scott, *Anne Brontë: a new critical assessment*, New York 1983.

NOTES Copy text: *The poems of Anne Brontë: a new text and commentary*, ed. Edward Chitham, London: Macmillan 1979. References to *The complete poems of Anne Brontë*, ed. Clement Shorter, London: Hodder and Stoughton [1920] are also given.

108. Text: Chitham, pp.63–4, Shorter, pp.3–4. Dated 26 January 1838. First published, 1902.

109. Text: *Poems by Currer, Ellis, and Acton Bell*, London 1846, pp.92–4, Chitham, pp.84–5, Shorter, pp.28–30. Dated 10 November 1842.

William Cowper] William Cowper (1731–1800), poet, whose work was an important inspirational source for several women poets, offering a network of common themes from the religious *Olney hymns* (1779), the didactic, satiric and idyllic *The task* (1785), the anti-slavery verse of the late 1780s, and the intense religious doubt and 'madness' accompanying it. See also **117**.

110. Text: *Poems by Currer, Ellis, and Acton Bell*, London 1846, p.125, Chitham, p.88, Shorter, p.34. Dated 30 December 1842.

111. Text: *Poems by Currer, Ellis, and Acton Bell*, London 1846, pp.149–50, Chitham, pp.92–3, Shorter, pp.41–2. Dated 31 October 1843 but 'mostly written in the Spring of 1842'.

The captive dove] On the captive bird theme in women's lives, see Mary Wollstonecraft's remarks in *Vindication of the rights of woman* (1792), in *The works*, ed. Janet Todd and Marilyn Butler, 6v. London 1989, v.125, 'Confined then in cages like the feathered race, they have nothing to do but to plume themselves, and stalk with mock majecty from perch to perch.' Helen Maria Williams, Mary Robinson, Ann Yearsley, Charlotte Beverley, Ann Taylor, Sara Coleridge, Caroline Norton and many other women also wrote poems on the theme. See Ellen Moers, *Literary women*, New York 1976, pp.245–51 and on this and other forms of (self) imprisonment, Sandra M. Gilbert and Susan Gubar, *The madwoman in the attic: the woman writer and the nineteenth-century literary imagination*, New Haven 1979. See also **50**.

112. Text: *Poems by Currer, Ellis, and Acton Bell*, London 1846, pp.80–1, Chitham, pp.111–12, Shorter, pp.68–9. Dated 20 May 1845.

113. Text: Chitham, p.113, Shorter, pp.66–7. Written spring 1845. First published, 1915.

CHARLOTTE BRONTË (later NICHOLLS) (1816–1855)
DNB; *FC*; *NCBEL*, iii.864–73; Davis & Joyce, 36; *LR*, i.90–1; *LLC*, vi. 17–31; GRO. Elizabeth Gaskell, *The life of Charlotte Brontë*, 2v. London 1857; F. E. Ratchford, *The Brontës' web of childhood*, New York 1941; Winifred Gerin, *Charlotte Brontë: the evolution of genius*, Oxford 1967; Tom Winnifrith, *A new life of Charlotte Brontë*, Basingstoke 1988; Irene Taylor, *Holy ghosts: the male muses of Emily and Charlotte Brontë*, New York 1990; Patricia H. Wheat, *The adytum of the heart: the literary criticism of Charlotte Brontë*, Rutherford, N.J. 1992.

114–115. Texts: *The poems of Charlotte Brontë. A new annotated and enlarged edition of the Shakespeare Head Brontë*, ed. Tom Winnifrith, Oxford: Basil Blackwell 1984, pp.241, 242.

114 Dated 24 December 1848.

115 Dated 21 June 1849. Emily Brontë died on 19 December 1848 and Anne Brontë died on 28 May 1849.

ELIZABETH BARRETT BROWNING (née BARRETT) (1806–1861)
DNB; FC; NCBEL, iii.435–9; Davis & Joyce, 39; *LR,* i.98–101; *LLC,* vi. 228–47; Frederic G. Kenyon (ed.), *The letters of Elizabeth Barrett Browning,* 2v. London 1897; M. B. Raymond and M. R. Sullivan (eds), *The letters of Elizabeth Barrett Browning to Mary Russell Mitford, 1836–1854,* 3v. Winfield, Kansas 1983; Sandra Donaldson, *Elizabeth Barrett Browning: an annotated bibliography of the commentary and criticism, 1826–1990,* New York 1993; Charlotte Porter and Helen A. Clarke (eds), *The complete works of Elizabeth Barrett Browning,* 6v. New York 1900 (repr. New York 1973); H. F. Chorley, 'Elizabeth Barrett Browning', *Athenaeum,* 6 July 1861; G. B. Taplin, *The life of Elizabeth Barrett Browning,* London 1958; Margaret Forster, *Elizabeth Barrett Browning: a biography,* London 1988; G. W. Hudson, *An Elizabeth Barrett Browning concordance,* 4v. Detroit 1973; Margaret Forster, *Elizabeth Barrett Browning,* London 1988; Dorothy Mermin, *Elizabeth Barrett Browning: the origins of a new poetry,* Chicago 1989; Ann Parry, 'Sexual exploitation and freedom: religion, race, and gender in Elizabeth Barrett Browning's "The runaway slave at Pilgrim's Point"', *Studies in Browning and his Circle,* 16 (1988), 114–26; Deborah Byrd, 'Combating an alien tyranny: Elizabeth Barrett Browning's evolution as a feminist poet', *Browning Institute Studies,* 15 (1987), 23–41.

116. Text: *NMM,* XLV (1835), 82. Reprinted as 'Stanzas on the death of Mrs Hemans', in *The seraphim, and other poems,* London 1838, pp. 271–6, where an epigraph was added, 'Nor grieve this christall streame so soone did fall / Into the ocean;—since she perfumed all / The banks she past—' (William Habington, 'To Castara, upon the death of a lady', in *Castara. The second part,* London 1634, p.55). Later reprinted as 'Felicia Hemans', in *Poems. New edition,* 2v. London 1850, ii.209–11, where the epigraph was dropped.

117. Text: *Poems. New edition,* 2v. London 1850, ii.190–8, First printed *The seraphim, and other poems,* London 1838, pp.207–20.

Epigraph] Trans. 'Now begins intellectual flight.' *Synesii Cyrenensis; Hymni.* ed. Nicolaus Terzaghi, 2v. Rome 19832, i.24. Another epigraph from Milton, '—Procul urbano strepita, seccibus altis / —Jucunda per otia ripae', was dropped in the revision.

Westminster Hall] Originally a banqueting hall where law courts were later established.

Newgate] The main prison for the City of London situated at the end of Holborn Viaduct. *The Newgate Calendar,* originally begun in 1773, continued throughout much of the nineteenth century and consisted of biographies of notorious criminals.

the young queen goes to parliament] Queen Victoria ascended the throne in 1837 and attended Parliament, 19 July 1837. Barrett wrote other poems in this period about her, 'The young Queen' and 'Victoria's tears', *Athenaeum,* 1 July (1837), 483, and *Athenaeum,* 8 July (1837), 506, reprinted, *The seraphim, and other poems,* London 1838, pp.323–7, 328–31, 'The crowned and wedded Queen', *Athenaeum,* 15 February (1840), 131, reprinted in *Poems,* 2v. London 1844, ii.136–41.

NOTES

Winged steed] Pegasus, the winged horse that sprang from the blood of Medusa and was ridden by Perseus. Later given to Bellerophon who attempted to ride to heaven but was thrown, Pegasus turning into a constellation.

Sabrina's chair] Sabrina, the Roman name for the river Severn, although Monmouth's *Historia Britonum* gives Sabra as the murdered daughter of Locrin and Estrildis who was later changed into a water nymph. Barrett probably has in mind Milton's *Comus* where she is a water nymph with the power to counteract Comus' spells.

Nereids] The fifty daughters of Nereus, an ancient Greek sea god, listed in Spenser's *Faerie Queene*, Book IV, Canto xi. St. 48–51.

118. Text: *The seraphim and other poems*, London 1838, pp.346–53. Reprinted, *Poems. New edition*, 2v. London 1850, ii.370–4, where the epigraph was dropped.

I will invite thee] William Habington, 'Elegy 8', in *Castara. The second edition. Corrected and augmented*, London 1635, p.166. See above **108n**.

119. Text: *Poems*, 2v. London 1844, ii. 173–9. First printed in a slightly different form, *Boston Miscellany of Literature and Fashion*, 2 November 1842, 197–9.

Wains] wagons.

Chimar . . . makes madder the centaur] Chimar was a Greek garment. In Sophocles' *The Maides of Trachis*, the centaur, Nessus, gave a poisoned shirt to the wife of Herakles for her husband, which drove him mad.

120. Text: *Blackwood's*, LIV (1843), 260–2. Reprinted, *Poems*, 2v. London 1844, ii.127–35, *Poems. New edition*, 2v. London 1850, ii.142–9. 'Report on the employment of children and young persons in mines and manufactures', R. H. Horne. A Greek epigraph was added in 1844. Trans. 'Woe, woe, why do you look upon me with your eyes, my children?', Euripides, *Medea*, line 1048.

Like the weeds] 'A commissioner mentions the fact of weeds being thus confounded with the idea of flowers' (EB).

Our Father] 'The report of the commissioners represents instances of children, whose religious devotion is confined to the repetition of the first two words of the Lord's Prayer' (EB). 'A fact rendered pathetically historical by Mr. Horne's report of his commission. The name of the poet of "Orion" and "Cosmo de Medici" has, however, a change of associations; and come in time to remind me (with other noble instances) that we have some brave poetic heat of literature still,—though open to the reproach, on certain points, of being somewhat gelid in our humanity' (EB, 1844). See also Sibella Elizabeth Miles, *An essay on the factory question, occasioned by the recent votes in the House of Commons. Addressed to the ladies of England* . . . , London 1844, and Caroline Norton's response in *The child of the islands*, London 1845.

121–122. Texts: *Poems*, 2v. London 1844, i.123, i.124. First printed, *Graham's Magazine*, 23 July 1843, 34; *Graham's Magazine*, 23 August 1843, 71.

122. The Seven] the seven angels.

123. Text: *The Liberty Bell* (Boston 1848), 29–44. Reprinted, *Poems. New edition*, 2v. London 1850, ii.129–41. A microfilm of the printer's copy, dated 1846, is in the British Library (M/538). Elizabeth Barrett

Browning contributed a further anti-slavery poem, 'A curse for the nation', in *The Liberty Bell*, (Boston 1856), 1–9. In a later letter she noted the link between slavery and women's status: 'Oh, and is it possible that you think a woman has no business with questions like the question of slavery? Then she had better use a pen no more. She had better subside into slavery and concubinage herself, I think, as in the times of old, shut herself up with the Penelopes in the "women's apartment", and take no rank among thinkers and speakers.' Letter to Anna Jameson, 12 April 1853, *Letters*, ed. Kenyon, ii.213.

A number of English women also contributed to *The Liberty Bell*: Jane Elizabeth Hornblower (née Roscoe), 'British West Indian emancipation', 1848, pp.139–40, 'Sonnet', 1849, pp.33–4; Mary Carpenter, 'Offerings of English women', 1848, pp.238–42, 'The ocean monarch and the pearl', 1849, pp.147–54; Lady Anna-bella Noel Byron (née Milbanke), 'To the anti-slavery advocate', 1849, p.105.

whippoorwill] American bird, so named after its cry.

cat of the glen] wildcat.

124. Text: *Blackwood's* (1846), p.490. Reprinted as 'A year's spinning', in *Poems. New edition*, 2v. London 1850, ii.403–4. On the theme of the fallen woman, see Sally Mitchell, *The fallen angel: chastity, class and women's reading, 1835–1880*, Bowling Green, Ohio, 1981; Helsinger, Sheets & Veeder, iii.111–70; Kathleen Hickok, *Representations of women: nineteenth-century British women's poetry*, Westport, Conn. 1984, pp. 92–116; Angela Leighton, '"Because men made the laws": the fallen woman and the woman poet', *Victorian Poetry*, 27 (1989), 109–27. See also notes to **80** and **82** above.

125–126. Texts: *Poems. New edition*, 2v. London 1850, i.353, i.354.

125. Text: *Blackwood's* (1847), 684.

126. Hiram Powers] American sculptor (1805–1873), resident in Florence from 1837 and a friend of the Brownings. His 'Greek Slave' (1843) was a female nude based upon the idea of Eve before the Fall, and in 1850 he produced a marble version, which was exhibited at the Great Exhibition at Crystal Palace in 1851.

APPENDIX

MARY BRYAN (née LANGDON) (1780 to after 1823)
She was born on 15 June 1780 at North Petherton, near Taunton, Somerset, the daughter of Edmund Langdon and Mary (Ballam), who had married 19 January 1778, at North Petherton. She was baptised along with her sister, Anna (born on 27 November 1781), on 3 April 1782. Another sister, Julia, was born on 27 July 1784 and baptised along with a brother, John Ballam (born on 28 March 1783), on 3 September 1784. The two sisters and her brother appear frequently in her poems. Anna possibly married James Bedingfield (to whom Mary Bryan dedicated her *Sonnets and Metrical Tales*, Bristol 1814), calling him 'the Friend also of my Parents—my Brother'. A poem, 'To Mrs. J–.B.', indicates that 'Dear Anna' is Mrs J[ames] B[edingfield] and that he was often at sea. In the dedication she also noted his 'professional advice' on her ill health and the Preface records her dying husband leaving Mary 'to your kindness—to your skill', indicating that he was perhaps a ship's doctor. The other sister, Julia, who features in several poems, died 17 February 1804 at Durston, near Taunton, Somerset. The unnamed brother, John Ballam, probably saw military service in the Napoleonic wars and later moved to Bethnal Green, London, where he married Ann Prior, 30 September 1827.

She married Edward Bryan on 30 May 1804 at St Cuthbert's, Wells, Somerset. In or about 1809, he set up as a printer and stationer, in the High Street, Bristol. From 1812 to 1814, the firm operated from the City Printing Office, 52 Corn Street and 19 Clarence Place. He probably died in 1814 (although there is no Bristol burial record) and the firm became known as Mary Bryan & Co. from 1815 to 1823. At this point Mary Bryan's involvement may have ceased since the firm changed to Bryan & Co. in 1824, and moved to Shannon Court in 1825. By 1826 it appears to have either ceased trading or changed hands.

Her date of death has not yet been established. Her burial record is not recorded in the Bristol Record Office up to 1837 (nor is Edward Bryan's). Nor is it recorded in the Somerset & Dorset Burials Index and there are no matches for a Mary Bryan of Bristol in the GRO, indicating perhaps that she died in another part of the country, or remarried, pre or post 1837.

1   TO W[ILLIAM] W[ORDSWORT]H, ESQ.

Thou! who dost well reprove the sordid fear,
    That spoils the springs of bliss—wasting life's powers,
O wilt thou *mourn* the ungenial influence here,
    One moment pausing o'er these withered flowers?

Like thee through many a darling haunt I strayed;
    And if to thee sublimer views were given,
Dear were the scenes my lingering steps delayed—
    As dear the silent grove—the starry heaven.

MARY BRYAN

Far in the sheltered vale, I never knew
   To mark great nature in her wonders dressed;
Around her child her tenderest charms she threw,
   And smiling, hid me in her tranquil breast.

No sordid wishes drew me from her bowers—
   Not such the passion that these strains reveal;
No sordid cares consume my wasting powers—
   My infant spoilers wear the bloom they steal.

—O, happiest of Poets, as of men,
   Who dost delight to show with feelings true,
The maiden, dearest in her native glen,
   Spontaneous graces blending with her view—

Hast thou ne'er watched her cheek's decaying bloom?
   Hide—hide it ever from thy cheerful ken—
The faded mourner should not ask a tomb,
   To chill thy breast—O, happiest of men!

Poet of Nature's—Reason's—Beauty's light—
   Who nobly scorned the Muse by custom dressed:
If too long dazzled, the bewildered sight
   Mark not her glories in her simpler vest;

The futile glare at length will cease to charm,
   At length awakening truth delight to find
A Muse with genuine hopes, and passions warm;
   Too wise for form—'Too pure to be refined.'

2   SONNET: THE SPINNING WHEEL

Oft has thy simple humming soothed my ear,
Musing on some rude bench where woodbines wove
Around the cottage window—hours so dear,
That more than skilful airs, thy changeless tones I love,
And there I heard a plaintive strain the while—
Some ancient ballad's warning history
Of banished youth, by cruel stepdame's wile,
Of fairest lady's fall, man's wicked perjury.
I thought, alas! of love and constancy,
While tears and smiles told all my bosom then,
O, falsest *****! I gave the smiles to thee—
The tears to damsels wronged by wicked men!
For, ah! what maid that heard thy winning tale,
Could dream that e'er such tears, should thy deceit bewail.

MARY BRYAN

3 THE VISIT

With feeble frame, by lingering sickness worn,
And painless languor, and that hectic cheek,
Death's flattering mask, his painted mockery
To native air and early friends restored—
Kind renovaters; and thou, most kind, most dear,
Maternal Aunt!—sadly I thought of one
Who was, in artless beauty, dear to each
Eye, each heart—alas! how changed! heedless now
Of home's dear scenes and smiles of kindred love,
Bestowed to stranger's care—a wildered one.
—Not yet had health returned with wonted strength,
Ere, sorrowing, I sought my childhood's friend,
Where dwell the living dead—dismaying sights!
Friend of my happiest hours! I sought her there.
—'Twas a long lonely way, yet every shrub
Of earliest verdure in full beauty bloomed,
On ev'ry hedge-row, while the bursting leaf
Or swelling blossom made a lovely show
Of later promise.—O, 'twere a cheering
Sight; but wintry gloom o'ercast the young morn:
Chilling and heavy sleets bent many a flower
So fair! alas, so fragile fair! to rise
No more. Like Sensibility's fond child
Pressed with untimely woe—unmeet to bear,
Yet all unwise to shun the ills that spoil
Its tender bloom! and ne'er shall genial suns
For either shine—cold is their early fate—
Cold the untimely tears that chill their gentle
Sweets—and e'er a smile will save them—they're gone!
————So mused the saddened mind,
Till, Castle Ne Roch, on thy wild scenes amazed,
I gazed! With slow and cautious steps the steeds
Pursued a broken path, that crossed midway,
The steep declivity—a dangerous pass—
Beneath, a fenny marsh extended wide—
Down the deep fall the dizzy sight,—with fear
Oft shunning, yet, again, involuntary
Turning,—viewed the black, vast waste; barren, or,
If a shrub grew—dark as its parent swamp—
Unsightly all—in vain the weary eye
Sought aught beyond.—Bounded by hazy mists
The murky scene seemed shut from light or joy.
Above a huge high cliff its rocky sides
Rude, torn, and bare, upreared—'Here,' said my Guide,
'The poor crazed inmates of yon mansion stray;
Their keepers watch their moody wanderings;
Yet oft in these wild heights unseen they lurk

MARY
BRYAN

Eluding all research.'—I trembled at the tale—
Oh, frightful haunts! lest a strange form
With sudden rage and demon strength possessed,
Swift from some jutting crag, with fell intent,
And horrid yell might rush, and hurl me down
The immense below! Urged by these terrors, soon
We gained the sullen dwelling—drear retreat!
The massy doors—the iron-grated lights
Appalled with very strength—I trembled there,
E'en in the terrible security.
Then, fearful wrecks of storms I ill endured,
Unmeet to greet a sympathizing guest,
The shriek—the long loud laugh—the desperate din
I scarce forbore to join. I clasped my dewy brows
Insensate of the pressure, chilling cold—
I thought or death or madness soon will seize
My trembling frame, and I shall never more
Behold aught fair, or good, or blest, or dear.
Instant I clasped them all; Oh, what a change
To love, and hope, and joy, one tender look—
One precious word of recognition—gave.
Now, all her own sweet self in loveliness,
Restored by kindest care and medicinal aid,
I saw my gentle Friend—mutual surprise
Of unexpected bliss! Dear news I brought—
Tidings of all she loved.—Enquiry o'er,
And calmed the sudden joy: "'Tis years,' she said,
'Dark years since we have met—dark years of grief,
And dark the future too—but these *will* pass—
These too *will* pass, and so we'll meet in heaven.
Nay, here we'll meet if, kind, my soon return,
Thou'lt wait amongst our native bowers—shelters
From many a storm, when rambling far we saw
The gathering clouds with fear—fond maids, nor shunned
The darker storms that early whelmed us o'er.—
One more request, and we will say Farewell—
Lest night o'ertake thee. Dost thou remember
Six years ago—past a few warmer suns
To give the summer ripeness—one evening
We lingered in the copse, plucking wild flowers
To weave us wreaths beseeming more, we said,
The brows of simple maids, than garden flowers
Flaunting so proud, in artificial hues—
Capricious idlers, so we moralized;
And this—for one afar you cried, bending
A pliant branch, on whose high top you hung
A varied garland—withdrawn the gentle force
Upsprung in air it waved its modest tints
So prettily, we, smiling, marked the while—

'Till roused by distant sounds, threatening and rude,
We turned and through the mazy thicket,
Ev'ry repelling branch or bent or torn,
Heedless of hurt, a tattered creature, wild,
Haggard, and wan, pressed on to where we stood
Silent and still with fear, nor time for flight;
In wrathful mood—mad Kattern hailed us loud;—
Then you with feigned composure forward stepped—
*This to Kate—sweet flowers for her—does any
Harm poor Kate—ought ail her.*'—Relenting, pleased,
She took the fragrant gift, muttered and passed,
'Poor Kate!—Rude boys had worried her to rage;
Harmless else, and sometimes happy too, for
Kate had long forgotten him who wronged her;
Blessed forgetfulness! O, falsest man,
Forgetting thee!'—Then, in those softest eyes,
Gleamed wandering fires—fires not their own—but soon
To tears they changed.—'How much,' she said, 'in fond
And idle talk, I wandering, lose myself,
Detaining thee! Tomorrow at this hour
Cross that low copse, and climb the ascent beyond—
So gay with yellow broom and purple heath,
I to you sullen heights will bend my way,
And if the day is fair I have a glass
Will show thee there—thy white kerchief waving
Though indistinct thy form I see, this sign
Will mark it thine—sweet consciousness.—Again
Each day return—the dearest hour I'll know
Till that I meet thee there.—Farewell—Farewell!
Each word of thine is treasured—O Farewell.

4   ON SEEING THE REPRESENTATION OF A VICTORY
    O execrable war!   Dr Adam Clarke

What spectacle of horror this! Victory!
Are these thy triumphs? Hero! these thy deeds?
Conqueror! hast thou pierced with thy brave arm
Hearts fearless as thy own?—'twas bravely done!—
Oh but these hearts were dear, as thine, were dear,
As brave, as generous hearts!—mine cannot
Welcome thee, for at the piteous sight, 'tis
Almost as cold as their's whom thou hast slain—
'T has not a throb—a pulse for victory!—
Now—now it bleeds with *that* trodden beneath
Thy horse's hoof—I am, methinks, the maid,
The miserable maid, that crushed heart loved;
How can I bless thee—so!—That mangled form—

MARY BRYAN

I loved with sister's pride, the gallant boy!
Oh that gashed head!—I am the mother whose
Breast did pillow it!—Mighty conqueror!—
I have much kindred here whom I must wail;
I cannot joy in thee, nor in thy work.—
Thou God of Mercy, I will look no more
Lest seeing thee not here, I should forget
My God!

5 **THE DREAM**
     C———H

The Winds around my cottage rudely blowing
  Bear on the midnight hour a fearful tone,
Near and more near—loud and still louder growing;
    Terrors shrill scream—
      And now—a feeble, dying moan:—
Awaking from a fevered dream—
  I listen to the howling storm!
Slow from the dark and haunted stream,
  Her shadowy arms uprise,
Till all, appeared a phantom maid;
  Ah not in beauty's wonted form,
As fair, and fond, but much betrayed,
  And weary of her ceaseless woe,
    She sought a sleep
      So still and deep,
Where, dark the waters flow.—
Blue vapours round her played
  She cannot rest in deep and night,
  And ever gleams a ghastly light
That haunts the unquiet shade.
Abhorring! from the light her eyes
  Still turn, but turn in vain;—
Methought on me a look they cast
  No eye might look again.
    And then, methought a fatal claim!
    'Come victim of as false a flame!'—
A murmur on the blast—
    So indistinct the tone
      That to the heart alone,
Spake, fearfully, and passed.
    Then, then, she sunk the deep below:
Yet, still a shadowy arm did wave;
To her unblessed, unhallowed grave
    Where dark the waters flow.

MARY BRYAN (née LANGDON) (1780–after 1823)
Dwelly's Parish Records, v.12, North Petherton Registers, West Ewell, Surrey 1923; *Somerset Marriage Index* (S&DFHS); *Somerset & Dorset Burials Index* (S&DHFS); *They lived in Bristol: an index to Bristol burials, 1813–1837*, Bristol Record Office; *Mathew's Bristol Directories, 1806–1830*; *Pigot & Co's London & Provincial Directory 1822–1823, 1824*; IGI; GRO.

1–5. Texts: *Sonnets and metrical tales*, Bristol 1815, pp.1–2, 19, 27–33, 35–6, 59–60.

1. 'Too pure to be refined'] 'Wordsworth's "Address to the Spade of his Friend"' (MB).

2. *****] person unknown.

3. Death's flattering mask, painted mockery] 'I am not quite assured, but believe this idea is in Dr Young's *Night Thoughts*' (MB).

Th'immense below] 'Since writing the above, a fatal accident occurred on this spot. Two persons passing in a gig were precipitated a fall of more than 300 feet' (MB).

mad Kattern hailed us loud] My fair country friends will recollect poor Kate Dwelly, who a few years since, during the summer seasons usually rambled from the village of North Curry round the adjacent country. When enraged by the clamour or pursuit of the peasant boys, her appearance was really formidable, and has often alarmed unprotected ramblers. Her form was very tall, she wore the parish woollen dress, and small mob cap, her hair prematurely grey, hung wildly over her eyes, and down her bare neck. Within the remembrance of many, Kate had been a comely woman, but her person then retained not a wreck of that comeliness, nor her mind a trait of that tenderness which had destroyed her reason' (MB).

4. O execrable war!] Exact source untraced. Probably from Adam Clark, *Commentary*, 8v. 1810–1826.

5. C–H] person unknown.

Index of first lines

A star has left the kindling sky—	156
Ah! what art thou, whose eye-balls roll	53
Amid a gloom more terrible than darkness,	100
Amidst the darkness of the ancient time,	98
And is there sadness in thy dream, my Boy?—	140
And like myself lone, wholly lone,	220
And there the island lay, the waves around	152
Another day, Ah! me, a day	56
As the freed bird from its prison springs,	194
Be hushed, ye angry winds, that sweep,	77
Blow on, ye death-fraught whirlwinds! blow,	80
Borne on by the wondrous power of steam	185
Bring flowers, young flowers, for the festal board,	118
Bring flowers to crown the cup and lute,—	153
Bristol thine heart hath throbbed to glory. Slaves,	32
By the side of the brook, where the willow is waving	67
By the soft green light in the woody glade,	133
Cease, Wilberforce, to urge thy generous aim!	43
Cold in the earth—and the deep snow piled above thee,	223
Come near, my children! till the hour of prayer	107
Come to me with your triumphs and your woes	134
Dark midnight o'er the stately city throws	187
Daughter of the Italian heaven!	121
Do I not love at midnight to gaze forth	102
Do ye hear the children weeping, O my brothers!	248
Dost question of my fate? I was of those	148
Gentle and lovely Form!	123
Hadst thou, beneath the cloudless skies	158
Hark! 'tis the note of joy; the trumpet's voice	74
Hark to the mingled voices of the storm!	147
Harp of wild and dream-like strain,	217
He listened at the porch that day	259
Herbless and crownless, with your foreheads bare	166
I am the only being whose doom	217
I dreamed I was alone on earth. Methought	174
I dwell amid the city ever,	237
I had a dream in the dead of night;	163
I have been lonely, even from a child	96
I saw her in her youth's bright dawn; her eye	180
I sit amidst the universe,	166
I stand beside the waves,—the mournful waves,—	208
I stand on the mark, beside the shore,	252
I stood beside thy lowly grave;—	122

INDEX

I stood within the grave's o'ershadowing vault;	211
I was within a home, where nature smiled,	103
I would that I might wander far away,	144
If Heaven has into being deigned to call	21
I'm happiest when most away	216
In a lofty room a lady fair	191
In St. Lucie's distant isle	27
In scenes untrod for many a year,	213
In summer's mellow midnight,	219
In the cold change which Time hath wrought on Love	195
In the dungeon crypts, idly did I stray,	224
Is it twilight from some bright former day,	106
It is a place where poets crowned	242
It is not pride, it is not shame,	218
It's over now; I've known it all;	216
It was a chamber faire, with arras dight,	160
'Lady, danger hovers around:'	179
Lamenting o'er her orphan child,	88
Like an enfranchised bird, who wildly springs,	208
Mountain winds! oh! whither do ye call me?	142
My bark floats on the sea of death,	213
My darling, thou wilt never know	233
My soul is awakened, my spirit is soaring	229
No coward soul is mine	225
Now falls the thick-descending rain,	48
O God! if this indeed be all	230
O Nature! thou didst rear me for thine own,	143
O Spirit-Land! thou land of dreams!	136
O Thought! O Memory! gems for ever heaping	143
Oft has thy simple humming soothed my ear,	App
Often rebuked, yet always back returning	226
Oh! for thy wings, thou dove!	137
Oh, stranger! heed the famished debtor's prayer,	93
Oh, what a waste of feeling and of thought	156
Once more the eternal melodies from far,	143
Peace to thy dreams!—thou art slumbering now,	141
Pent in the city's darksome walls, I pine	98
Poor restless dove, I pity thee;	230
Repose, sweet babe! thy crying cease;	89
Seest thou my home?—'Tis where yon woods are waving	139
Shall Earth no more inspire thee,	221
She plies her needle 'till the lamp	176
She stood alone; but on her every eye	151
Sister, a rapid year has fled,	184
Source of our first affections; sacred Home!	145

INDEX

Sweet are thy strains, celestial Bard;	228
Swift, e'er the wild and dreary waste	64
That wind is from the North, I know it well;	227
The altar, 'tis of death! for there are laid	156
The hollow winds of Night, no more	12
The knights returned from Holy Land,	82
The morning, unconscious of horrors, arose,	47
The mystery of life—oh how it weighs	99
The poet hath the child's sight in his breast,	260
The seraph sings before the manifest	252
The visions that beset the couch,	170
The wind, I hear it sighing	219
The winds around my cottage rudely blowing	App
There is a tongue in every leaf!	105
'There is no God,' the foolish saith,—	245
There's little joy in life for me,	233
They say Ideal Beauty cannot enter	260
Thou bay-crowned living one—who'er	235
Thou hast a charmed cup, O Fame!	125
Thou! who dost well reprove the sordid fear,	App
Though to my living eye be still denied	96
To thee upon the waters! a green wealth	146
Transpierced with many a streaming wound,	91
'Twas but a dream!—I saw the stag leap free,	126
'Twas in the mazes of a wood,	70
'Twas in youth, that hour of dreaming;	209
'Twas mine to watch the dreary night,	92
'Twas night; mysterious silence reigned;	90
Up now, my little Margaret!	112
We stood at eve where the flashing waves,	146
What spectacle of horror this! Victory!	App
When fallen man from Paradise was driven	195
When weary with the long day's care,	222
Where rocks tremendous frown on either side,	97
While on my lonely couch I lie	231
Why shrinkest thou, weak girl? Why this coward despair?	94
Wildly and mournfully the Indian drum	119
With feeble frame, by lingering sickness worn,	App
With stammering lips and insufficient sound,	251
With swelling heart, I hear thy stifled sigh,	82
Ye trees, does your foliage delay,	49
Yes, she has left us. She, whose gifted lays	182
Yes! there are sympathies fate cannot part,	100

Selected thematic index

abandonment 20, 81, 124
bereavement 7–8, 11–12, 19, 114–15
birds 50, 85, 88, 90, 111
children/child labour 1–2, 4, 19–20, 25, 38–9, 52, 87, 120
the city 10, 38–9, 82–3, 87, 120
William Cowper 109, 118
death 10–14, 19, 21, 23, 43, 46, 66, 72–4, 79–80, 91, 97, 104, 114–15, 116, 118, 123
dreams 26–7, 49, 52–3, 63, 72, 75–6, 96, 102, 113, App. 5
factories 38–9, 87, 120
fame 42, 45, 53, 64, 73, 75, 78–9
female characters 4, 9, 11, 16, 18–20, 25, 41–6, 48, 53, 64–7, 70–1, 77–81, 83–4, 98, 114–16, 123–4
Felicia Hemans 37, 66, 70, 80, 116
flowers 40, 48, 61
graves 43, 91, 104, 118
home 35, 47, 51, 59, 69, 93
Ireland 7–9
love 4, 9, 11–12, 19–20, 25, 32, 41, 46, 67, 81, 85–6, 88–9, 104, 114–15, 123–4
madness 9, 13, 46, App. 3
marriage 12, 67
mothers 1–2, 4, 10, 19, 20, 25, 77, 123
poetry 37, 42–3, 45, 55, 64, 66, 70, 78–80, 90, 96, 103, 109, 116, 118, 122, 125, App. 1
prisons 10, 24, 33, 83–5, 88, 105, 108, 111
sea 1–5, 14–16, 23, 64–5, 69, 72, 74, 89, 92, 110, 123
seamstresses 77, 83–4, 124, App. 2
sickness 55–6, 92
slavery 1–5, 10, 22–3, 25, 123–6
solitude 27–9, 30, 33, 34, 58, 62–3, 72, 75–7, 83–6, 89, 99–101, 108, 111
travel 10, 13, 25, 28, 41, 60, 65, 69, 82, 94, 117
war 6–8, 10, 11, 12, 14, 17, 19, 23, 44, App. 4
women poets 37, 43, 66, 70, 80, 114–16